ENLIGHTENMENT MADE SIMPLE

AN INTRODUCTION TO ADVAITA VEDANTA

Rory B. Mackay

Lead us from ignorance to truth,
From darkness to light,
And from death to immortality.

Brihadaranyaka Upanishad

This work is licensed under a Creative Commons Attribution 4.0 International license. This license allows for redistribution, commercial and non-commercial, provided the author is credited and no modifications are made to the material. For contract details, visit https://creativecommons.org/licenses/by-nd/4.0/

Copyright © 2024 Rory B. Mackay, some rights reserved.

First edition

Published by Blue Star Publishing

UnbrokenSelf.com

The right of Rory B. Mackay to be identified as the author of this work has been asserted by him in accordance with the Copyright, Designs and Patents Act, 1988.

Enlightenment Made Simple / Rory B. Mackay — 1st ed.

ISBN 9781739608958

For Ishvara, and for you.

Contents

Introduction   i

Part 1: The Problem of Suffering
Chapter 1: When Life Doesn't Work   1
Chapter 2: The Curse of the Limited Self   13
Chapter 3: Life's Highest Goal   29
Chapter 4: Vedanta: Roadmap to Freedom   41
Chapter 5: Preparing the Mind   55
Chapter 6: Values and Dharma   75
Chapter 7: Karma Yoga   101
Chapter 8: The Entry Point   119

Part 2: The Power of Self-Knowledge
Chapter 9: Self-Enquiry   125
Chapter 10: The Self   149
Chapter 11: God, Maya and the Creation   171
Chapter 12: Devotion   191
Chapter 13: The Three Energies   217
Chapter 14: Keys to Self-Knowledge   239
Chapter 15: The Three Orders of Reality   267
Chapter 16: Karma and Rebirth   283
Chapter 17: The Ultimate Truth in 3 Words   303

Part 3: From Knowledge to Freedom
Chapter 18: The Enlightenment Protocol   321
Chapter 19: Vedantic Meditation   351
Chapter 20: Troubleshooting, FAQs & Pitfalls   369
Chapter 21: A Life of Freedom   389

Appendices
Appendix 1: Tattva Bodha   417
Appendix 2: Nirvana Shatkam   429
Appendix 3: Resources   431
About the Author   437

ENLIGHTENMENT MADE SIMPLE

Introduction

To manifest one's Divinity is the goal of life.
Swami Chandarashekarendra

Enlightenment! The coveted goal of spiritual seekers the whole world over; heralded by sages and mystics across the ages as the pinnacle of human attainment.

But what exactly is enlightenment?

You'll find surprisingly little consensus in spiritual circles. Definitions differ wildly between the various teachings and traditions; invariably resulting in a lot of confusion and misdirection.

While there are certainly places you can engage in spiritual discussion, from Facebook groups to various sub-Reddits, it's difficult to hold a meaningful and informed dialogue when just about everyone has their own idea of what enlightenment is.

Some see enlightenment as a kind of superhuman state, replete with quasi-magical powers. New Agers take it to mean "ascension", in which the very atoms of the body are somehow transformed into light.

Yoga philosophy suggests enlightenment is the merging of a lower self into a Higher Self. Buddhists talk about nirvana; a state in which all thought and desire is extinguished. Taoists aim for physical immortality through the creation of a "light body".

Some people take enlightenment to be the destruction of the ego or a state of fully inhabiting the Now. A New Age lady once, rather unhelpfully, told me that enlightenment is "different for everyone" and it can be "whatever you want it to be."

Indeed, in the absence of a coherent and logical definition, many people cobble together their own ideas which, sadly, rarely hold up to scrutiny.

It's perhaps little wonder that, of all the many people ardently seeking enlightenment, so few ever find it.

In order to reach any destination you need two things. Firstly, you need to know exactly where you're going and, secondly, you need to know how to get there. That's where Advaita Vedanta comes in!

A Map to Freedom

Rooted in India's ancient Vedas, possibly the world's oldest scriptures (and the basis of what we call Hinduism), Vedanta can justifiably be called the grandfather of enlightenment traditions.

If you want a clear understanding of something it's usually best to go to the source rather than rely upon second hand knowledge subject to bias and distortion. Unlike many traditions, Vedanta has been closely guarded over the millennia in order to prevent distortion and alteration of its teaching. In fact, the complex and sophisticated way the Vedas are composed and recited ensures their incorruptibility.

Spiritual seekers, rebellious by nature, often have a certain disdain for tradition and structure when it comes to teachings. Many like to believe they can find their own way to enlightenment; flitting between different teachings like a spiritual butterfly, piecing together their understanding based on what "resonates" (which is to say, what fits with their existing beliefs).

It's an appealing notion, which unfortunately doesn't work in practice.

The reason is simple. According to the Vedas, the problem of "unenlightenment" is ignorance, specifically, self-ignorance.

We don't know who and what we truly are. We make assumptions about our identity based on the limited knowledge we have.

Ignorance is an intractable foe; particularly self-ignorance, to which we not only yield, but often wilfully cling to as though our lives depended on it.

Without some way of neutralising this ignorance and discriminating the true from the false, our cognitive biases will forever blindside us, distorting our perception of reality and, most crucially, of our own self.

The fact of the matter is this: if you were capable of figuring it out all on your own, you'd likely have done so; years, or even decades ago.

In the absence of a clear destination and a legitimate map of the territory, you'll likely remain lost. Worst case scenario is you end up wasting decades of your precious life on teachings that lack clarity, cohesion and perhaps even basic logic and still be no closer to enlightenment.

Vedanta provides the necessary map.

Neither a religion nor a philosophy as such, Vedanta is a means of knowledge. It's a tool for removing self-ignorance and bringing your understanding of yourself into alignment with who and what you truly are.

It provides not only a clear and logical definition of what enlightenment is but also the means of attaining it. Arguably, Vedanta is the closest the world has to an actual science of consciousness and enlightenment.

The proof, as always, is in the pudding.

Vedanta has been around for thousands of years. It's lasted all this time for a simple reason. It works; and, like any science, its results are replicable.

With breathtaking scope, cohesion and logic, this ancient body of knowledge has been setting minds free for millennia, providing nothing less than a roadmap to freedom.

The Definition of Enlightenment

Freedom, incidentally, is the name of the game.

The term enlightenment is a loaded one and, like the word God, comes with a great deal of baggage and misunderstanding.

The Vedic term for enlightenment is *moksha*, which means "liberation."

Bingo! That's what enlightenment actually is—liberation from suffering.

The suffering we're referring to doesn't relate to politics, family matters or concern over the stock index. It's not about the state of the world, your body, or the various trials and tribulations of worldly life.

We're talking about the pervasive sense of insufficiency, lack and limitation common to virtually all human beings. It's the deeply ingrained sense that who and what you are is never enough; and that, in order to be happy, you have to be, become or acquire something more, different and better.

Peoples' goals in life are many and varied. One person may want a promotion at work, a relationship, or a new car, while another might simply be struggling to put food on the table.

No matter how diverse our goals, however, we're all united by a singular imperative: the desire to be free. Whether it's freedom from sorrow, poverty, illness, or even boredom, freedom is the innermost yearning of the human soul.

Why do we seek freedom?

Only a fool seeks what they already have.

We crave freedom because, in spite of whatever tangible or intangible blessings we may have in life, at the core of our being, we feel desperately unfree. We're driven by a deep and gnawing sense of lack and insecurity; a relentless and insatiable hunger we can never fully satisfy.

Such is the predicament of the human being.

Misplaced Seeking

What sets humankind apart from our animal friends is our ability to self-reflect; our capacity to be aware of and to form concepts and judgements about that self.

The downside of this capacity is clear. The self that we become aware of, and with which we identify, may not be a whole, happy and complete self. It may, in fact, be a limited, lacking and incomplete self—and such a self is simply not acceptable to us.

Driven by this diminished sense of self, we frantically seek scraps of joy and happiness outside of ourselves. Because the senses are naturally hooked to the external world of objects and experience, that's where we seek our happiness. We see the world as both the source of our misery and the doorway to our liberation.

Desperately seeking freedom by manipulating our environment and fulfilling our various desires and goals, we become embroiled in the seesaw of duality; life with all its ups and downs, pleasures and pains, gains and losses, victories and defeats.

Alas, trying to bend the world into alignment with our personal will is perhaps the least effective way of attaining freedom. As the saying goes, "you win some, you lose some." Because all things phenomenal are subject to duality, it doesn't matter how much you "win" at the game of life; how popular you are, how large your bank balance and how flash your Lamborghini.

There's no freedom to be found in an ephemeral, time-bound world forever subject to the law of duality. To put it another way, there's no way to beat the system within the system.

The wise, mature person will eventually acknowledge this fact and, with luck, take a different approach to happiness. If lasting happiness cannot be found outside of ourselves, then surely it must be found within?

That's when you hopefully turn to what the Vedas proclaim life's highest goal: enlightenment.

You open yourself to the teachings of the scriptures and the seers and sages across the ages. Their message is radical yet clear. The happiness and wholeness you seek is not to be found in the world outside of you, but within you; as the very core and essence of what you are.

That may seem a revolutionary idea. It may fly in the face of everything you've ever been taught, not to mention contradict your current experience.

But what if it's true?

What if the freedom you crave is already present and available to you, right this very second?

Removing Self-Ignorance

Vedanta establishes that the true problem isn't that you're not getting what you want from life. The secret to happiness lies not in *getting* what you want but in understanding *why* you want in the first place.

You want because you feel a sense of lack. Burdened by a diminished, lacking sense of self, you've been driven by a deeply rooted need to be more, to have more, and to become more than you are. Again, the source of this misery is ignorance of your true nature. You've been victim to a crippling identity crisis shared by virtually all human beings.

Vedanta resolves this error by removing self-ignorance, enabling you to appreciate yourself as you are in actuality. You come to realise that, far from lacking and limited, your nature is pure Awareness or Consciousness; always whole, always complete, always present.

Freedom comes from Self-Knowledge; from knowing who and what you truly are. Believe it or not, you've actually always been free, for freedom is the very essence of your being. It's simply been hidden from you by ignorance and the mind's inability to see reality as it actually is.

When properly understood and integrated, Self-Knowledge brings lasting liberation from suffering; the goal of all beings.

That's enlightenment in a nutshell.

How To Use This Book

Vedanta can potentially seem intimidating to the newcomer. It's a comprehensive body of knowledge with its own specific terminology; a great deal of which is in Sanskrit with no direct English equivalent.

This book is written as an accessible introduction, using as little Sanskrit as possible. The aim is to help both those new to the spiritual path and those who may have spent considerable time with other teachings yet still haven't made the breakthroughs they're looking for.

Like the teaching itself, this book has been structured in a precise and methodical way. Rather than dipping in and out, it's important to start at the beginning and work your way through in a sequential fashion.

Don't feel compelled to rush. Instead of simply reading the words, allow yourself to reflect deeply upon what is being said until you have a clear enough understanding to move onto the next section.

More than simply a book, this serves as a foundational course in Vedanta. You'll find a number of guided exercises and meditations which I encourage you to do. They form the basis of a solid spiritual practise and will help you to grasp the teaching at a deeper level; allowing this timeless wisdom to come alive in your own immediate and direct experience. Audio recordings of these meditations can be purchased online from the author.

The book is divided into three sections.

The first section explores the nature of human suffering and its solution. Delving into the Vedas' ancient and timeless psychology, you'll learn about the four human goals: security, pleasure, virtue and liberation. We'll then go on to examine what enlightenment is and isn't and the necessity of preparing the mind for Self-Knowledge.

The middle section unfolds the core principles of Vedanta. It includes topics such as self-enquiry, Consciousness, the individual, the nature of God and the creation, devotion, the qualities of matter, karma, and the essential oneness of existence.

The final section draws everything together, providing the necessary tools and methods for actualising this Knowledge. It lays out the benefits of enlightenment and includes a section on troubleshooting and avoiding the pitfalls inherent in the spiritual path.

By the end of the book, you'll not only have a clear understanding of this ancient teaching but will also know how to convert this Knowledge into true and lasting liberation.

That's no idle promise.

Vedanta's time-tested method has been working for sincere and devoted seekers across the millennia—and, with the appropriate time, dedication and perseverance, it can work for you too.

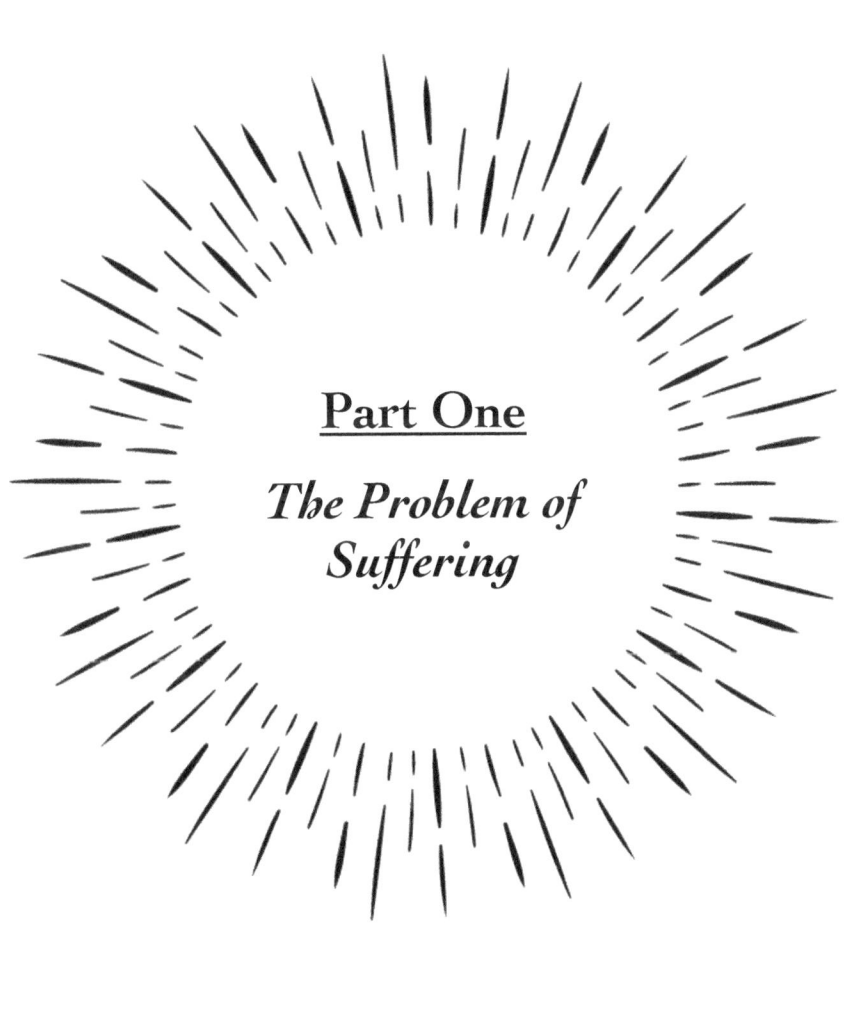

Part One

The Problem of Suffering

1.
When Life Doesn't Work

The ignorant stumble through life, goaded by the senses,
addicted to passing pleasures and blind to the true
goal of life.
Katha Upanishad

I'd like to introduce you to Mike.

Mike is in his mid-fifties and the first thing he does each morning is reach for a vodka bottle. A functioning alcoholic, Mike has to force himself out of bed to work at a job he hates. If he wasn't reliant on the income he'd most certainly quit in a heartbeat. Not that he truly believes he can do (or deserves) much better.

As a child, he was filled with dreams for the future. An imaginative and introverted kid, Mike lived out multiple lifetimes in his head. Life seemed full of exciting possibilities. He yearned to set off and travel the world, exploring each and every continent with wide eyed wonder. He wanted to be an artist, an inventor, an engineer; and felt certain he could change the world in some way.

Of course, life didn't turn out quite as he imagined.

He struggled at school, having little aptitude for the classroom curriculum. He also suffered a degree of social anxiety, although it wasn't called that back then; he was simply dismissed as being shy and awkward.

Often subject to bullying, Mike developed low self-esteem; something that only got worse as he hit adolescence. Rather than staying on to finish his final year, he made a break from school the moment he was old enough.

His dreams of childhood fell by the wayside and he took the first job he could find. Life became a matter of simply getting by; turning up at the office for another day of drudgery, trying to get along with colleagues he didn't particularly like, and endeavouring to make himself seem more impressive than the lowly image he had of himself inwardly.

Nevertheless, he worked hard and eventually moved through the ranks of his accounting company. He went from renting apartments to eventually owning a small house of his own.

Dating wasn't easy. He felt he had to bluster his way to impressing the ladies; too afraid to let them see what he truly thought of himself. During his teenage years, he'd learned to craft a persona; a social mask he presented to the world; an idealised version of who he wanted to be. Over time, he became pretty good at it, too; projecting what he thought others wanted to see.

After a number of failed relationships, he eventually found the woman he would marry and, for a time, was happy. He had a good, if unfulfilling, job, he had a decent house and, best of all, somebody to love and support him. A year after they married, his first child was born, and then another, two years after that. He liked being a father even if he didn't feel particularly prepared and confident in the role of parent; doubly so when it became clear that one of his kids had learning needs and required specialised education and support.

Mike already knew that life rarely remained rosy for long. Every upside seemed to come with an inevitable downside and, after a time, his relationship with his wife deteriorated as the strain of parenting took a toll on their marriage.

He began seeking solace in alcohol. Several drinks at the local bar would dull his emotions and he began channelling his discontent into gambling—and, worse, by hitting on women.

At first, it was simply a way boosting his self-esteem; which it most certainly did when they reciprocated his advances. Of course, he never had any intention of actually cheating on his wife because he didn't see himself as that type of person. One evening, however, after a few too many drinks, that's exactly what happened.

Although he desperately tried to keep it a secret from his wife, she knew something was up and, as a result, their marriage deteriorated rapidly.

This only increased Mike's reliance on alcohol and he began having an affair with a woman from his office. Although he hadn't set out to hurt anybody, least of all his wife and kids, that's what happened when the truth spilled out one day and his wife learned of Mike's infidelity.

Mike tried to defend himself and justify his actions as the product of stress at work and his admitted reliance upon alcohol.

His wife, however, wouldn't hear a word of it. She immediately left him, taking the kids along with her. Perhaps most heartbreaking of all, when the kids learned of their father's betrayal of their mother, they wanted nothing more to do with him.

Now alone with nothing but his dreary job and an empty house, Mike's addiction to both alcohol and gambling has only worsened. He's given up hope of finding love again because he decided that, at least in his current state, he had nothing much to offer anyone.

Life, he concluded, is nothing but a succession of disappointment and failed dreams. Even when he did have everything, he still managed to mess it up because he simply couldn't control his own mind and its compulsions and addictions. He's now unsure what life might hold for his retirement other than loneliness, self-pity and alcohol.

Samsara: A Universal Problem

It's a sad story and one that's not at all uncommon.

While the details differ from person to person, the nuts and bolts are the same. We all want to be happy and complete. With that in mind, we set about trying to make life work for us.

We desperately try to get what we want and avoid what we don't want, with particular emphasis on attaining security and pleasure; only to find that life rarely plays a fair game.

For all the victories we attain, we're likely to experience just as many failures, if not more.

There's simply no getting around this fact.

We want life to be a certain way but, in spite of all the motivational slogans in the world, our ability to force circumstances into alignment with our wants and desires is limited at best.

We are, after all, simply human beings. We are not God; we didn't create the stars and galaxies and the world with everything in it. While it's true that we have a degree of volition and control, it's always limited because, simply put, there are trillions of factors, both known and unknown, over which we have no control.

Mike's story is the story of *samsara*: the worldly suffering experienced by human beings across time, the entire world over.

A Sanskrit word with no direct English equivalent, samsara refers to the cycle of lack, desire, attachment and suffering experienced by virtually every human being you'll ever meet.

A *samsari* is somebody who seeks happiness outside of him or herself. Acutely aware of an inner sense of lack and emptiness, and driven by various attachments and addictions, compulsions and neuroses, the samsari pursues happiness by manipulating the things of the world; by trying to force reality to conform to his or her personal demands.

It's a futile task, because in a world of duality, there can be no gain without loss, no pleasure without pain and no happiness without sorrow.

Indeed, the universe didn't go to the immense bother of existing simply to cater to the desires and whims of the little humans living on one particular rock in space. Our preferences and predilections don't, unfortunately, factor into the cosmic equation.

Even if they did, the objects of the world are inherently impermanent. They don't last. Nothing stays the same indefinitely, for life exists in a constant state of flux. What seemingly brings happiness one day can just as easily bring sorrow the next.

What's worse, try though you might to hold onto things, there's ultimately no way to escape the fact that everything in the phenomenal world is finite and time-bound. In other words, every gain is subject to eventual and inevitable loss.

You must think I'm real fun at parties, right?

Hear me out, though. It's not until you accept this inherent downside to life that you can overcome your dependence on external objects and experiences for your happiness—and, therefore, begin to break free of samsara.

The First Human Pursuit: Security

It's important to understand what drives human behaviour. The Vedantic scriptures, about which we'll learn more in Chapter Four, outline four basic human goals or life pursuits. You might think of it as an ancient take on what psychologists today call Maslow's Hierarchy of Needs.

Let's take a look at the first two goals of human life: security and pleasure. While there are another two, higher goals, many human beings will never actually move beyond these two primary motivating factors.

In common with all forms of life, whether human, animal, vegetable or mineral, our primary goal relates to security and basic physical survival.

The urge to survive and, hopefully, thrive is common to all lifeforms.

Nobody has to tell you that it's a good idea to stay alive. Above all else, you want to be alive and to avoid physical harm and danger. All beings know that they exist and, unless there's something terribly wrong, given the choice, they want to continue living.

Anything that contributes to our basic survival and material needs falls into the category of this first life pursuit.

That includes having food to eat, shelter and warmth, clothes to protect us from the elements and the avoidance of anything that might endanger our survival, including injury and illness.

Obviously, as a child, it falls upon our parents to provide these things for us. When we reach maturity, however, we begin taking care of such necessities ourselves.

That's why our early years are focused on education which then, with a little luck, prepares us to enter the workforce, find employment and make the necessary money to provide for our worldly needs.

This corresponds with what the Vedic system outlines as the student or educational stage of life. The culmination of the educational stage leads into the householder stage, in which we are traditionally expected to settle down, find a spouse and start a family.

In our example, Mike had these bases covered. It might not have been a job he enjoyed, but he nevertheless had employment and didn't have to worry about his basic material needs. He also got married, had kids and provided for them, thus moving from the educational to the householder stage of life.

Until you've taken care of your basic security needs, not least having a roof over your head and food to eat, you won't be in a position to progress to the subsequent life pursuits.

The Second Human Pursuit: Pleasure

When basic security is no longer an issue, one's attention naturally gravitates to the second human pursuit: pleasure or enjoyment.

Indeed, for those who don't have to worry about basic survival, pleasure often becomes the most important aspect of living. For some, life becomes an exercise in hedonism and getting the most amount of pleasure for the least amount of effort.

What constitutes pleasure obviously varies from person to person. One person's idea of enjoyment—say, gaming or mountaineering—may well be a source of misery to another. Our pursuit of pleasure is, therefore, an individualistic choice determined by our temperament, culture and our personal likes and dislikes.

Many of us are blessed to live in affluent countries with no shortage of comfort and luxury. All forms of entertainment fall into the category of pleasure pursuits; whether it happens to be television, cinema, music or theatre. It's worth noting that the entertainment and hospitality industries are among the most prominent and profitable on the planet.

Once our friend Mike had taken care of his need for employment, money and a roof over his head, his attention turned to pleasure. He sought a partner and found pleasure through relationships and starting a family.

Of course, some of his attempts at pleasure seeking weren't altogether healthy, for he succumbed to excessive drinking, gambling and womanising.

The way we pursue these first two goals, security and pleasure, can most certainly be imbalanced and unhealthy. Some people obsess over money and security while others fixate on pleasure and enjoyment to an unhealthy degree, perhaps becoming addicted to alcohol, drugs, sex or food. All things have the potential to become problematic when taken to excess.

It's for that reason that we'd all do well to observe the next and, arguably most important, goal of human life.

The Third Human Pursuit: Dharma

When you've taken care of both your material needs and your desire for comfort and enjoyment, you may begin wondering if there isn't more to life than simply surviving and gratifying the senses.

That's when the third human pursuit begins to take prominence: the desire to live according to a sense of morality and ethics; and a commitment to doing the right thing by oneself and others.

This life pursuit is called *dharma* in Sanskrit. A word with no direct translation, dharma has a number of different meanings depending on the context. With regard to life goals, dharma means the desire to contribute something back to the world; to do what is right and proper in each situation and to live with integrity. A simple translation of dharma might be "virtue".

Part of Mike's problem is that, while he had no problem pursuing goals relating to security and pleasure, he didn't have a complete enough understanding of dharma.

Indeed, some people are so invested in their own desire for wealth and enjoyment that they actively violate dharma. Rather than doing the right thing in a situation, their desires and compulsions are so strong that they end up hurting others and perhaps even themselves just as long as they get what they want.

A thief, for instance, is so focused on the first two life goals, wealth and pleasure, that they pay scant regard to dharma. Quite the contrary, they wilfully violate dharma; something that always brings undesirable consequences.

All but the most damaged of human beings have an innate understanding of dharma. We know what is right in any given situation based upon mutual reciprocity, or how we expect others to treat us.

For instance, we know that it's wrong to harm others because we, ourselves, do not want to be harmed. We know that it's good to be honest, kind and straightforward because we, in turn, expect others to behave that way toward us.

Dharma, then, relates to a sense of shared values.

That's why we're naturally inclined to follow established rules of conduct and behave with integrity, honesty, kindness and compassion.

All our goals, whether they relate to security or pleasure, should be governed by a commitment to dharma.

When we live by dharma, we won't go about lying, cheating and harming others. Instead of living solely to gratify our own wants and needs, we live with generosity and consideration for all beings. We see it as our imperative to give at least as much as we take from life

THE FIRST THREE HUMAN PURSUITS

and to do what we can to make the environment around us a better place.

If Mike had followed dharma, he would have done something to tackle his alcohol and gambling addictions and would certainly never have cheated on his wife.

The virtuous, dharmic person doesn't simply act out their desires and whims without question. They first make sure that what they want is, in fact, the right thing to do.

In that respect, following dharma protects you and others and keeps your life on track. By acting with integrity and pure intent, and living in harmony with your own highest nature, you generally avoid the negative consequences that come from causing harm and injury to oneself and others.

By living with dharma, we grow as human beings and develop psychological and spiritual maturity. In time, we hopefully become primed for the fourth and final human goal, which will be the focus of the remainder of this book: enlightenment.

Summary

- We all want to be happy and complete. Most people seek this happiness and completeness by attempting to manipulate the world into alignment with their personal likes and dislikes.
- Samsara is the cycle of lack, desire, attachment and suffering experienced by virtually all human beings.
- Samsara is seeking happiness outside of ourselves.
- Unfortunately, life doesn't factor our personal wants and desires into the equation. Furthermore, everything in life is subject to duality, change and finitude.
- That's why seeking happiness outside of ourselves is a recipe for continual frustration, disappointment and sorrow.
- There are four basic human pursuits that motivate our lives, desires and wants. The first three are security, pleasure and

dharma.

- Once our basic survival and security needs are met, people tend to focus on pleasure, entertainment and enjoyment.
- The third, and arguably highest, life pursuit is dharma. Dharma means a commitment to doing the right thing at the right time in the right way. It means living with compassion, kindness and consideration for others; and being willing to contribute to life rather than being a constant taker.
- We all have an innate and intuitive understanding of dharma. Not everyone behaves according to dharma, however. Some peoples' desires and aversions are so strong that they are willing to violate dharma in order to get what they want. This always leads to problems and suffering, for oneself and others and the world.
- By living in alignment with dharma, we grow as people, psychologically and spiritually, and become primed for life's final and ultimate goal: enlightenment.

2.
The Curse of the Limited Self

> Worlds apart are truth and ignorance. The former leads to
> Self-Realisation; the latter estranges one ever further from
> one's own Self.
> *Katha Upanishad*

In order to be free, and that's always our true goal, it's necessary to understand what binds us in the first place; what causes us to feel limited, lacking and incomplete.

That's why this chapter explores the mechanics of samsara, the seemingly endless cycle of suffering experienced by virtually all human beings. This is very much the "bad news" chapter, so buckle up! Once we've fully explored and understood the problem, however, we're then ready to move onto the exciting part: the solution.

As stated in the previous chapter, whatever our goal, whether it relates to security, pleasure or virtue, it's ultimately driven by the underlying desire to be free. Whether it's freedom from poverty, freedom from insecurity, loneliness or discontent, you can guarantee that every desire is, at heart, a desire to be free of limitation.

We want to be free of limitation because limitation is not natural to us. If it were, if limitation were an inherent part of our nature, we'd happily accept it. But we find limitation in any form unacceptable because, as long as we are subject to limitation, we cannot be free. To be free is to be happy and happiness is the goal shared by all beings.

Unfortunately, ignorance makes us believe that happiness and freedom can only be found outside of us in the world of objects. We believe that the only way to remove our innermost sense of discontent is to rearrange the circumstances of our lives by desperately trying to get more of what we want and less of what we don't want.

It's an understandable mistake because it seems to be true in our own direct experience.

In the next few pages, however, we're going to examine why this approach does not and *cannot* work—and why, no matter what you try to achieve, acquire or attain in life, nothing outside of you can deliver true and lasting happiness.

The Never-Ending Search For Happiness

Why do you want what you want—and why do you do what you do?

In large part, our desires, values and goals are programmed into us by societal expectations and norms. The culture we're born into obviously sets the template and plays a dominant role in what drives us to attain and acquire.

Certain goals tend to be universal. For instance, education is naturally a priority for children. We all have to learn the ways of the world and the society into which we are born. This isn't knowledge we are born with, but something we must acquire.

As a child, it was likely drilled into you by your parents, teachers and other authority figures that success and happiness in life come from scholastic achievement; from passing exams and graduating with as high a grade as possible.

So, you likely did your best and once you finished primary or elementary school, you moved onto high school and then possibly college or university. Upon graduation, you felt happy and satisfied with yourself: *I did it! I made it! I graduated!*

Was this a lasting happiness?

Probably not.

Almost immediately, the goal posts shift as you realise that education is only the beginning of the road to success. After all, what use are qualifications without doing something with them?

Your focus turns to employment and, with a little time and luck, you manage to find and secure the job of your dreams. You work hard over the subsequent months and years, again most likely to an initial sense of satisfaction and accomplishment.

What happens next is probably inevitable. Your joy and satisfaction are eclipsed by the demands and stresses of the job. Sure, you might be making good money now, and you may even have your own home, car and holidays in the sun. But it comes at a cost: the cost of time, energy, sacrifice and varying degrees of stress.

When it becomes clear that education and career aren't enough in themselves to provide lasting satisfaction, you perhaps figure that what you really need in order to feel whole and complete is somebody to love you.

Your focus moves to finding Mr or Mrs "Right". After trawling the dating apps, frequenting singles bars, and possibly enduring a few failed relationships, let's say that you find your ideal partner—again, to an initial burst of euphoria. It might seem like you've finally found the love, joy and contentment you've always been seeking, first through education, then career and now through romance.

Unfortunately, the intoxicating rush of hormones you experience at the start of a relationship rarely lasts long. It's only a matter of time before the rose-tinted spectacles come off and you come to realise that, much to your horror, your partner is a human being after all, complete with their own issues, quirks and downright flaws.

After a time, the relationship is no longer fully satisfying in itself. Assuming you don't decide to end it and find another partner, you might conclude that what you need in order to be truly happy is to get married.

Yes, that'll do it! A fairytale wedding.

So, you get down on your knee, pop the question, and, assuming your partner agrees, you then set about planning the wedding to end all weddings. When the big day arrives, you experience another burst of joy—which will hopefully last at least the duration of the honeymoon before it, too, eventually wears off.

Like most things in life, you find that married life has its ups and downs. Even if you're generally happy with your partner, it's likely you still haven't found that permanent sense of joy, peace and satisfaction.

At this point, you conclude that, in order to be truly complete, what you need is to start a family. So, you have a child; and then perhaps another, and maybe even more after that.

Parenthood, you find, brings both tremendous joy and its own particular stresses, anxieties and sleepless nights.

After a time, you're still not convinced that you've hit the jackpot and found that elusive, everlasting happiness (which you still resolutely believe must exist somewhere!).

Perhaps your goals now centre on your kids; on getting them the best education and helping steer them toward a good career and then a marriage and family of their own. Maybe *that's* where true happiness lies?

When that's all taken care of, and your kids have families of their own, your focus likely shifts to your own impending retirement. You assume that when you retire and can do what you want all day long, you'll finally, *finally* have found lasting happiness...

Chasing Rainbows

It's a frustrating cycle. You've been sold dreams of lasting happiness only to discover that happiness to be limited and fleeting in nature.

As you adapt to your new circumstances, your focus shifts to the next goal, and then the next, in the vain hope that this might finally solve your problems and erase your sense of lack and craving.

Seeking lasting happiness through worldly attainment is like chasing rainbows. The rainbow might be beautiful and alluring, but no matter how hard you try and what lengths you go to, you will never reach it. The moment you try to grab hold of it, you're left holding nothing but empty air.

All things exist in a constant state of flux. Everything is constantly changing. People change, our environment changes and even our own moods, desires and values fluctuate over time.

Pleasure is, like anything phenomenal, temporary and liable to give way to pain. Many of us learn in our college days that a wild night out drinking and socialising with friends will be followed by a day spent in bed with a crippling hangover. Pleasure is by no means an unqualified blessing. You invariably must pay for it in some way.

Seeking permanency in an impermanent world is a source of great sorrow, as is the assumption that you should always get what you want.

Even if you do get what you want, the human mind is wired in such a way that we're rarely satisfied with what we have for long. Subject to the mind's inbuilt novelty bias, we tend to quickly take what we have for granted.

Sociologists call this hedonic adaptation. Put simply, we quickly become accustomed to our new car, new job, partner or lottery win. As the novelty wears off and we begin taking things for granted, we come to see the defects in the supposed objects of our dreams.

It's then only a matter of time before the mind gets restless and finds a new object of desire upon which to pin all of our hopes and dreams. After all, isn't the grass always greener on the other side?

That's why you can achieve all of your dreams and goals, become a multimillionaire and have everything that money can buy, and yet still find yourself miserable, unfulfilled and yearning for something better.

We can only conclude there are two ways to be unhappy in life. The first is to not get what you want. The second is to get what you want—and realise that, as with all things in life, it comes with a downside and doesn't, in fact, resolve your deep rooted dissatisfaction with yourself and life.

Quite the conundrum.

Perhaps it's becoming clear that, as long as you have life's basic necessities, the solution to your existential suffering is not an external one.

It doesn't matter what you do or don't do. As long as your attention is fixed solely outside of yourself, upon objects, attainments and achievements, whatever they might be, there's no way to find permanent and lasting happiness.

Fulfilling your various desires and whims does not address the underlying problem of want.

Happiness Doesn't Come From Things

The Maitiri Upanishad, one of the source texts of Vedanta, dating back at least two millennia, speaks of the human predicament:

> The human soul is conditioned by the threefold qualities of matter and thus falls into delusion. Because of this delusion [samsara], the soul is unable to realise the shining Self, pure Consciousness, dwelling within; the power by which one lives and breathes. The soul is whirled along the rushing stream of muddy waters, confused yet unyielding and prideful, unable to see with clarity and subject to endless frustrated desires. Fixated on the sense of "I" and "mine", it binds itself like a bird in the net of a snare.

This basically sums up the problem of samsara, the existential suffering of humankind, introduced in the previous chapter. The word samsara literally means to "revolve", as if mounted upon a wheel, through successive states of birth, death and rebirth.

What keeps us bound to this wheel of samsara is worldly attachment and desire. Like an old millstone, this particular wheel steadily grinds us down as we vainly seek infinite happiness in the finite world of objects and experience.

The samsari looks to the outside world to provide them with happiness, wholeness and fulfilment. They do so by hungrily pursuing, acquiring and devouring various objects, experiences and possessions.

Of course, it's only natural that we want certain things. This is a transactional reality. We live by taking action in the world. That's what enables us to live, function and hopefully thrive. We are hungry, so we eat. We are tired, so we sleep. We need money, so we work. We're a goal oriented species and we naturally crave company, community and meaning.

The problem is clear, however. If your happiness is dependent upon external factors then it's a highly precarious happiness.

Why?

Well, for a start, we have only limited control of external variables. Not only that, but as we've established, everything in this world is subject to duality and, as such, is highly changeable and impermanent.

Objects themselves are neither inherently good nor bad. It's the human mind, driven by its accumulated likes and dislikes, which superimposes certain values onto an object. It then becomes either "good" or "bad" to us; desirable or undesirable.

It's also important to understand that the happiness we experience when we get what we want is not actually coming from the object itself.

Consider this. If happiness was inherent to a particular object, that object would bring equal joy to each and every person.

That's clearly not the case. One person's idea of bliss might be sitting in a library reading books, while another person is illiterate, can't stand books and instead gets their kicks from extreme sports. A child may experience joy watching Saturday morning cartoons, while an adult might find those same cartoons unwatchable, instead preferring to watch historical documentaries (which most kids would find interminably boring).

The joy we experience is, therefore, never in the actual object or experience itself. It's superimposed onto the object as determined by our personal values and likes and dislikes.

We Seek Freedom From Desire

At best, the objects of our desires are proxies. They seem to bring us joy because the moment we get what we want, the desire that prompted us to seek it has been extinguished. For that instant, we are temporarily freed from our aching sense of lack, insufficiency and want—and we experience the bliss and peace of desirelessness.

You've probably never thought of it this way before but, make no mistake, desire is suffering.

We only want things when we are driven by a sense of lack; and such limitation is painful to us. To want is to suffer; to be lacking and incomplete. Freedom from want is experienced as bliss.

As we'll explore in later chapters, this bliss is actually a taste of our own essential nature. Where else would it come from? It doesn't come from outside of us, although that might certainly seem to be the case. It comes from within; when the mind is sufficiently calm and free of the turbulent waves of dissatisfaction and want.

Unfortunately, as long as our focus remains strictly object oriented (and Vedanta defines "object" as anything perceivable by the mind and senses), you can guarantee the pleasure will be temporary.

The moment it wears off, our inner sense of lack again returns and we shift our attention to the next object of our desire.

It's little wonder that our happiness always seems to be just over the horizon—only, try though we might (and we *really* do try), we can never reach it.

The Price of Samsara

Samsara, the compulsion to seek happiness outside of ourselves, comes with multiple problems.

1. Attachment

By superimposing certain desirable qualities onto an object, we easily become attached to that object. We see it as essential to our happiness; as something we cannot live without; something we must acquire, possess and keep no matter the cost. Here lies the root of psychological addiction. Something appears to bring us pleasure, so we want to keep hold of it and never let it go. If you've ever seen a dog with a bone, you'll know exactly what I mean when I speak of attachment.

2. Mental Disturbance

Such attachment inevitably leads to mental disturbance. Our mind gets clouded and we fail to see things as they actually are, free of the qualities we're superimposing onto them. This compromises our ability to see and deal with life objectively.

When we're under the delusion that X, Y or Z will bring us unending happiness and satisfaction, we're out of touch with reality. We're seeing what we want to see rather than what's actually there.

We expect certain objects to continually fulfil us, to bring us pleasure and joy, and we're quite unprepared when we have to deal with the inevitable downside to those objects, not least the fact that we cannot hold onto anything indefinitely.

3. Anxiety and Grief

Attachment inevitably leads to suffering. When we become attached to an object, the fear of losing it can generate tremendous anxiety and that's to say nothing of the grief we experience if and when we do.

Human psychology isn't actually as complex as you might think. When it comes to our attachments and aversions, like children, we basically want what we want, when we want it. When we don't get it, we experience upset, whether in the form of tears and tantrums, bitterness or rage, depression or anxiety. Much of our sorrow basically boils down to life not giving us what we want.

4. Delusion

The resultant anger, sorrow and grief leads to delusion. This delusion, in time, can incapacitate our mind altogether.

An incapacitated, grief stricken mind is unable to think and process reality objectively. At worst, we lose the capacity to discriminate between right and wrong, between what's truly important in life and what only seems important in the context of our desires and attachments.

Like the snake devouring its own tail, the samsari self-destructively expects the world to deliver more than it's capable of delivering—and then suffers like hell when it doesn't. This relentless cycle of seeking, acquiring and losing objects is most certainly not the solution to the problem of self-lack.

Samsara is the false expectation that, if you can just bring the world into alignment with your desires and aversions—if you can get what you want and avoid what you don't want—you'll get your "happy ever after" ending.

Let's look at this from another angle.

How can you be happy if your happiness is dependent upon external variables?

For a start, you're never truly in control of anything outside of yourself. All objects in duality are, by nature, finite and fleeting. Try though you might, you can never hold onto anything for any length of time. There's simply no permanence to be found in an impermanent world.

The stronger your attachment, the more your mind will be a bubbling cauldron of desire and anxiety. You become an addict; hopelessly dependent upon objects and experiences for temporary bursts of happiness. You seek experience after experience, always desperate for the next hit.

You may even become so addicted to your desired objects that the very thought of losing them is akin to death. You may have heard the stories of Wall Street brokers jumping out of their windows when the stock market collapsed in 1929. Those poor souls were so identified with their jobs and with money that they simply couldn't conceive living without it.

5. Violating Dharma

Another danger when you become addicted to objects is that your desire for those objects may supersede your commitment to dharma.

Dharma manifests our inherent sense of right and wrong. It means doing the right thing and responding appropriately to life in any given situation or circumstance.

People whose desires have spiralled into uncontrolled attachment may be liable to do all kinds of questionable things in order to get their way. At best, they might simply cut corners and bend the rules here and there. At worst, they may be willing to break the law and actively harm others. Basically, their desire becomes so strong that they end up causing untold suffering to both themselves and others.

This can be seen at both an individual and collective level. The human race is so deeply enmeshed in samsara that we've been living in an insanely self-destructive manner; willing to sacrifice the planet upon which we depend, and all our children's futures, for whatever short term monetary gains we can acquire.

The Problem is You

Let's forget about the world for now, though. The fundamental problem, the very root of your suffering, is not the world even with all its strife and turmoil. It lies much closer to home.

The source of your sorrows is—you.

Samsara is born of a deep sense of personal lack; the feeling that what you are is somehow deficient and inadequate; that you don't have enough and that you aren't good enough.

That's what you're ultimately seeking in life: the basic sense of being sufficient, adequate, whole, worthy and complete.

As subsequent chapters will explore in some depth, your dissatisfaction with yourself is based upon ignorance; delusion.

The delusion in question?

Because you experience a body, sense organs and a mind, you've assumed that this must be what you are: a crude merging of mind and matter, subject to birth, death and all kinds of limitations in between.

By superimposing your sense of self onto the body and mind, you've contracted the vastness of your being into a limited, time-bound entity called a "person".

Regardless of personal circumstances, human beings universally make the same misidentification and are united by the same sense of limitation and incompleteness.

This sense of limitation gives rise to desire; which then spurs us to seek completeness wherever we can.

Because the senses are automatically hooked to world of objects, that's precisely where we channel our search for wholeness. It's also hardly surprising when, from a young age, we are bombarded by advertisements and media messages convincing us that we need certain objects and experiences in order to be happy.

The greater our sense of lack and self-limitation, the stronger our desires and the more desperate our search to find love, wholeness, validation and happiness outside of ourselves.

Driven by misplaced desire, we become obsessed with getting what we want and avoiding what we don't want. Our lives become an exercise in manipulating the world to our fancy.

Human beings are naturally goal-seeking creatures. So, it's absolutely fine to want to improve your life situation and there's no problem at all with pursuing material objects and experiences.

However, if you're attempting to overcome your basic sense of self-dissatisfaction by simply rearranging the circumstances of your life, it's very much a wasted endeavour. It doesn't ultimately matter how much money you make, how many luxury holidays you go on a year or how successful you become in business or love. It won't fix the underlying problem.

The issue is not that "your life" isn't the way you want it to be.

There are people out there who lack any form of material wealth and who still live happy and fulfilled lives, irrespective of their situation. Conversely, some of the richest and most successful people on the face of the planet suffer crippling despair, anxiety and unrelenting misery.

The problem, therefore, is not your life. The root of the problem is the idea you have about yourself; this notion that what you are isn't enough.

Whatever object you happen to want, it's never the object itself you're really after. What you want is to feel better, to be different, to be whole, complete and free of lack.

That's the fundamental human want; the need to feel whole and complete. You cannot be happy in the absence of this.

Your attempts to find wholeness outside of you are doomed to constant failure. While you certainly have it in your power to achieve and accumulate certain things, there's no way you can get what you want all the time. Life simply isn't set up that way.

That's both bad news and good news.

It's bad news for the wanting, needing little person ravaged by desire and fear. It's good news when you realise that, although life isn't here to fulfil your every wish, it is here to wake you up; to break your heart open and reveal that deep within, you already have and are everything you could ever possibly want.

The Solution is You

The crucial takeaway here is the acknowledgement that your suffering is not caused by the fact you're not getting what you want from life.

The real problem is self-ignorance.

You have assumed yourself to be something limited and lacking; a person subject to all kinds of limitation, want and sorrow. You have taken yourself to be what you are not. That's the fundamental message of Vedanta. You've imagined yourself to be a beggar when you are, in fact, a king or queen.

In time, you may actually be glad that you didn't manage to hold God to ransom and force Him to deliver your long list of worldly desires and demands. Instead, you'll be grateful that you finally came to realise that the true treasure is within; that the freedom you long sought was always and only within you as the very essence of your own Consciousness.

There's no way to "win" at samsara within samsara. The only solution is to break free of it altogether, and, as we'll see in the next chapter, that's what the fourth and final life goal, enlightenment, is all about.

Summary

- We all seek freedom because limitation is not natural to us. To be free is to be happy and happiness is the goal of all beings.
- Ignorance makes us seek lasting happiness outside of us when, in actuality, happiness can only be found within.
- Desire is suffering. Freedom from desire is experienced as bliss.
- The cost of samsara is great. It causes attachment, mental disturbance, anxiety and grief, delusion and the tendency to violate dharma, hurting both ourselves and others.
- The real problem is our innermost sense of lack and insufficiency; the sense that who and what we are is not enough.
- This is caused by a misidentification; by identifying ourselves with the body and mind rather than with the Consciousness we are.

3.
Life's Highest Goal

Knowing the Self to be limitless, deathless and free, delusion is vanquished, freeing the soul from bondage to the things of this world. That is enlightenment.

Bhagavad Gita

We've now ascertained that the core human problem is the suffering caused by self-ignorance.

In short, we have assumed ourselves to be nothing but a body/mind/ego subject to the ravages of time and fate. Consumed by a fundamental sense of lack and want, we've tried to break free by focusing upon the world of objects and pursuing various desires, attachments and addictions.

This, of course, comes with many downsides; not least the fact that all objects are ultimately impermanent, changeable and rarely under our direct control. What's worse, when our desire eclipses our commitment to dharma, we may even find ourselves inclined to harm others and the environment around us in our desperation to get what we want. Needless to say, this does nothing but generate more suffering, both for others and ourselves.

Fortunately, there is a way out of this quandary. For Vedanta reveals a fourth and final human pursuit; the highest of all goals and the ultimate purpose of life. It's called *moksha*, which translates as liberation, freedom or enlightenment.

THE FOUR HUMAN PURSUITS

The Fourth Human Pursuit: Enlightenment

For the average person, life generally revolves around the first two human pursuits: security and pleasure. The mature, refined human being also makes the third goal, dharma, a priority, as it should be. Indeed, dharma, which entails doing the right thing in every situation, should always form the basis and foundation for our entire life.

Precious few, however, will ever truly commit to life's final and highest goal. Many people aren't even aware that it legitimately exists. Even those who know of enlightenment, and may be actively pursuing it, are often hampered by the many misconceptions and contradictory ideas that exist around it.

When we lack clarity with regard to a topic, the mind will tend to fill in the blanks itself. Because the unenlightened mind is driven by ignorance, our thoughts, beliefs and assumptions will, therefore, be conditioned by ignorance. We automatically create our own meanings and definitions; and we cling to them, even if they have little basis in empirical fact.

In order to understand something, we must first reach a consensus about what it actually is. That's why it's essential to clearly define what enlightenment is; and, just as importantly, what it isn't.

What Enlightenment Isn't

As noted in the introduction, the modern spiritual scene is swamped with enlightenment myths. Some are plainly wacky whereas others might seem to make perfect sense until you apply a little logic and they begin crumbling apart.

Although by no means an exhaustive list, here's a brief rundown on what enlightenment is *not*.

1. Superhuman States and Cosmic Bliss

Many seekers have the appealing yet erroneous notion that enlightenment means attaining some kind of superhuman state; a kind of endless cosmic orgasm in which you experience permanent bliss and various omniscient powers.

Such people are in for a tremendous disappointment, not because states of heightened spiritual consciousness aren't possible, for they are, but because no experience lasts. All states are finite and subject to a beginning and end.

What's more, the need to chase these exalted spiritual states is actually an impediment to liberation. The reason is simple. If your freedom is dependant upon achieving and maintaining a certain experience, however subtle and sublime, then it's not freedom at all, because the moment the experiences changes, as it most certainly will, your freedom goes out the window along with it.

Although there's certainly nothing wrong with seeking spiritual highs, it potentially comes at a cost: namely, attachment, addiction and dependence; the very essence of bondage. Being a spiritual junkie can distract you from the nuts and bolts of what enlightenment actually is.

True liberation must be independent of whatever experience you happen to be having, or it's not liberation at all. Enlightenment is unconditional, permanent and not dependent upon any extraneous factor, or it isn't enlightenment at all.

2. Cessation of Thought

Some teachings paint enlightenment as the attainment of no-mind, or a thought-free state. However, enlightenment isn't about emptying the mind of all thoughts.

It's true that, upon liberation, your relationship to mind and thought will change. You become more detached toward the content of your mind, no longer identifying with the various thoughts, beliefs and ideas you hold about yourself and others. You'll likely also experience a quieter, more tranquil mind and periods where mental activity slows right down or even suspends altogether.

That isn't enlightenment in itself, however. It's simply the mind at rest; purified, refined and undisturbed by the relentless barrage of desire and fear that characterise the mind of a samsari.

Thought itself isn't the enemy. After all, it's the nature of the mind to think. That's fine; let the mind think! The secret is the quality of your thinking. In order to be free, all that's necessary is to weed out thoughts conditioned by ignorance and replace them with thoughts of truth. That's what Vedanta will teach you to do.

3. Destruction of the Ego

The idea that enlightenment means the destruction of the ego is another misconception. The ego doesn't need to be destroyed. Which is just as well, because without it you wouldn't be able to function in the world. Whenever somebody called your name you'd be unable to respond because you'd have no way of associating that name with you.

So, it's neither necessary nor possible to destroy the ego. All that's necessary is to disidentify from it. The ego is part of you, but is *not* you. It's a component of the subtle body (which, as we will see in later chapters, is comprised of the mind, intellect and ego). The ego is not the enemy as long as you see it for what it is; a tool enabling Consciousness to function in matter. The only destruction involved in enlightenment is the destruction of self-ignorance.

4. Mindfulness and Present Moment Awareness

Mindfulness, the ability to be fully present in the here and now, is an important quality to develop in life.

As long as we are fully in touch with the present moment we are unlikely to be swept away by the mind's various storms, stories and fantasies. This relates to mastery of the mind and is one of the important qualifications for attaining liberation, as we shall see.

It doesn't equate to enlightenment in itself, however. Simply putting your attention on the present moment is a wonderful practice and a rewarding way to live, but it won't resolve the fundamental problem of samsara.

Only Self-Knowledge can do that by eradicating the ignorance that causes us to feel empty, lacking and addictively attached to the world of objects.

5. Kundalini, Energy Bodies and Ascension

Some traditions, such as Taoism and certain forms of yoga, purport enlightenment to be some kind of energy shift.

Taoists often focus on the cultivation of spiritual energy, Qi or prana, which they believe is then used to construct a kind of immortal energy body. Yoga practitioners may dedicate themselves to the raising of the kundalini and various mystic experiences that come with it. Similarly, New Age teachings talk of ascension, whereby you supposedly merge your "lower self" into a "higher self".

These ideas are based on the presupposition that enlightenment is a process of becoming; becoming something different, something better, something more exalted and holy. Such concepts are subtly, or not so subtly, rooted in the dualistic notion that what you are is some kind of lower self, or ego-self, which must then be transformed into a greater spiritual Self.

Vedanta negates this idea. There's nothing you have to *do* or *become* in order to be free. The scriptures are very clear on this. There is only *one* Self—and you are already That! What else could you be? Only ignorance of your nature has prevented you from apprehending what you truly are.

So, fortunately, you don't have to do, achieve or transform anything in order to "become" your Self.

Which is just as well, because any action is subject to the laws of duality and will, therefore, be inherently limited and finite. It's impossible to create a limitless result from a limited action. Not only that, but anything that has a beginning will necessarily have an end.

The solution, then, does not involve adding something to yourself in any way. Enlightenment is a process of removal—specifically, the removal of ignorance. As the great sage Ramana Maharshi said:

> Is there any moment when the Self is not? It is not new. Be as you are. What is new cannot be permanent. What is Real must always exist.

What Enlightenment Is

Enlightenment means freedom; freedom from limitation, lack and the innermost sense of self-dissatisfaction that universally blights human beings.

The radical contention of Vedanta is that you don't need to go anywhere or do anything in order to gain that freedom.

It's not something that you can acquire and add to yourself.

Which is just as well, because anything that can be gained can be lost.

Fortunately, although this may not seem to be the case, the freedom you seek is already within you. For freedom is the nature of the Self, and, whether you realise it or not, it's this very Self that you've been looking for your entire life.

Well, look no further.

The Self is already present, attained and always available. Although it might seem to be hidden, that's simply the effect of ignorance.

You've known all along that you exist; that you *are*. You just haven't known *what* you are.

The problem all along was ignorance. Your entire life, ignorance has covered the mind like an impenetrable cloud, obscuring your perception of reality and distorting your vision of who you are.

Through ignorance, you superimposed your innermost sense of Self, of "I am-ness" onto the instruments of the body, mind and ego.

This naturally generates a tremendous sense of lack and limitation. Why? Because the body, mind and ego are subject to suffering, mortality and the ravages of time and fate.

This misapprehension compelled you to seek wholeness by manipulating the things of the world; by acquiring various objects, attainments and experiences. Of course, the joy of acquisition is temporary at best and everything in duality is subject to an inevitable downside.

Perhaps you can now see that if ignorance is the problem, and it is, the only solution can be knowledge.

That's why we have Vedanta, the ancient science of Self-Knowledge.

Fortunately, Vedanta isn't telling you anything you don't want to hear. In fact, the news is pretty darn wonderful.

Whereas before enlightenment, your experience of life was one of unsatisfactoriness and inadequacy, Self-Knowledge liberates the mind, intellect and heart, as you come to realise that all these limitations were false. They were caused by self-misidentification. You were never the body, mind or ego, nor some conglomeration of thoughts, beliefs, emotions, desires and fears.

You were always and only *the Awareness* in which these objects are experienced.

If you think about it, the essence of a room is not the objects it contains, but the space in which the objects are arranged. You can remove each and every object and the room will still remain the room. The objects are incidental; the space inside the room is the pervading essence.

In the same way, you are not your body, mind, nor your thoughts and feelings. You are the Awareness, the Consciousness; the very light in which these things are experienced and known.

Self-Knowledge, when firmly established in the mind, yields freedom.

It's worth repeating: this freedom isn't something that you have to add to yourself. Anything that can be added can be removed.

Instead, you realise that you were always free.

Freedom is your very nature; your very essence.

Only the mind, under the spell of ignorance, makes it seem otherwise.

By committing to this teaching and allowing Self-Knowledge to take root in the mind, your sense of identity will gradually shift from the body, mind and ego to the Awareness in which they appear.

As a result, you finally experience freedom from the lack and incompleteness that has ravaged your mind and heart for years, decades and, yes, even lifetimes.

This fundamental cognitive shift changes both nothing and everything.

Outwardly you will still appear to be the same person. Inwardly, however, you know that you are far more. You realise that, in spite of the limitations inherent in matter, you are free of suffering, sorrow and any sense of limitation. These pertain to the body and mind, but not the Awareness in which they are contained.

Awareness is free—and you are Awareness!

Objects and experiences still arise and subside in the substratum of your Awareness. You are free to enjoy them, but you're no longer compelled to desperately seek, grasp and attach yourself to them.

You have nothing to prove to anybody, because you know, with the entirety of your being, that you are already whole and complete. Nothing can be added the totality of what you are and nothing can be taken from you either. Because you are other than the body and mind you are no longer subject to their defects and dysfunctions. They are but instruments through which you, Awareness, express yourself.

Once again, although this might be hard to grasp, enlightenment isn't a process of attainment as such. This Self, pure Awareness, is not something you have to attain or become. It's already present, fully existent—and, as the ancient Vedantic proclamation *Tat Twam Asi* states, I Am That (or, literally, "That, You Are")!

Unenlightenment is merely ignorance; the failure to apprehend the true nature of your Self and Reality.

Your old concept of yourself was distorted by ignorance and this ignorance generated tremendous suffering. It's as though you've been living with a blindfold over your eyes your entire life, forcing you to grope your way through the dark when, in actuality, it's daylight all around.

Enlightenment is the application of Self-Knowledge to the mind and intellect. It's a radical revision of who you think you are. We will explore this in much greater detail as we progress, so don't worry if it's not clicking at this early juncture.

Knowledge, of course, can only be gained with the appropriate means of knowledge. In order to see objects in the visual field, you require eyes and the capacity for sight. To register sound, you require ears and the capacity for hearing, and so on with taste, touch and smell.

When it comes to the Self, our means of knowledge is Vedanta.

An ancient body of Knowledge, not attributable to any particular person or group of people, Vedanta is a tool to eradicate ignorance and reorient you to a full and lasting appreciation of your own essential nature.

The next chapter explores the origin of Vedanta, how it works and how it can be used to remove self-ignorance and open the door to enlightenment.

Summary

- According to the scriptures, enlightenment, or liberation, is life's highest goal.
- Very few will ever realise, understand and commit to this goal. They either aren't aware that it exists or they are hampered by the many misconceptions and contradictory ideas that exist around the topic.
- In order to understand what enlightenment is, it's helpful to be aware of what it isn't.
- Enlightenment isn't some kind of superhuman state complete with cosmic powers and heightened states of consciousness. Liberation isn't about experience; it's about being free regardless of your experience.
- Enlightenment is not about the cessation of thought or the destruction of the ego. Thought and ego are not the problem; identifying with them is the true problem.

- Mindfulness does not equate to enlightenment, although it is a highly beneficial and recommended practice. Enlightenment is also not about kundalini, energy bodies, states of cosmic bliss.
- Many enlightenment myths are based on the notion that you have to do some action in order to "become" the Self. Vedanta reveals you already are the Self.
- Enlightenment is freedom through Self-Knowledge.
- Self-Knowledge destroys our misidentification with the body, mind and ego and all of their problems and suffering.

4.
Vedanta: Roadmap to Freedom

The subject matter of Vedanta is a single desire: the desire for liberation. The fulfilment of this desire is not through actions, which are many, but through Knowledge, which is singular with regard to that which is to be known—oneself.
Swami Dayananda Saraswati

What if I told you that great the mysteries of existence—the nature of reality, God, Consciousness, humankind and our purpose in life—had already been solved thousands of years ago?

Indeed, life's supposed unanswerables were unravelled with breathtaking scope and clarity back in India's Vedic period, dating from pre 500 BCE.

The crowning achievement of the Vedic age, the Vedas, are quite unparalleled in the history of the world and represent nothing less than a Divine gift to humanity. It's from these ancient scriptures that we find the Upanishads, the primary source texts of Vedanta.

The Vedas

The Vedas are a voluminous collection of hymns, prayers, rituals and dialogues which form the basis of Sanatana Dharma, or the "Eternal

Truth". (Today, we use the term Hinduism, although Hinduism isn't a religion as such. "Hindu" was a geographical term originally used to describe the people living around the Indus River, or the Sindhu River as it was called in Sanskrit; mispronounced by the Persians as "Hindu".)

It was during this age of antiquity that ancient mystics devoted their lives to understanding and unravelling the mysteries of creation. They did so by purifying their minds and turning their attention inward, meditating deeply upon the nature of God and Reality.

Over many years, the knowledge gained by their intense and profound spiritual explorations gave rise to the Vedas.

The Vedas (which mean "Knowledge"), constitute a science of life, society, duty and metaphysical discourse.

Long before the advent of written language, the mantras of the Vedas were recited and shared orally from generation to generation.

The sage Vyasa is credited with compiling the Vedas into four distinct volumes: the Rig Veda, the oldest and largest of the four, as well as the Yajur Veda, the Sama Veda and the Atharva Veda.

Crucially, according to tradition, these monumental works are not a product of the human intellect. No particular person or group of people authored the Vedas. Rather, they are considered "revealed knowledge", or divine revelations. The seers, or *rishis*, who received the knowledge, are said to be intermediaries. Rather like a radio set, they tuned their exceptionally pure, subtle minds into particular sound frequencies and then shared them in the form of Sanskrit mantras. These same mantras have been recited with exacting precision (using certain mnemonic techniques to prevent distortion or alteration) down the centuries and millennia.

A great deal of debate exists over when the Vedas were composed, with some dating the Rig Veda to around 11,000 BCE, while more conservative scholars suggest 1,000 BCE.

Either way, the knowledge is considered timeless. While much is specific to Vedic culture, its themes—the nature of God, Reality and humankind—transcend time, place and culture.

Back at a time when human beings lived in much closer alignment with the natural world, the elements and forces of nature are personified as deities, such as Agni, god of fire, Varuna, god of the sky, rain and water, and Surya, the sun deity. While some might dismiss this as primitive, the Vedas are, in fact, highly complex and advanced, displaying a remarkable understanding of the cosmology of the universe, the workings of nature as well as human psychology, health and physiology.

Among other things, the Vedas categorise four stages of life, or *ashramas*, that all humans must go through.

The first is the student stage, in which education and learning are a priority, followed by the householder stage, in which a person pursues a career and typically starts a family. In time, this leads to the retirement stage in which one gradually withdraws from social life and obligations. This is followed by the final and highest stage of human development: the quest for enlightenment.

Also outlined are the *varnas*; four divisions of vocation based upon a person's constitutional and psychological makeup.

The priest class is considered the highest, highlighting the immense regard Vedic culture had for spiritual knowledge as the guiding light for all of society. Next up, are the administrative class; government leaders, advisers and the people who defend the society. Then come the merchant class and the labour class, those who are essentially the arms and legs of society.

A key theme of the Vedas is dharma, a topic we've already introduced and will explore later explore in greater detail.

The word has multiple meanings depending upon the context, but essentially refers to the inherent, essential nature of a given thing.

All things were created to contribute to the universe a certain way, including human beings. Dharma means to follow your own nature and to adhere to the underlying cosmic order; to do the right thing at the right time in the right way. The Vedas make it clear that we must all learn to recognise and play our appropriate part in the game of life.

The Upanishads

The Vedas can be broken into two particular sections. The first section deals with the first three human pursuits we outlined: security, pleasure and dharma. These sections offer countless prayers and rituals to be employed in daily life to help us achieve various ends relating to worldly living, success and enjoyment.

The final section of each Veda is exclusively devoted to the fourth and final human goal: enlightenment. This takes the form of the Upanishads.

The word Upanishad literally means to "sit by the feet of" the teacher, or guru, and thus allow the sacred Knowledge to flow from the Master to disciple.

The Upanishads, like the Vedas, take the form of Sanskrit mantras and, through various dialogues and poetic stories, explore a range of topics, including the nature of Consciousness, God, the individual soul, the process of Creation, life and death, reincarnation, meditation, worship and, of course, enlightenment.

Over two hundred Upanishads are known, of which a hundred and eight are considered canonical and ten are deemed "major", or primary, Upanishads.

These primary Upanishads are the Katha Upanishad, Kena Upanishad, Mandukya Upanishad, Isha Upanishad, Prasna Upanishad, Mundaka Upanishad, Chandogya Upanishad, Brihadaranyaka Upanishad, Aitreya Upanishad and Taittiriya Upanishad.

The primary topic is Brahman, or the universal Self; the singular, all-pervading Reality from which all name and form has its root and eternal basis.

The highest truth of the Upanishads is the inherent oneness of Reality and the non-difference between the individual and God. In other words, all things are Divine, even if not all things outwardly express that Divinity.

The purpose of life, according to the Upanishads, is to realise our oneness with the Divine Self and, by doing so, resolve all worldly bondage and sorrow.

Vedanta: The End of Knowledge

The Upanishads are synonymous with and, indeed, form the very basis of Vedanta.

The term Vedanta is a compound taken from the words *Veda* (knowledge) and *anta* (the end of). Vedanta can be taken to mean "the end of the Vedas" because the Upanishads comprise the end portions of each Veda. It can also be translated as "the end of knowledge", for it is, in fact, the knowledge to end all knowledge; that by knowing which, one understands the essence of all things.

Vedanta might be considered the systematic distillation of the teachings of the Upanishads. It deals primarily with the question of self-identity and finding liberation from worldly suffering through Self-Knowledge; which is to say, knowledge of our inherent Divinity as pure, limitless, unchanging Consciousness.

In addition to the Upanishads, two other sources form part of Vedanta's "triple canon". The first is known as the Brahma Sutra, or the Vedanta Sutra. This work is credited to Badarayana, who lived sometime between the 5th century BCE and the 2nd or 3rd century CE. A somewhat involved and intricate treatise, the Brahma Sutra summarises and clarifies the main teachings of the Upanishads and seeks to resolve various arguments and conflicts with other teachings.

The third primary source text of Vedanta is the Bhagavad Gita. This famous and highly beloved scripture is a part of the quasi-historical epic Mahabharata. Composed by the sage-scribe Vyasa, the Mahabharata remains one of India's crowning achievements; a sprawling tale covering an immense span of time and detailing a momentous civil war between two powerful families.

The Bhagavad Gita forms a brief but central part of the Mahabharata narrative. It takes the form of a dialogue between the warrior-prince Arjuna and his Divine mentor, Krishna, on the eve of a bloody battle. Dealing with topics of action and duty, meditation, devotion and the true nature of the Self, the Bhagavad Gita is a perfect manual for both daily living and the attainment of enlightenment. Adi Shankara believed that if a person was to only read a single Vedantic text, it ought be the Bhagavad Gita.

While the Upanishads, Brahma Sutra and Bhagavad Gita form Vedanta's primary source texts, a range of other sutras expound the teaching in short, simple verse form. These secondary scriptures unfold some of the more complex and intricate aspects of the teaching with remarkable clarity and succinctness.

The Visionary Shankara

Perhaps the most pivotal contributor to Vedanta was the eighth century visionary Adi Shankara, also known as Adi Shankaracharya (*acharya* meaning "great teacher").

With an unparalleled intellect and a fierce commitment to reform, Shankara set out to eradicate an element of corruption and distortion that had crept into the priest cast and lineage holders at that time.

Shankara took the teaching and consolidated it into a clear and fully realised vision in a way nobody had done before. His commentaries on the Vedantic texts, and his own contributions, are considered landmark works.

He traveled the length and breadth of the country, establishing schools, engaging in public debates, countering the rise of Buddhism and re-establishing the Vedas as the primary spiritual and religious heart of India. Indeed, the decline of Buddhism in India and the resurgence of Sanatana Dharma and Vedanta, is attributed to Shankara's razor sharp intellect and profound spiritual writings.

While a few other schools of thought later emerged based upon the Vedantic teaching, including dualistic interpretations, Shankara's school, Advaita Vedanta (Advaita literally means "not-two", or Non-dual) remains the primary and most celebrated lineage of Vedantic thought.

Shankara stressed the Non-dual nature of Reality. In spite of appearance, which makes us seem to be living in a world of subject-object based duality, all experience, perception and knowledge presupposes a perceiver; a Self that experiences and knows the various objects presenting themselves in the world of form.

The nature of this Self, the Upanishads declare, is pure Consciousness/Awareness. This Consciousness is not personal, but universal in nature.

A helpful metaphor is to think of the sun. The same sun shines upon all the reflective surfaces in the world. If we only see the reflection, we might conclude that the light shining on a window is different to the light shining in a puddle or a lake. However, although the reflecting mediums are many in number, the light is actually one. So, too, with the Self.

This universal Consciousness, which animates and enlivens all the bodies and minds, is called *Brahman* in Vedantic terminology; or the Eternal Self. This Self, without limit or differentiation, is of the nature of Existence, Consciousness and the Bliss of limitlessness.

While the world of form exists as a kaleidoscope of perpetual change and motion, and our bodies and minds are subject to constant modification and eventual death, the Self is eternal and unchanging. It is unaffected by anything in the world of form because it occupies a different order of Reality.

The full realisation of this Self, and the shifting of our centre of identification from the limited body and mind to this limitless Consciousness, liberates the individual from worldly suffering.

This freedom from bondage is called enlightenment or liberation; the highest goal available to humanity and the ultimate purpose of life.

The Three Stages of Vedanta

Vedanta is taught in a deliberate and carefully structured way. The teaching progresses through a certain sequence of logic and it's important to fully grasp each step before moving onto the next. We start small and gradually expand to the bigger, full picture.

There are three essential stages to the teaching: listening, reasoning and contemplation. Let's take a brief look at each.

1. Listening

The first stage is simple enough, at least in theory. All that you require is a capable teacher and an open, reasonably calm and focused mind. The teacher teaches with the aid of various Vedantic texts and the student listens. Simple though it is, that alone can pose a significant challenge to many.

Vedanta isn't for everyone. A certain degree of mental preparation is necessary and this will be covered in detail in the next chapter.

As with many things in life, whether a university course or a particular job, certain qualifications are necessary. Once the entry requirements have been met, all you need to do is sit, clear your mind of preconceptions and listen as the teacher unfolds the teaching from beginning to end.

Bear in mind that it's necessary to have a teacher; one well versed in the teaching methodology and established in their nature as the Self. Ideally, the teacher should be part of a recognised lineage and not somebody with their own teaching and interpretations of the scriptures.

A lot of modern teachers mix and match elements of the teaching, borrowing a little from this and a little from that, attempting to cobble together their own teaching. That rarely works, for it's all too easy for subjective biases to creep in and distort the purity of the teaching.

The Vedantic teaching has been carefully guarded over the centuries in order to keep it pure and fully aligned with the vision of Shankara and the visionaries who transcribed the Upanishads.

People often think they can go it alone and read their way to enlightenment. Again, that rarely yields fruit. Your own pre-existing ideas, assumptions and prejudices—not to mention the issue of confirmation bias and the mind's tendency to simply want to confirm what it already believes—will almost certainly trip you up. It's vital that you approach Vedanta on its terms and not your own.

That's why it's essential to approach both the teacher and the teaching with a mindset of openness and humility. It's necessary to discard your pre-conceived notions in order to fully hear what is being said.

Don't make the mistake of measuring the teaching against what you think you already know. Harsh though this may sound, if your knowledge was already on point, you'd no longer be seeking enlightenment; you'd be there already.

Vedanta works when you approach it with what the Zen tradition calls a "beginner's mind"; when you are open to listening with a mind that's keen and eager to learn.

This first stage of Vedanta might last months or years. You simply expose your mind to the teaching, over and over again, until it gradually begins to click. Don't be in a hurry to rush to the end. Be patient, for you have all the time in the world. Resist the urge to skip over the bits you don't find as interesting, eager to get to the "juicy" stuff. Each topic feeds into the next, as the teaching is unfolded in a carefully considered, sequential manner.

A traditional Vedanta teacher uses Vedantic scriptures as the basis of the teaching. This may include beginner texts such as Shankara's Tattva Bodha (Knowledge of Truth), or the Bhagavad Gita, the Upanishads or any number of secondary texts such as Atma Bodha, Vivekachudamani and Panchadasi. Each verse is recited and then explained in some detail, allowing the student to gradually build their understanding and knowledge.

2. Reasoning

The next stage, which can run concurrently with the first, is to make sure that you understand what is being taught.

It's not enough to simply listen and accept things on faith alone. Vedanta isn't about blind faith. Of course, a certain degree of faith is required in order to commit the necessary time and energy. If you don't trust both the veracity of the knowledge and the skill and integrity of the teacher you won't get far at all.

It's not, however, a case of simply taking somebody's word for it. You must actively contemplate what's being taught and ensure that you understand the logic.

This is where you begin to see the necessity of a teacher. You need somebody to guide you and help you work through any doubts, blocks and misunderstandings. Regardless of your education and mental acuity, you can guarantee there will be concepts or ideas that you struggle to "get", at least to begin with. Doubts are a silent killer and must be resolved. It's important to be able to dialogue with your teacher and ask the necessary questions. Be honest and open; they are there to help you.

Believe it or not, there are no questions that haven't already been asked and resolved by Vedanta teachers over the centuries. Just about every conceivable doubt or objection has been dealt with in advanced texts such as the Brahma Sutra. If you find yourself stumped at any point, either keep listening, because there's a good chance any questions will be dealt with as the teaching progresses—or ask. In general, Vedanta teachers don't bite!

3. Contemplation

The third and all-important final step is to convert your newfound Self-Knowledge into conviction. Until the knowledge has been fully assimilated it won't lead to liberation from suffering; which is, of course, the entire point of the teaching and the reason Vedanta exists.

If you've been studying Vedanta for some time and understand everything that's been taught but still aren't experiencing the fruits of that Knowledge, it's a sure sign that you need to devote more time to this final stage: the deep contemplation of the basic truth, "I am not the body-mind, but the Consciousness/Awareness pervading them."

This contemplation takes the form of Vedantic meditation; the art of reconditioning the mind to dis-identify from the false self, the body/mind/ego, and claim your identity as pure Consciousness.

A mere intellectual understanding of the teaching is insufficient. Until this Self-Knowledge is fully integrated into the mind, heart and psyche, there's no escaping the emotional and psychological problems inherent to identification with the ego-self.

This isn't a one-time task, either. The key is to continue applying Self-Knowledge until all the ignorance-based conditioning is eradicated and replaced by a full appreciation of Truth. Much more will be spoken of this in the third section of this book.

Neo Advaita and The Necessity of a Complete Teaching

Even if you know little about Vedanta, it's likely many of the concepts and ideas will be familiar to you. Indeed, a great many modern spiritual teachers have appropriated the key elements of Vedanta and repackaged them into what often gets termed "Neo Advaita".

Given that the term is generally viewed as a pejorative, you probably won't find any teachers who advertise themselves as Neo Advaitins. They're more likely to call themselves teachers of Non-duality or Advaita; and they are exceedingly common in the spiritual marketplace.

These teachers generally teach by *satsang*, whereupon they maybe offer some inspiring words and then simply answer questions from the audience. Some of them are even quite good at what they do and can be highly inspiring.

What they lack, however, is a complete teaching. They take the ultimate truth of Vedanta, our identity as Awareness or Consciousness, and skip the rest of the teaching.

This doesn't work. The context and foundations have been stripped away and you truly need a solid foundation if you hope to attain enlightenment. It's not enough to simply wax lyrical about the nature of the Self. You also need to understand the nature of the phenomenal world and how the Eternal Self relates to the apparent self; the body/mind/ego entity.

Vedanta alone provides these answers. It employs multiple, refined teaching methodologies, each with a slightly different way of looking at and helping us understand Reality.

The tendency of modern Advaita teachers is to simply declare, "You are Awareness—you just need to *get* it!"

"Getting it", however, may not be as easy as it sounds owing to the vast amounts of conditioning and ignorance governing the psyche.

Ignorance is stubbornly tenacious. You can guarantee that it won't be defeated in a single battle. It's an ongoing war and you need the appropriate tools in your arsenal; something only Vedanta provides when it comes to Self-Knowledge.

There's certainly no lasting harm listening to non-traditional teachers. It can provide a preparatory introduction and enable people to go on to find an actual Vedanta teacher. It can also, however, waste a tremendous amount of time on dead-end teachings that simply aren't enough to ferry you to true Self-Realisation and liberation.

So, don't sell yourself short by accepting the first Non-duality teacher that comes along. Check the credentials of the teacher. Make sure they are from a recognised Vedantic lineage, are well versed in the scriptures and capable of wielding this knowledge rather than simply offering flowery words of encouragement and little else.

It's easy as pie to simply talk about the Self and affirm that's what you are. Mere talk is rarely enough, however. A teacher needs to be able to guide students through every nuance of the teaching; to recognise the pitfalls and blindspots and help them to understand and contextualise the relationship between the Self, Awareness, and the world of form we all so intimately experience. That's not as easy as it sounds. It requires subtlety and skill.

If you have a medical condition, you'll only want to deal with a proper, qualified doctor. I'm certain you'd avoid somebody who had just picked up bits and pieces online and cobbled together their own personalised understanding of medicine.

Similarly, a teacher of enlightenment must be qualified and have a firm understanding of the intricacies of Vedanta. You owe it to yourself to make sure that you are in capable and competent hands.

Summary

- Vedanta ("the end of knowledge") is the essence of India's ancient Vedas, specifically the end portions which we call the

Upanishads. This vast body of knowledge is considered revealed knowledge and not the product of human thought.

- The subject matter of the Upanishads is the nature of the Self, God and the creation.
- According to Vedanta, our suffering comes from not knowing who, or rather what, we are. The key to liberation is Self-Knowledge.
- In spite of the appearance of duality, reality is Non-dual and is of the nature of universal and limitless Awareness/Consciousness, which the scriptures call Brahman, or the Self.
- The nature of the Self is Existence, Consciousness and Bliss. All beings and all creation is the product of this one, changeless Consciousness.
- Vedanta is a means of knowledge, specifically Self-Knowledge, and a tool for revealing our oneness and non-separation from the one, universal Self.
- Vedanta has three stages: listening, reasoning and contemplation.
- Many modern teachers and teachings, particularly of the Neo Advaita variety, cherry pick the key elements of Vedanta but lack a complete and cohesive teaching. This rarely leads to liberation.
- It's preferable to find a traditional Vedanta teacher from a recognised lineage who can share the complete picture.

5.
Preparing the Mind

Ultimate success in spiritual endeavours is determined chiefly by the mental preparedness of the seeker. All other considerations are secondary.
Adi Shankara

Have you ever tried growing plants from seeds?

The process is generally simple. You find a suitable pot, fill it will soil, sow the seeds, add a little water and place it in a suitably sunny location. *Et voilà!* Over the next few days, you can be on the lookout for signs of growth.

While most take it utterly for granted, this is one of the everyday miracles of life. Isn't it remarkable that a tiny seed somehow contains all the necessary intelligence and energy to grow from a dormant speck into a living, growing and hopefully thriving plant?

There are, however, times when the seeds simply won't germinate. It doesn't matter how patient and attentive you are, or how much water and sunlight you provide; nothing happens.

As anyone familiar with horticulture will attest, plants will only grow if the conditions are right.

That's why, as with many things in life, preparation is essential.

Prior to planting a single crop, a farmer will send a soil sample for laboratory testing to check the pH, texture and fertility levels. The land must then be tilled and irrigated. Although a long and laborious process, this vital preparation cannot be skipped. For it's only when the conditions are right that the seeds can be planted and allowed to work their magic.

The same is true of enlightenment.

It doesn't matter how determined you are and how many years, or even decades, you spend pursuing spiritual liberation. Like the farmer's field, your mind must first be prepared and cultivated. It's only when the mind is appropriately receptive and fertile that the seeds of Self-Knowledge can take root, grow and flourish, bestowing you with the sweet fruits of liberation.

This isn't something that most modern spiritual teachers will readily admit. People don't want to hear it. These days, even spiritual seekers are looking for more or less instant gratification.

The scriptures are clear, however. Success or failure with regard to enlightenment is determined not by the capricious hand of God, but by the quality of a person's mind; and, specifically, the presence or absence of what we call the fourfold qualifications.

Why Are Qualifications Necessary?

Many things of importance in life require qualifications; whether it's a job, a university course or driving a car.

Vedanta is no different.

Nobody will disagree that worldly life is inherently stressful. We face not only immense outer demands made of us, but also the turbulent inner world of our various psychological complexes and deep rooted attachments and aversions.

That does not lend itself to a peaceful mind. Quite the contrary, the woes of samsara are endless, as evidenced by the widespread emotional and psychological distress afflicting persons of all ages and walks of life.

In order to work, Vedanta requires a reasonably clear, open and tranquil mind. After all, if you are overcome by stress and strain, whether it's work issues or relationship or financial problems, your attention probably won't remain upon the teaching for any great length of time.

You'll find it hard to focus and and impossible to devote the necessary time and contemplation the teaching requires.

A muddled mind invariably yields muddled results.

Vedanta was not traditionally taught to the wider public. Candidates were carefully selected by the teacher based on their mental and psychological eligibility. If they didn't meet the right criteria, the teacher wouldn't accept them as students.

That might seem shockingly inegalitarian. It was actually to save both the student and teacher a whole lot of time and energy. Returning to the seed analogy, it's a waste of time planting seeds in arid, infertile soil. The conditions must be right or the process simply won't work.

There's good news, however. Even if one's mind doesn't currently fit the eligibility criteria, which we'll outline below, these qualifications can be cultivated.

What Are the Qualifications?

One of Vedanta's classic introductory Vedanta is *Tattva Bodha* (Knowledge of Truth) by Adi Shankara. This text will be referenced throughout the course of the book and is included in its entirety in Appendix 1.

Tattva Bodha lays out the basics of Vedantic teaching and provides a foundation for understanding many of the key terms and concepts.

It begins by first detailing the qualifications necessary for all seekers of enlightenment. These qualifications are sometimes referred to as the four "D's":

1. **Discrimination**
2. **Dispassion**
3. **Discipline, or the Sixfold Inner Wealth**
4. **Desire for Freedom**

Discrimination

This first qualification lies at the heart of Vedanta's methodology.

The Sanskrit term is *viveka*, which generally translates as "discrimination". Unfortunately, that term has a negative connotation in today's world. An acceptable alternative might be "discernment", for it relates to our ability to clearly discern or differentiate one thing from another.

Discrimination is essential for a simple reason: nothing is ever what it seems to be in life. Taking appearance to be real is the gravest of errors and the source of all our sorrows. Conditioned by ignorance, the average human being takes him or herself to be nothing but a body and mind. This assumption lies at the heart of samsara and from it comes our attachment to objects as a means of attaining happiness.

The ability to discriminate the real from the unreal, Truth from falsity and the fleeting from the Eternal happens to be our ticket out of samsara.

In fact, one of Vedanta's key practices is the art of discriminating the Self from the not-Self; reality from appearance, and what you actually are from what you merely appear to be.

When you lack discrimination, you're unable to process reality with the necessary clarity and objectivity. Incapable of determining right from wrong and what seems good from what's actually good, you're blindly led by the mind and senses; your actions unconsciously impelled by your conditioned attachments and aversions. Such a life is mired in constant frustration and sorrow.

It's only by exercising proper discrimination that you become clear about your true values—and resolute that your ultimate goal is enlightenment. You're able to see the limitations inherent in worldly seeking and understand that only enlightenment offers lasting, durable happiness.

Discrimination keeps you on track spiritually, serving as a torchlight, piercing through the murky veil of samsara and helping you to see and respond to life with clarity, purpose and resolve.

Dispassion

When you're able to discriminate between the fleeting and the Eternal, between the world of appearance and the Awareness in which it appears, you naturally begin developing a more dispassionate attitude toward the world of the senses.

This dispassion happens to be the second vital qualification.

When you lack dispassion, you remain hooked to the mundane world. You'll never muster the required time and energy necessary for attaining liberation. This is an important point. It generally does take considerable time and effort to break free of ignorance and reorient the mind from the false self to your actual Self.

Dispassion helps you see that attachment to worldly objects and the crazed need to pursue, grasp and acquire objects is not the solution, and is, in fact, part of the problem.

While you may obviously have a range of worldly duties and responsibilities, dispassion enables you to shift your priorities. You're able to deal more effectively with your worldly life, while knowing that your ultimate goal and the key to lasting freedom is spiritual liberation.

Once again, the word "dispassion" may carry a negative connotation for some. It might be misconstrued as being cold, aloof or uncaring.

This is not the case at all. Dispassion simply means withdrawing the excess emotional and psychological attachment you've placed upon objects in the hope they will deliver lasting happiness.

When you're no longer attached and even addicted to relationships, career, possessions and so on, you're actually far freer than ever before to enjoy them.

You needn't fear that you'll somehow become less loving to others. If anything, dispassion will allow you to become more loving because you're no longer seeking anything back from the other person. Vedanta teaches you to derive your happiness from within and not without. This liberates both you and the other person from the terrible burden of expectation induced anxiety.

Shankara defines dispassion as freedom from attachment to sensory pleasure and from attachment to the fruits of your actions. You worry less about the fruits of your actions because discrimination and dispassion enable you to see that happiness doesn't come from getting what you want. You're still free to enjoy and appreciate life and all of its finer things. But your value for them will naturally lessen as you learn to derive your joy from the one thing nobody can ever take from you—your own Self.

Discipline, or the Sixfold Inner Wealth

The cultivation of discrimination and dispassion naturally lead to the third qualification; the ability to discipline and master the senses. This discipline is sixfold in nature:

1. Discipline of the mind
2. Discipline of the senses
3. The ability to withdraw from sense objects

4. Endurance
5. Faith in the teaching and teacher
6. Concentration of the mind.

Some people may balk at the word "discipline". "That doesn't sound like much fun," they complain. "It sounds like repression and denial!"

Admittedly, words like discrimination, dispassion and discipline may give the impression that Vedanta is some kind of dour, life denying nihilism, when, in fact, quite the opposite is true!

Vedanta is, however, uncompromising.

It is a means of knowledge intended for mature human beings; people who've already concluded that there's no permanent solution to existential suffering to be found in the world of impermanent objects.

What Vedanta promises is lasting inner happiness. However, in order to realise and access this vast inner wealth, it's first necessary to bring the mind and senses under control.

The Katha Upanishad provides a wonderful analogy, comparing the human being to a chariot. The Self, Consciousness, is the chariot passenger. The chariot itself represents the physical body and the intellect is the chariot driver. The reins represent the mind and the horses are the senses.

As the Upanishad states:

> Those who lack discrimination and whose minds are undisciplined find their senses galloping hither and thither like wild horses. But for those with both discrimination and a disciplined mind, the senses fall into line like a well trained horse.

Human beings have limited time and energy. Both are precious commodities that should never be squandered. We each possess the instruments of a body, mind, intellect and senses; all necessary tools for transacting with the world. It's imperative that these instruments remain under our control, lest we be controlled by them.

When you fail to control your faculties, you become like a charioteer who has lost control of the chariot, helplessly at the mercy of the galloping senses and their insatiable appetites. You lose the capacity to see and think clearly and become overpowered by various desires, compulsions and addictions.

Basically, you lose control of your life and destiny.

When that happens, you can barely function in the world, much less attain enlightenment.

What I'm about to say isn't fashionable and it certainly isn't sexy or fun, but you really must learn to control, or, at the very least manage, your mind and senses.

If you fail to do that, you will be utterly dominated by them. As the saying goes, the mind makes a wonderful servant but a terrible master. It's possible that a lot of the mental health problems afflicting people today come down to a simple problem: we're not taught how to understand the mind and keep it in check. Rather than the controller, we become the controlled.

The ability "to withdraw from sense objects" means overcoming our attachment to objects and sense pleasures, whether material or subtle. Again, this may not anybody's idea of a good time, but it marks another essential component of self-mastery.

It's important that we never be governed by our appetites, desires and attachments. Desires naturally arise in the mind, but we alone get to decide whether it's necessary and appropriate to act upon those desires.

A gluttonous, alcoholic, chain smoking drug addict will never get far in terms of enlightenment. Why? Because until such a person masters their addictions, the mind will be completely dominated and controlled by them.

If you fail to discipline the mind and senses there's no way you will be able to develop the necessary discrimination and dispassion required to set the mind free.

The next quality, endurance or forbearance, means the ability to weather life's inevitable storms and hiccups. Let's face it, there are no shortage of these. Duality being duality, things don't always go according to plan and we often must deal with setbacks, challenges, stresses and traumas. That's part and parcel of being human. As a seeker of enlightenment, it's essential that you develop resilience and the ability to bend with the wind. Like the branches of trees, when people become too rigid and brittle, it doesn't take much to make them snap.

Next up, we have faith. It's necessary to have faith in both the teaching and the teacher. That doesn't mean blind faith. Vedanta is not some religion seeking to indoctrinate and brainwash you into believing something you can never verify in your own direct experience. On the contrary, you will be encouraged to exercise your intellect and question things until you finally begin to understand this new vision of reality.

An initial faith is necessary because you otherwise wouldn't commit the necessary time and effort to your journey toward liberation. The moment you got bored or found that things weren't "clicking" as quickly as you'd like, you'd be off searching for salvation elsewhere.

Many spiritual seekers indulge in a relentless merry-go-round of teaching after teaching, never sticking at anything for any length of time and dismissing each one the moment they hit a bump on the road.

It may, indeed, take some time for this teaching to click for you, and that's okay. Vedanta's vision of reality is radical and may initially seem counterintuitive. Yet it's important that you stick with the threefold process of listening, reasoning and contemplating for as long as it takes. You can trust Vedanta. It has been around for thousands of years. As I said before, it's longevity is down to a simple reason: it works.

Last but not least, the final component of discipline is the ability to concentrate the mind. Today's world is one of constant distraction. Our attention has become accustomed to rapidly flitting between all kinds of stimulus. The advent of smartphones, social media and our addiction to scrolling has had an enormous impact on peoples' ability to focus and process and retain information.

Studies indicate that our attention span is deteriorating. Recent headlines suggest that some younger people, addicted to the video shorts of TikTok, are finding themselves unable to focus on videos lasting more than a couple of minutes.

This erosion of focus poses a real problem, particularly for students of Vedanta. It's necessary that you be able to focus the mind and keep it upon the topic for a sustained period of time. If your mind is unfocused, restless and prone to buzzing about like a bee in a jar, you'll struggle to follow the teaching, much less be able to integrate it into your heart and mind.

Therefore, if you're at all uncertain about your concentration skills you would do well to sharpen them. That will help you not only when it comes to your Vedantic studies, but also in many other areas of your life.

Desire for Freedom

While desire is often seen as an impediment on the spiritual path, that's not entirely the case with Vedanta. There is, in fact, one desire that we actively encourage you to strengthen—the desire for liberation.

Once you've developed the qualities of discrimination and dispassion and gained a degree of mastery over the mind and senses, this naturally leads to the final qualification.

With keen discrimination, you've already ascertained that while the world has its many pleasures and joys, there's no lasting solution to the problem of samsara to be found outside of you. All worldly gains, however great and enticing, come with an upside and downside and are ultimately fleeting in nature.

The only way to be free is to resolve the sense of lack, inadequacy and limitation at the core of your being. That's precisely what Vedanta does. It provides Self-Knowledge; the medicine that will, once and for all, destroy the self-ignorance at the heart of your sorrow and dissatisfaction.

The caveat? You have to want to be free. And I mean really, *really* want to be free!

Very often students have a desire for enlightenment, but it's just one desire among many. If that's the case, the desire for tangible worldly things will inevitably supersede the spiritual goal. It simply won't work in the long run. Your desire for freedom must be so strong that it becomes and remains your top priority and highest value. Anything less and you are selling yourself short and dooming yourself to spiritual failure.

The desire to be free is analogous to the heat that cooks a meal. If the temperature of the oven or stove isn't high enough, the ingredients will remain such as they are. The food simply won't cook. You really must fire up your desire for freedom because that's what ignites everything and provides the necessary energy, motivation and determination to pursue and attain enlightenment.

Even then, it's never an overnight process. For the majority of students, it may may take years to work through the three stage process of Vedanta. It's a case of repeatedly applying Self-Knowledge to the mind in order to rewire its many layers of ignorance induced conditioning. Even though it's inherent to your very nature, liberation is, for the mind, a battle hard fought and well earned. The end point is infinite freedom; which, being an infinite gain, is, therefore, worth any amount of effort.

It's easy to muster excitement and enthusiasm at the beginning of an endeavour. What we often find, however, is that our initial excitement quickly wears off. That's why it's crucial that you stay motivated and committed over the long haul.

Instead of giving up when you don't appear to be getting expedient results, you need to be like a dog with a bone. Anybody who's ever had a dog knows that it's futile trying to get between a dog and its bone. No matter the distraction, that dog will absolutely refuse to relinquish its prize until it has chewed the bone to bits. As a seeker of enlightenment, you require a similar level of single pointed devotion.

So, how do you fan the flames of this most singular desire?

The desire to be free can be bolstered by consciously contemplating the cost of not being free; which is to say, the pain inherent in samsara. Behavioural scientists have found that people are generally more motivated by pain, and the desire to remove or avoid pain, than by pleasure. So, while understanding the benefits of liberation are likely to encourage you, it's contemplating the pain of *not* being free that will really motivate you to stick to the path.

So, be very clear about the lifetime of pain you've experienced by seeking happiness and wholeness outside of yourself in the world of objects and form. Take time to contemplate the downside of samsara and the disappointment and futility of pursuing object based happiness. All those things you thought would bring lasting happiness—the romances, the jobs, the endless goals and scheming—what did they really bring but eventual disappointment and disillusionment?

Isn't it true that the moment one thing failed to work out, you simply set your sights on a new objective; one that you believed would finally, truly be different?

Aren't you fed up of the hamster wheel of samsara? So much time, energy and life spent getting nowhere? If you aren't fed up with it yet, why not? How much suffering do you need before you finally decide to draw the line and take a different approach?

When your desire to be free is strong enough, the attainment of liberation will naturally become your highest value and greatest priority (something we'll talk about in the next chapter).

It's only when something is regarded with sufficiently high value that it overrides all other desires and you are motivated to pursue it with all your heart, mind and soul.

Once you've kindled the burning desire for freedom (and it has to be burning!)—you're set to go.

How to Attain the Qualifications

So, you might be wondering, that's all well and good, but how do I actually attain these qualifications?

The answer is simple: through spiritual practice.

Indeed, that's what spiritual practice is for.

People often assume that the practices themselves, such as meditation, mantra, prayer, yoga, and so on, are what lead to enlightenment. That isn't the case. What they do is prepare the mind for Self-Knowledge. It's Self-Knowledge alone that leads to enlightenment.

Why is knowledge alone the solution? Because the entire problem of samsara is one of ignorance. Knowledge destroys ignorance as light dispels darkness.

Before we dive into the teachings on Self-Knowledge in the next section, we first need to explore some of the tools that will help prepare the mind for that Self-Knowledge.

Whatever your goal in life, whether it's to climb a mountain, cook a meal or get enlightened, preparation is essential.

The sad fact is that some people can spend years studying Vedanta and still remain firmly in the grip of samsara. Other, rarer souls, might dive straight in, spend a little time immersing themselves in the teaching and then—bam! Enlightened! Their seeking ends and they come to know the resplendent light of their own being.

So what is it that determines success or failure when it comes to enlightenment? Why, out of so many spiritual seekers, are there so few finders?

The answer in short is: the presence of absence of the mental qualifications listed above. The mind must be sufficiently refined and purified in order for the seeds of Self-Knowledge to sprout, ripen and grow.

If the mind isn't qualified, it doesn't matter how long and how hard to try to "get it"; the teaching will never be more than idle words and concepts and your suffering will continue.

That's why this is undoubtedly one of the most important chapters of the book. It's telling you something that most spiritual teachers will never admit. You have to be ready. Your mind must be prepared. Fortunately, we have the tools to do just that.

These tools include:

1. An understanding of and commitment to following dharma and dharmic values, as we'll explore in the next chapter.
2. Karma yoga: the key practice for neutralising the mind's conditioned attachments and aversions. Karma yoga is a practice that will rapidly transform your life if properly understood and correctly implemented.
3. Devotion: cultivating a devotional, worshipful mindset, thereby transmuting emotional difficulties into devotional love.
4. Meditation is an excellent tool for calming the body and mind and sharpening one's ability to focus. Vedanta particularly recommends upasana meditation, something that will be explained in Chapter Twelve.

5. Learning to manage and balance the three basic energies or qualities of matter (called the *gunas*).

Each of these will be unfolded over the course of the book.

If you've been already been learning and applying Vedanta for some time with no tangible results, you likely need to work on your mental qualifications. When you develop the necessary discrimination, dispassion, disciple and desire, you'll find the teaching more or less does the work itself.

Even if you happen to have no interest in enlightenment whatsoever, the cultivation these qualities will transform your life for the better, for they relieve anxiety and stress like nothing else.

Living with discernment, dispassion towards the world of the senses, and maintaining a degree of mastery over your mind, thoughts and emotions, is by far the healthiest and sanest way to live. Certainly more so than being a victim to fate, helplessly subjugated by your wayward desires, attachments and addictions.

You were bestowed the gift of life. It's up to you how you choose to live that life. If your life isn't currently working as you would like, it's never too late to change that. It may not be an easy and expedient ride. It may, in fact, take considerable effort; and yet it is effort most certainly well spent.

The Two Paths

According to the scriptures, two paths are available to the human soul: the path of fleeting pleasure and the path of lasting freedom.

The Path of Pleasure

The first path, fleeting pleasure, is referred to in the Bhagavad Gita as the "path of dark". This is the path of the sensualist; the one whose goals in life pertain to pleasure seeking and sensory gratification. Despite it's obvious allure, this path is governed by ignorance and leads to continued immersion in samsara; which is to say, suffering.

Those whose lives are an orgy of overindulgence with little regard for the long term cost are immature both psychologically and spiritually. Their desires are so strong they are blinded to the suffering they're creating for themselves. Extreme examples include alcoholics, drugs addicts and, in fact, addicts of any kind.

We've already explored the downsides of object based happiness. Aside from the issue of attachment, there's no getting around the fact that all things in the world of form are subject to duality. Pleasurable experiences always taste sweet in the beginning. If, however, indulged to excess, you can guarantee the sweet nectar will eventually turn to poison.

Think about eating a lavish four-course banquet. While you may be in culinary heaven as you shovel the food into your mouth, the pleasure turns to pain an hour or two later when you're suffering indigestion and heartburn. Another example is alcohol, which may bring enjoyment at the time, but too much and the hangover the next day will be anything but pleasurable.

Sensory pleasure should never be one's primary goal in life. A lifetime spent pandering to desire, overindulging the senses and hankering after material objects is, in spiritual terms, a wasted life.

The Katha Upanishad warns of this:

> The path of the pleasurable holds allure to the senses, but the path of what is preferable leads to lasting bliss. Both prompt the soul to action. Those who follow the preferable reap the rewards; those who choose only what is pleasurable miss the true goal of life.

Shankara is even more brutal in the text Vivekachudamani. He highlights how rare and precious a human birth is, particularly in combination with a mature temperament, the desire for liberation and access to the scriptures. He says:

> If such a person, so richly blessed, is foolish enough not to strive hard for Self-Realisation, they commit spiritual suicide by clinging to things that are unreal. Is there a greater fool?

The Path of Freedom

The second path, lasting freedom, is called the "path of light", for it brings illumination and knowledge, leading the soul to spiritual liberation and release from suffering.

Those upon this path devote themselves to life's highest goal: enlightenment. As we saw in the Katha Upanishad quote above, while the first path is preferable to the senses, the second is preferable to the soul, for it leads to lasting freedom and is the true goal of life.

The first path appeals to most human beings because it promises expedient pleasure and sense gratification. The second path, on the other hand, requires discipline and self-restraint and its rewards are less immediate.

The former tastes like sweet nectar upon drinking, but the taste soon turns bitter. The latter is the other way around. It may initially taste bitter, but the long term rewards are, according to the Bhagavad Gita, "the sweet nectar of happiness, born of the clarity of Self-Knowledge."

As a seeker of liberation, it's essential that you're able to discriminate between the two and make your choice wisely.

The path of lasting happiness may call for a certain sacrifice in terms of time and effort. Upon analysis, it is, however, infinitely preferable than remaining in the bondage of samsara.

Freedom or bondage? The choice is yours.

The Necessity of Spiritual Practice

Before we close this chapter, let's touch upon an issue that's become something of a controversy in the modern spiritual scene. That topic is spiritual practice.

This may be particularly divisive for those who may have been exposed to Neo-Advaita. You may recall, Neo-Advaita is a largely Western appropriation of the core teaching of Vedanta, which cherry picks the general principles but strips away the contextual framework.

Neo-Advaita teachers often dismiss spiritual practice as unnecessary. "You're already free," they insist. "You're already the Self, so what is there to practice?"

That's true from the Absolute perspective (which we'll go on to explain in subsequent chapters). You are the Self. That Self cannot be gained through action because it's the truth and essence of what you are. It's the one thing that can never be gained or lost.

The problem isn't with the Self, however. The Self was never unenlightened.

The problem is with the mind, specifically the intellect. Blinded by ignorance, the intellect has distorted your vision of reality and of yourself. That's where the problem lies, so that's where the work needs to be done.

Ultimately, liberation of the mind is achieved only through the deep contemplation of the Self-Knowledge as revealed by Vedanta.

As we've emphasised throughout this chapter, in order to be receptive to Self-Knowledge, the mind must first be sufficiently tamed. An untamed mind is a disturbed, restless and distorted instrument, easily overcome by the push and pull of desire and aversion, and incapable of accurately reflecting the light of truth.

The idea that spiritual practice is unnecessary is a seductive but dangerous fallacy. It's only true if the seeker happens to possess an uncommonly pure, clear, restrained and discriminating mind. Again, such souls are exceedingly rare given the stresses, strains and compromised values of the modern world.

In the Bhagavad Gita's sixth chapter, Krishna advises:

> To succeed, you must lift yourself up by yourself. The mind can be your greatest asset or your worst enemy. By cultivating self-mastery, you ensure that your mind works for and not against you.

This self-mastery does not happen by itself. It would be nice if it did. But for all but the most saintly of souls, it takes consistent effort and discipline to tame the mind and make it your faithful servant rather than your wayward master. That's why spiritual practice is absolutely necessary for the vast majority of seekers. At least, until it isn't.

Summary

- Just as seeds require the right conditions in which to grow, the Self-Knowledge that leads to liberation requires a sufficiently pure and fertile mind in order to take root.
- The presence or absence of the fourfold mental qualifications is what determines one's success or failure with regard to enlightenment.
- The fourfold qualifications are discrimination, dispassion, discipline of the mind and senses and desire for freedom.
- Discrimination means the ability to differentiate one thing from another and, specifically, that which is fleeting (unreal) from that which is Eternal (real).
- Dispassion is freedom from attachment to sense objects and freedom from anxiety over the fruits of your actions.
- Discipline is sixfold in nature and includes discipline of the mind, discipline of the senses, the ability to withdraw one's

attention from sense objects, endurance, faith and the ability to concentrate the mind.

- Finally, one must possess a sufficiently strong desire for liberation.
- If these qualifications are currently lacking, then don't worry. They can be cultivated through commitment to dharmic values, karma yoga, a devotional mindset and balancing the three energies.
- Two paths exist for the human soul; one is the path of pleasure and the other is the path of freedom. The first is driven by the desire for sense gratification and the feeding of desire, while the second is a commitment to the pursuit of enlightenment as life's highest goal. One leads to continued bondage in samsara and the other leads to liberation from samsara.
- Some modern teachers assert that spiritual practice is unnecessary. This is untrue for all but the most advanced seekers. The mind must be made reasonably pure, tranquil and open or Self-Knowledge will never translate to freedom.

6.
Values and Dharma

> Dharma is that which upholds and supports the world.
> *Mahabharata*

It's impossible to overstate the importance of values, particularly for those on the path to liberation.

The dictionary defines values as one's "judgement of what is important in life"; "the regard, importance and worth one holds for a certain thing", and "what one considers good or bad, and desirable or undesirable."

Values are the lynchpin around which our lives pivot.

It's perhaps not a topic the average person gives much consideration, but our underlying values lie at the root of all our desires, ambitions and goals. After all, you cannot desire a thing without first having a clear value for it. The value always precedes the desire.

On the topic of desire, a famous verse from the Brihadaranyaka Upanishad reads:

You become what your deepest, driving desire is.
For your desire determines your will,
Your will determines your deed,
And your deed determines your destiny.

Therefore, your desires are born of what you value; and your priorities are born of what you desire. Your priorities then inform your actions and your actions shape the entire trajectory of your life. In short, your values serve as an inner compass guiding you through life.

Because values can be both healthy and unhealthy, dharmic and adharmic, it's wise to always be clear about the values underpinning your desires and actions.

This is sound advice for anyone, but it's particularly important for the seeker of liberation. The reason? Until liberation becomes your highest value, superseding all materialistic, worldly values, your priorities will be muddled at best, and muddled priorities cannot lead to anything but a muddled life.

In order to prepare the mind for liberation (and, in fact, to live a happy life in general), your values must be brought into full alignment with dharma.

The Law of Dharma

Values have their basis in dharma. We've already spoken about dharma; a term with no English equivalent. It's a Sanskrit word derived from the root *dhr*, meaning "to hold, maintain and nourish" and *dharman*, which means "bearer" or "supporter".

You might think of dharma as the moral law woven through the entire creation. Inherent as the innermost nature of all things, dharma is intrinsic to the smooth functioning of the cosmos, the world, nature, society and everything in it.

Everything has its own dharma. It's the dharma of the stars to shine and the planets to spin in orbit; the dharma of rivers to flow, flowers to bloom, birds to fly and fish to swim.

Contrary to the idea that this is a disorganised, chaotic universe, it's actually a highly ordered, lawful creation. That's courtesy of the law of dharma, which supports and sustains the entire cosmos in perfect equilibrium.

With reference to human life, dharma means "right action". It means doing the right thing, in the right way, at the right time.

Dharmic actions are those aligned with the natural order of life.

Animals and plants effortlessly follow dharma because they follow their own nature. They have no option but to be what they are. A fish will always swim. It'll never try to fly, crawl or walk.

Only human beings, possessing the capacity for free will, are capable of contravening dharma and committing what we call adharma, or "wrong action". This always leads to adverse consequences.

We each have an instinctual understanding of dharma. It's built into us as our innermost sense of right and wrong. Because we all want to be treated with non-injury, kindness and honesty, these qualities form the basis of our ethical standards of conduct. In simple terms, we, ourselves, don't want to be harmed by others, so we know that it's wrong to harm other people.

That's why dharma is described as our protector.

If we behave according to dharmic principles, we can generally be assured that others will treat us the way we want to be treated. Dharma protects us, as long as we protect dharma by upholding right action at all times.

The Yajur Veda states that, "Nothing is higher than dharma."

This means that dharma is even more important than enlightenment. One can survive without enlightenment, but without dharma, society would degenerate into chaos.

The Three Types of Dharma

There are three basic types of dharma: universal dharma, situational dharma and personal dharma.

1. Universal Dharma

Universal dharma relates to the fundamental values shared by all beings.

Foremost among these is non-injury. No living creature, from the human being all the way down to the tiniest amoeba, wants to be harmed. That's why we know that it's wrong to harm others.

We also want and expect others to treat us with truthfulness, kindness, sympathy and generosity.

These form our core, universal values. Failure to adhere to such values creates problems, both for the perpetrator and the victim.

Violating dharma always incurs a cost. If people violate dharma on a mass scale, society eventually disintegrates, and that's why laws are created to uphold dharma.

2. Situational Dharma

Life is rarely black and white, so dharma is also relative and may vary depending on the situation.

For instance, if a psychopath takes a knife and attacks somebody, they will rightly be imprisoned. On the other hand, if a surgeon takes a scalpel and cuts into somebody, they will be rewarded with a handsome salary.

Both took a knife to somebody; but one intended to harm and the other intended to heal.

Each situation has its corresponding dharma; certain rules that should be observed and not broken. If you go to a talk, for example, it's the dharma of the audience to sit quietly and listen. On the other hand, it's obviously the dharma of the speaker to stand up and talk. It simply wouldn't work if the positions were reversed; if the attendees were chattering and the speaker remained silent.

So, dharma can be specific to each situation and circumstance, and this dharma must be followed in order for things to function smoothly.

3. Personal Dharma

We each have a personal dharma, too. Our personal dharma is not self-chosen but is determined for us by our own essential nature.

We are each born with a particular temperament and inherent proclivities, skills and strengths. These point the way to our personal dharma.

Once upon a time, a person's career would be determined by the family line. That's no longer the case in the modern world, so many people struggle to figure out what they're meant to do in life.

The answer, as always, lies within.

Some of us are by nature artists, while others are mathematicians, healers, leaders, businesspeople, scientists, spiritual seekers, and so on. Our life path is coded into us as the very essence of who we are at a personal level. All we need do is look within and figure out what's most important to us; what we're good at; and what interests, captivates and compels us.

Just as the sun shines and birds sing, all beings must follow their nature. They cannot be happy otherwise. That includes human beings. We must adhere to our nature; to our dharma. In doing so, we effectively contribute to life and this brings fulfilment, happiness and peace of mind.

Unfortunately, people often find themselves in conflict with themselves and at odds with their own nature. They perhaps have difficulty accepting themselves because they're trying to live up to some artificially imposed ideal of what they think they "should" be. This leads to nothing but sorrow, disillusionment and grief.

Indeed, the Bhagavad Gita warns that, "It is better to be imperfect at one's own dharma than to excel at the dharma of another."

Following our personal dharma requires self-acceptance and the confidence and determination not to yield to the erroneous judgements of others. Above all, we must honour ourselves and follow the path of our dharma, which is written into the very essence of our being. That's how we can best contribute to life.

Violating Dharma

Following dharma feels good. You experience a sense of satisfaction and inner peace when you do the right thing by yourself and others.

Violating dharma, on the other hand, always leads to both inner and outer conflict. Even the smallest transgressions of dharma come with consequences.

Sometimes the consequences are swift. Let's say you hit me in the face and I hit you right back. You violated universal dharma, non-injury, and you immediately paid for it with injury in kind.

Sometimes, the karma takes longer to fructify. Perhaps I go to the police and a few days later you get a court summons on the charge of assault. Either way, even the slightest violation of dharma will cause ripples and karmic consequences.

If dharma is innate and feels good, what is it, you might wonder, that causes people to commit adharma?

The problem is one of self-will. When we fail to manage our ingrained desires and aversions, they can become so powerful, so overwhelming, that they have the capacity to overrule dharma. We experience a conflict between what we want and what we know is right—and we end up doing what we want, regardless of the consequences.

A mature person recognises the importance of doing the right thing regardless of their personal desires and preferences. They know that if you transgress dharma, the result will always be undesirable karma in some form or another. Keeping that in mind, wise people are able to discriminate between what they should and should not do.

The immature person, on the other hand, lacks this crucial discernment. Their desires are so overpowering that they may not have a problem with lying, cheating, stealing or harming others as long as they get what they want. That's the power of unbridled desire. It overrules morality.

There's always a price to pay, however. Adharma causes both inner unrest and outer turbulence. Retribution, either from other people or the law itself, is often swift. Even if it isn't, even if you seem to get away with a transgression, you'll have no peace of mind because you'll constantly be looking over your shoulder, just waiting for the consequences of your actions to catch up with you. An adharmic life is a life of stress and conflict, both inwardly and outwardly.

Incidentally, just because a person chooses to violate dharma, it doesn't mean that they don't understand dharma. The most ruthless of thieves still know that it's wrong to steal. We know this because they, themselves, don't want to be stolen from. That's why they hide their loot. Even a serial killer knows that it's wrong to harm others, because they don't want to be harmed themselves. That's why there's no escaping dharma and values, even if a person conveniently chooses to ignore them.

Dharma is based on mutual reciprocity. We want and expect people to treat us with honesty, kindness and openness, and we should, therefore, be willing to reciprocate that in the way we deal with others.

Some people, however, hypocritically expect others to treat them well while being willing to lie, cheat and harm them in return. That happens when a person's personal values are not aligned with universal values.

Half Values

According to Swami Dayananda Saraswati (whose book "The Value of Values" serves as the template for much of this chapter), a value is only a value to you if you're convinced of its value to you.

In other words, in order to adopt a value as your own, you must fully assimilate that value. You need to be clear as to both the importance of upholding it and the cost you incur by violating it.

A partially assimilated value is sometimes as good as no value at all, because you're liable to jettison it the moment it gets in the way of your agenda, whatever that might be.

We might term a partially assimilated value as a "half value".

Half values invariably lead to conflict. An example of a half value might be honesty. On the one hand, you hold others to that value, and expect them to be honest with you. But on the other hand, if it's only a partially assimilated value, you might be willing to lie to them if you believe that lying benefits you more than telling the truth.

Let's say somebody offered you half a million in currency in exchange for telling a lie. What would you do?

Given that many people have a partially assimilated value for honesty and a fully assimilated value for money, you might be sorely tempted to tell the lie and take the money. After all, the benefit of taking the money is clear to you (extra money to spend on whatever you want) and the consequence of telling the lie may not be immediately apparent (they might never find out that you lied!).

However, there's no escaping the conflict this will generate in the psyche. Although you may have reasoned it away, that half value for honesty will still eat away at you, causing guilt and agitation. You'll find it hard to shift the feeling you've done something wrong because honesty is a value shared by all. Again, even hardened criminals, who seem to lack even a basic sense of morality at all, suffer when they violate dharma; even if it's just because they're fearful of being caught and punished.

Be Clear About Your Goal

Half values are a particular problem for seekers of liberation.

If you're reading this, you obviously you have a value for enlightenment. It may, however, only be a partially assimilated value; at odds with other more worldly values, such as the desire for money, relationships and status.

The value for liberation must be fully assimilated. You must wholeheartedly realise that seeking permanent happiness in the impermanent and ever-changing material world is a recipe for perpetual disappointment and sorrow.

Your desire for freedom must override worldly desires that will otherwise co-opt your time and energy.

Nothing sabotages the quest for liberation quite as much as muddled, partially assimilated values. So be sure to catch yourself if you find yourself thinking, "Sure, I want to be liberated—but I also want a new relationship, a bigger salary, a fancier car and a holiday in Barbados."

There's nothing inherently wrong with any of those things. But the desire to be free must be paramount. After all, you only want those other things because you think they'll make you feel free. Why not go for freedom itself, irrespective of whatever objects you want or don't want?

In order for Vedanta to really work, you must want to be free with every ounce of your heart and soul; and be willing to fully commit yourself to the process. Settle for nothing less. If you do, you're cheating yourself of the liberation that is your birthright.

Values To Be Rooted Out

In order to prepare the mind for Self-Knowledge, it's helpful to conduct a values inventory. This helps you see which values underpin your desires, intentions and actions.

Bear in mind that are two types of value: those in line with dharma and those not in line with dharma.

Values not in line with dharma include gratuitous desires and fears.

Desire itself isn't the enemy. In fact, if you want liberation, it's important to cultivate a burning desire for freedom which will provide the necessary energy, motivation and determination to see you through.

Excessive and frivolous desires, however, should be rooted out. They distract and unsettle the mind, robbing you of the attention, energy and focus that can otherwise be directed to your ultimate goal of liberation.

Fear is a negative desire capable of distorting and incapacitating the mind. The practice of karma yoga, which will be explained in the next chapter, is an excellent tool for neutralising fear.

Other unhealthy values to root out are egotism, dishonesty, greed, unwarranted anger, selfishness, arrogance, jealousy, guilt and regret, pride and vanity.

It takes a great deal of self-awareness and honesty to be aware of such values when they come into play in the mind.

That's where mindfulness can be an exceptionally useful tool. Instead of letting the mind drag you along, unquestioningly believing every thought you think and assumption you make, it pays to be the witness and to calmly, objectively observe what's going on in your mind.

Are your desires and reactions rooted in these detrimental, adharmic values? If so, stop, take a few conscious breaths and reconsider your trajectory.

You are the charioteer of your mind; you direct it where you want to go. The mind is your instrument; your tool for transacting with the world. It's important you learn to be the master of your mind or you'll forever be its slave.

Consciously rejecting harmful values, such as greed and dishonesty, and replacing them with healthy, dharmic values, frees the mind of tremendous stress. This, along with the practice of karma yoga, are keys to qualifying the mind for Self-Knowledge and the three stage process of Vedanta.

Values For Enlightenment

The Bhagavad Gita, an essential resource for all seekers, outlines the main values necessary to prepare the mind for enlightenment in verses seven to eleven of the thirteenth chapter:

> Those who know [Truth] are free of conceit and pretence. They commit no injury, are generous, straightforward, devoted to their teacher, inwardly and outwardly pure, steadfast with mastery of the mind and dispassionate towards the objects of the senses. Free of pride, they realise the limitations and suffering of birth, old age, disease and death. With no sense of ownership, they do not get compulsively entangled in the affairs of family and home and retain evenness of mind regarding pain and loss. Their unswerving devotion to God is accompanied by a keenness for solitude and indifference to social life. Firm in Self-Knowledge, they know that seeking the Self is the true goal of life and all else is ignorance.

From these verses we can extrapolate a checklist of twenty core dharmic values. They are as follows.

1. Freedom From Conceit or Pride

This first value relates to the absence of egotism and our tendency to want and demand the respect and adulation of others.

When we live aligned with worldly values and have no understanding of God and the transcendent nature of the Self, we basically inflate the ego to godlike status. The desire to feed the insatiable ego becomes our primary *modus operandi* in life.

The human ego primarily wants two things. It wants to be right and it wants to look good. So, until the ego is brought under control, be aware that many of your actions may, consciously or unconsciously, be motivated by the desire to make yourself look better in the eyes of others, bolstering the opinion others have or you and, by extension, the opinion you have of yourself.

Of course, the problem is you then become hostage to the fickle opinions of other people. Because you have no control over how other people think, behave and react to you, you open yourself to tremendous insecurity, hurt and a sense of diminishment.

You can remedy this by learning to be secure in yourself; to be authentic and to validate yourself rather than seeking scraps of validation from others.

Instead of living with pride and conceit, you adopt an attitude of humility. This comes easily when you realise that everything you have and everything that you are belongs not to you, but is given to you by the same Divine creative force responsible for the creation of the entire universe (a topic we'll explore in depth in Chapter Eleven).

2. Absence of Pretence

Pretentiousness is similar to conceit and pride in that it manifests as self-glorification. However, whereas conceit is based upon actual accomplishments or qualities we may have, pretension means pretending to be something or someone you are not.

Perhaps, as a spiritual seeker, this means dressing a certain way and trying to convey a sense of being highly "spiritual" and "advanced", when, in fact, this is just an attempt to make yourself look good.

The basic human problem is that we're not happy with ourselves as we are. We don't feel good enough. So, the tendency is to seek validation from others. If we cannot do that through our own merits, then we may "fake it" by acting pretentiously; by trying to appear as more than we actually are.

Such pretension leads to stress and insecurity. What we're selling is basically a lie and we know that we can potentially be found out at any moment. Pretension is, therefore, a tendency that should be avoided at all costs.

Instead, it pays to cultivate the value of self-acceptance. Nobody in this world is perfect. We must be willing to accept ourselves as individuals, to let go of self-condemnation and present ourselves to the world with open-hearted honesty and integrity.

3. Non-injury

Non-injury is perhaps the fundamental aspect of universal dharma.

No living creature wants to be harmed. Even the tiniest microbes seek to avoid injury. Because we all have a fully assimilated value for non-injury with regard to ourselves, this should be extended to others as well.

If you want to be treated by others with kindness, respect and non-injury, it's essential that you treat others according to those qualities.

This means being aware of your thoughts, words and deeds and never knowingly causing harm to another. The Biblical statement, "Do unto others as you would have them do to you" sums it up nicely.

Non-injury is the hallmark of ethical living. It means treading lightly upon the planet, and always ensuring that your actions are tempered by kindness, consideration, empathy and compassion. Seek to help rather than harm others, animals and the planet.

4. Accommodation

This value is nicely summarised by the words of the Serenity prayer: "Grant me the serenity to accept the things I can't change, the courage to change the things I can change, and the wisdom to know the difference."

To be accommodating means to calmly accept those things in life which may not be ideal, and may not have be as you'd have chosen, but which you cannot change.

Since life presents no shortage of changeless situations, this is an essential value to cultivate. It leads from stress and emotional reactivity to the simple acceptance that, "It is what it is, until it isn't."

As we've repeatedly stressed, in order to be receptive to Self-Knowledge, the mind must be as calm and pure as possible. This simply isn't possible when overcome by turbulent emotion. That's why it's recommended that you cultivate accommodation; the ability to accept the things you cannot change in life; relinquishing friction and resistance for calm, even-minded acceptance.

5. Straightforwardness or Truthfulness

Truth is another aspect of universal dharma. Nobody likes being lied to. That's why truthfulness should be a value that we all seek to uphold.

Straightforwardness means that your thoughts, words and deeds are all perfectly aligned. When they fall out of alignment; when you think one thing but say or do another, you lack integrity.

This lack of integrity generates inner turmoil and can lead to outer conflict too, for you may become known as a liar and somebody not to be trusted or relied upon.

6. Service to the Teacher

This quality means having the appropriate respect and value for both the teacher and teaching. Service to the teacher is expressed by honouring the dharma of the student-teacher relationship, behaving with courtesy and consideration, and by devoting yourself to the teaching with impeccable resolve.

7. Cleanliness

The value of cleanliness relates to both outer and inner cleanliness. As the old saying goes, "cleanliness is next to Godliness."

Obviously, it's important to ensure that your body, clothes and environment are kept clean and tidy. It's equally important to keep your mind clean and tidy. This means taking note of your thoughts, emotions and habits and replacing harmful, negative ones with more positive substitutes.

A person's entire experience of the world, others, and life in general, is filtered through the mind. A murky mind, filled with festering resentments, grievances and negative judgements, conditions your entire experience of life, rendering it similarly dark and distorted. This applies not only to the way that you see others but also the way that you view yourself.

It's important to take stock of what's going on with you mentally and psychologically and be willing to work on healing, in time replacing any unnecessarily negative, harmful or self-destructive thoughts with a positive alternative. This may not be easy initially, but the more you learn to question your thoughts and to replace harmful thoughts with constructive ones, the easier it becomes.

8. Steadiness or Perseverance

This is a quality essential for many endeavours in life, not least the attainment of enlightenment. Liberation rarely happens overnight. For the vast majority of seekers, re-education of the mind takes time and consistent effort. Be dogged and determined and keep applying Self-Knowledge to the mind until such time as it completely eradicates all ignorance and the suffering associated with it.

9. Mastery Over the Mind

Once again, it's worth emphasising that the condition and quality of your mind determines how you experience life; and how qualified you are for liberation.

Krishna talks about mind management in the sixth chapter of the Bhagavad Gita:

> The mind can be your greatest asset or your worst enemy. By cultivating self-mastery, you ensure that your mind works for and not against you. Such a mind remains tranquil and composed in both pleasure and pain, light and dark, and praise and criticism. For the one who lacks self-mastery, the mind remains a great enemy.

The battle to tame the mind may be one of the hardest battles of your life. The mind can, at times, seem a relentless and implacable foe. We all face adversity and trauma as we go through life, and we must deal with conditioned habits of thought and behaviour that may not always be conducive to our wellbeing.

Alas, nobody can do the job of taming your mind for you. It's a battle you must fight yourself. Fortunately, with the right tools in your arsenal and enough determination and grit, it is possible to attain mastery of the mind and to ensure that this most precious instrument works for and not against you.

10. Dispassion Toward Sense Objects

This value may go against the grain for most of us, because our hyper-materialistic culture tends to promote the very opposite.

Human beings are generally conditioned to believe that, in order to find happiness and fulfilment, we have to get our wallets out and buy, consume and enjoy whatever takes our fancy. Still not satisfied at the end of it? Then you need more, different and *better!*

It's telling that governments and corporations don't even tend to refer to us as "people" anymore. Instead, we're called "consumers", because that's exactly what we've been trained to become. We hungrily devour sense objects because that's where we believe happiness is; the indulging of the senses.

This value, dispassion with reference to sense objects, relates to the qualification of dispassion introduced in the previous chapter. It's an essential quality to cultivate if you want to progress on the spiritual path. If you can't control the mind and senses, you simply won't be able to devote the necessary time, attention and energy to the pursuit and implementation of Self-Knowledge.

This dispassion can be kindled by the knowledge that what you're ultimately seeking is not the object of your particular desire. What you really seek is freedom from want, lack and limitation. The only true and lasting antidote to this malady is liberation from samsara.

11. Absence of Egotism

We're all brought up to view ourselves as a separate little individual; as a person consisting of a body and mind; one among billions of others.

Because this personal self, which we might call the ego-self, is subject to limitation, lack, injury and death, we experience perpetual suffering, insecurity and sorrow. This ego-self always feels limited; and limitation is unacceptable to us, particularly self-limitation.

Most people try to solve the problem of self-limitation by bolstering their ego. They seek to elevate themselves in the eyes of others and themselves. This is generally done by pursuing whatever goals, attainments and accomplishments they think will solve the problem of self lack. Whether they're seeking material possessions, power, status or prestige, what they're actually doing is attempting to fortify and enhance their ego.

Vedanta teaches that the key to freedom lies not in elevating the ego, which is never satisfied by any attainment for long, but in negating it through Self-Knowledge. As we'll see in Chapter Nine, the ego is a component of what we call the subtle body. It exists, but it's not who and what we are. Knowledge of that fact is the doorway to freedom.

12. Recognising the Limitations of Samsara

This value relates to being aware of the painful limitations inherent in samsara; such as birth, death, pain, disease and suffering in general. These pains come part and parcel of duality and there's no escaping them.

This might sound like a spectacularly negative value. It's essential, however, that you acknowledge the limitations of samsara and object-based happiness. The solution to samsara is not to be found within samsara. It really doesn't matter what you manage to attain and achieve materially in life—life is a mixture of gains and losses, victories and defeats, joy and sorrow. Whatever you gain can be lost and, as if that's not bad enough, nothing satisfies the samsaric mind for long.

The only solution is to exit samsara. Time is precious, so it's imperative that you use it wisely. Instead of wasting your time chasing rainbows, commit yourself to liberation through Self-Knowledge. This is, according to the scriptures, the only way to lasting happiness.

13. Absence of Ownership

The concept of ownership is hardwired into us, but just how much do we actually own? Do we really own anything at all?

Almost everyone, without exception, makes the assumption that they *own* their body. But, if you think about it, your body was actually made out of your mother's body and your father's. Couldn't they legitimately claim ownership of it? What of all the bacteria that make up your body? There's only one of you and many trillions of them? Who's to say you own the body and not the bacteria?

You didn't actually have a say in the creation of your body and you're not even responsible for its functioning. Respiration, heart rate, circulation of blood, digestion and countless other processes are all done for you by the innate Intelligence responsible for the creation and maintenance of this wondrous vehicle.

At best, you're a trustee, not only of the body, but of pretty much anything else you could claim ownership of in life.

This value helps cut the ego down to size by negating the concept of ownership. Nothing is actually owned by or owed to you. Everything that you have is a gift from the cosmic Intelligence some call God (the subject of Chapter Eleven of this book).

14. Absence of Excessive Attachment to Loved Ones

This can be a difficult value for many people to understand. It's only right and proper that we love our family and friends. However, just as the previous value negated ownership, it's important to realise that others do not belong to us; including our own flesh and blood, such as our children and parents.

Love and attachment are not the same thing. Love gives, while attachment clings. Love free us, and others, while attachment disturbs the mind and robs us of both objectivity and equanimity.

The ideal is to love and care for our nearest and dearest with an absence of clinging and attachment; allowing them to be who and what they are, without any sense of ownership or entitlement.

Excessive attachment, as happens in codependent relationships, must be avoided. Seeking wholeness through relationships with others causes bondage, making you a prisoner to those relationships. Your happiness becomes dependent upon that person behaving and acting in a certain way.

Ultimately, freedom and wholeness can never be found outside of yourself. It must be found within; and only then will you be in a position to lovingly share that freedom with others.

15. Even-mindedness

This is a key qualification for preparing the mind for Self-Knowledge. There's no escaping life's dualities; no good without bad, no heat without cold, nor day without night.

Instead of being pushed, pulled and utterly contorted by the play of opposites, and driven entirely by your desires and aversions, it pays to take an objective approach to life; seeing things with objectivity and dispassion.

Rather than projecting "good" and "bad" onto the various circumstances and events of life, it's best to reduce things to objective facts, helping you cultivate evenness of mind, equanimity and equipoise. This reduces stress like nothing else and enables you to function with far greater ease and effectiveness in life.

16. Devotion to God

Without devotion to God, or a higher ideal, the human mind defaults to the ego and its various wants, desires, attachments, fears and aversions. This must be resolved if the mind is to be a fit receptacle for Self-Knowledge and liberation.

Many people now balk at the word "God". It's a word that's been subject to such abuse and misuse over the centuries that some cannot accept it at all. The bottom line is, however, there is no getting away from God. To deny God is to deny one's own existence.

Chapter Eleven will unfold the ironclad logic for the existence of God, albeit not the kind of God spoken of in the Abrahamic religions; ie., the bearded old man sitting in the clouds casting judgement upon us. As we shall see, Vedanta uses the term *Ishvara* to refer to the Divine Intelligence responsible for the world of creation. Perhaps those with an aversion to the word God will find that term easier to use. Or you can use any other term you feel comfortable with.

Vedanta encourages us to adopt a devotional attitude to life and to the world; to see the Divinity of all things. God is not something outside of us, but is the very universe itself; both the form of it and the Intelligence inherent therein. This bestows us with a kind of Divine vision, whereby all things are seen as sacred.

The fire of devotion burns off our attachment and addiction to material objects and reorients us inward, where we come to know the Wholeness and Divinity that is the core of our being. A God-centred life brings tremendous joy and peace, whereas a life driven exclusively by materialistic ends leads to frustration, emptiness and grief.

17. Appreciation of Solitude

Love of solitude may be an alien concept to many worldly people, who cannot bear being alone with themselves for any length of time. Such people must constantly seek distraction from their own dysfunctional minds and perpetual emotional storms. Simply having to sit in a room by themselves with no distractions can be a tortuous experience for such souls.

The spiritual seeker, however, comes to love solitude. For solitude provides the opportunity to turn within and bask in the light and peace of the Self; something that can only be found in the quietude of a serene mind and heart.

18. Absence of Craving For Company

This follows on from the previous value. A cultivated, refined spiritual seeker is someone comfortable in his or her own company and has no craving to be amongst the crowd. Extroverted tendencies are sublimated into a beautiful introversion, whereby we relish the Wholeness of our own being.

19. Constant Practice of Self-Knowledge

We haven't yet reached the chapters on Self-Knowledge, so this value will make more sense in retrospect. We have established that the key to liberation from samsara is not through action, as such, but Knowledge. We suffer because we falsely identify with the finite instruments of the body and mind, oblivious to the fact our true nature is pure Awareness or Consciousness.

The only remedy to ignorance is Knowledge; therefore, only Self-Knowledge can neutralise the suffering wrought by self-ignorance. This is not a one time process. The full integration of Self-Knowledge into the mind, intellect and psyche takes time and consistent practice until, finally, the truth of our actual identity sinks in and eradicates our suffering.

As a seeker of liberation, you must be determined and unerring, making the most of your precious time and never squandering it on unnecessary indulgences. Freedom must be your highest goal and, as we shall see, that freedom is attained through the practice of Self-Knowledge. Be diligent and always committed to liberation!

20. Always Keeping the Truth in Mind

A fierce and uncompromising devotion to spiritual Truth is essential to keep you on track. In order to succeed spiritually, your entire life must be oriented around the attainment and realisation of that Truth. Your aim is to pierce the illusion of being a small, limited, lacking entity, and come to know your own essential nature as Awareness. Don't worry if this doesn't entirely make sense to you yet. The next section of this book delves into the heart of Self-Knowledge.

In the meantime, what you need to do is be clear that liberation from samsara is your primary goal in life. Liberation happens only via Self-Knowledge; therefore, this Knowledge must be your highest of priorities.

If you're serious about enlightenment, it cannot be one among many goals. It must be your primary goal. A poor to middling commitment will yield poor to middling results. So, never lose sight of liberation as your highest goal. Make sure that it's of sufficient value to you and that it supersedes all other goals.

Taking A Values Inventory

We've now explored unhelpful values and discussed in some detail the values Vedanta outlines as necessary to prepare the mind for Knowledge.

The next step is to conduct a values inventory and see how your existing value system measures against the list of values highlighted by Vedanta.

This isn't always as easy as you might think. It's a task that requires a great deal of objectivity, dispassion and self-honesty.

Let me say straight up: the aim is not to judge or berate yourself.

Perfection is unnecessary; you aren't trying to become a saint.

What you simply need to do is weed out any particularly materialistic, ego-driven, self-destructive or self-insulting values and replace them with the spiritual values listed above.

Remember that a value only becomes a personal value if you see its value to you. You have to be convinced that it brings you benefit or you'll never have the motivation to live by it. At best, it'll be a partially assimilated value; a half value. That isn't enough. You need to truly understand the value of enlightenment, of liberation from suffering, if you ever hope to attain it.

We stress the importance of values because a healthy value system is pivotal to prepare the mind for Self-Knowledge. In the absence of a sufficiently receptive, qualified mind, the Knowledge simply won't stick. Even if you happen to "get it" at an intellectual level, if the mind is incapable of assimilating the Knowledge, it'll never be more than just another set of ideas, concepts and beliefs.

Here's something else to consider when it comes to values.

Even if you don't proceed to the three stage process of Vedanta and the unfoldment of Self-Knowledge, adopting these dharmic values will unquestionably transform your life for the better. You'll find yourself enjoying a happier, more peaceful, fulfilling and altogether less stressful life.

How to Adopt a New Value

The best way to adopt a new value is through a process of self-enquiry.

Take a good, hard look at the current, less than healthy values you've identified. Examples might be greed, anger, lust, having to be right, wanting to get your own way all the time, vanity, jealousy, pretentiousness, and so on.

Ask yourself whether the belief or assumption at the heart of the value is, firstly, true, and, secondly, of benefit to you.

For example, let's use the example of greed. In order to be greedy, you must have the belief that greed, having more than you need, brings you some benefit; that it makes you happy and fulfilled.

But is that really true?

Does greed bring happiness or does it actually cause unhappiness?

Is that *really* how you want to live your life?

Is this *really* the type of person you want to be?

If the answer is "no" to any or all of those questions, you'll immediately be open to adopting the opposite belief, and the list above will help guide you in the right direction. If you want to eradicate greed, then adopt the value of dispassion toward the objects of the senses. See how that changes your life in a positive way and makes you feel better about yourself.

It'll likely take a degree of introspection, self-discipline and focused intention to replace one value with another. The mind is a remarkably conservative mechanism, so don't beat yourself up if you find it difficult.

The key is your intent and resolve.

Remember that by consciously purifying and refining the mind, you enable Self-Knowledge to blossom into liberation. What nobler endeavour is there than erasing ignorance and aligning yourself with the emancipating Truth of what you are, enabling you to shine as a beacon of light for others? It all starts with being resolutely clear about what you truly value.

Once cultivated, these dharmic values ready the mind for Self-Knowledge and, in the words of Swami Dayananda:

> The teaching of Vedanta is [then] like the meeting of gas and fire. Knowledge ignites in a flash!

Summary

- Values are our judgement of what is most important and what we truly want in life. It's impossible to desire a thing without first having a clear value for it. The value always precedes the desire.
- Dharma, the inherent moral law of creation, is intrinsic for the smooth functioning of everything from the universe to the natural world, human society and all our lives. Everything has its own innate dharma, built into it as part of its essential nature.
- Dharma might be thought of as "right action"; as that which should be done. The opposite of dharma is adharma, or "wrong action". Following dharma protects and supports us, society and the world. Violating dharma always leads to adverse consequences.
- There are three basic types of dharma: universal, situational and personal dharma.
- Our values should always be brought in line with dharma.

- Dharmic values are based on mutual reciprocity. We desire others to treat us a certain way, so we know that it's right to treat others that way.
- A partial or half value is when you haven't fully assimilated the value of a value. You may, for example, have a half value for honesty. This means that you expect others to be honest with you, but you may be willing to be dishonest with others if it suits you.
- It's essential that you be clear as to your true values. The value for enlightenment must supersede all other values.
- Adharmic values, such as greed, dishonesty, egotism, pride, and so on, should be weeded out and replaced with dharmic values.
- The Bhagavad Gita outlines twenty core dharmic values that will prepare the mind for Self-Knowledge. These are: freedom from conceit and pride, absence of pretence, non-injury, accommodation, truthfulness, service to the teacher, cleanliness, perseverance, mastery over the mind, dispassion toward sense objects, absence of egotism, recognising the limitations of samsara, absence of ownership, absence of excessive attachment to loved ones, even-mindedness, devotion to God, appreciation of solitude, absence of craving for company, constant practice of Self-Knowledge and always keeping spiritual Truth in mind.
- It's recommended you regularly take a values inventory. See how your existing value system matches up with these dharmic values. Root out any negative or unhelpful values and consciously cultivate the opposite, spiritual value.

7.
Karma Yoga

A life of karma yoga creates a tranquil heart and dispels the delusions of the mind.
Bhagavad Gita

We've now established that, in order to work, Vedanta requires a calm, disciplined and focused mind. It's the presence or absence of the mental qualifications outlined in Chapter Five that determine success or failure when it comes to liberation.

Traditionally, the pursuit of enlightenment has been seen as the purview of renunciants; called *sannyasis* in India. Stepping away from worldly life, the sannyasi takes a vow to relinquish all property and possessions, as well as all societal and family obligations. Living as wandering ascetics, they're able to devote themselves entirely to spiritual liberation.

This may seem extreme to some. There is, however, a reason for withdrawing from society. By freeing themselves from worldly concerns and material attachments, such renunciants find it far easier to cultivate the pure and refined mind necessary for Self-Knowledge.

That isn't to say that enlightenment isn't possible for those with worldly karma. Far from it. It will, however, likely take more time and effort to tame the mind while juggling various work, family and social duties.

In its truest sense, renunciation doesn't mean abandoning all your possessions and social duties. It means giving up attachment to such things. That can only happen when you relinquish the belief that happiness comes from worldly objects and from getting what you want.

If there's a single motivation behind all human endeavour it's the desire to be happy and free.

As we saw in the first few chapters, most human beings seek this happiness, firstly, through security and wealth and, secondly, through pleasure. The more mature person also seeks happiness through dharma, or performing virtuous actions for the good of oneself and others. The fourth and final motivation behind human behaviour is, of course, the subject matter of this book: enlightenment or liberation.

The Problem With Action

If you happen to be reading this, you've probably already concluded that the best way to gain freedom is not to seek it by proxy, via objects, but to seek it directly.

That's done by going through the three stage process of Vedanta. You acquire, understand and then integrate the Knowledge revealed by the scriptures; and this alone leads to lasting liberation from suffering.

If, like most seekers, you aren't by temperament or by circumstance a renunciant, your greatest challenge will be balancing the demands of worldly life with the need to keep the mind appropriately pure and fit for Self-Knowledge.

Life without enlightenment is inherently stressful. Driven by samsara's signature stamp of insecurity and lack, you undertake action after action, hopefully in line with dharma, in order to free yourself of limitation.

The problem is that you don't have a say in the result of those actions.

This highlights the basic uncertainty common to all. You have a choice with regard to the actions you take, but no real choice over the results.

The thing about samsara is that if you don't get what you want you suffer; and if you do get what you want there's still no end to the anxiety. After all, in a world of constant change, what you gain one day you can just as easily lose the next. Or worse still, the object of your heart's desire can change and cease delivering the same happiness and satisfaction. It may even become a source of unhappiness.

As a seeker of liberation, you need some way of managing your karma. Otherwise, the stress and uncertainty of daily living will rob you of the dispassion, discrimination and discipline required for the assimilation of Self-Knowledge. That, in turn, will destroy any hope of attaining liberation in this lifetime.

Fortunately, Vedanta provides a solution to this predicament. It teaches a method of transacting with the world that minimises stress and should, if properly applied, render the mind fit for self-enquiry. This method is called karma yoga.

The Three Steps of Karma Yoga

As you will recall, karma means action. Everything that we do is karma and everything that happens as a result of these actions is karma. Our actions today are determined by the sum total of our past actions, and they also sow the seeds of future actions. Life in the phenomenal world is basically the never-ending dance of karma.

Karma yoga, which is explained in detail in the Bhagavad Gita, is a way of navigating life and performing our various duties in as stress-free a way as possible. It's both a practise and a mindset that helps us to neutralise the mind's entrenched desires and aversions, thereby cultivating as peaceful and undisturbed a mind as possible.

The Gita states that the mind can be either our greatest friend or our worst enemy. What follows is a foolproof technique for managing the mind, rendering it a friend rather than foe.

Karma yoga can be broken down into three simple steps:

1. **Cultivate gratitude.**
2. **Offer your actions to God.**
3. **Relinquish the outcome.**

Let's explore each of these three steps of karma yoga.

1. Cultivate Gratitude

Life is a precious gift. If you think about it, you've been given everything you'll ever need. That includes a body, a mind and all the necessary resources and conditions for them to survive and, hopefully, flourish.

At the start of each day, you don't need to go out in search of oxygen. You've already been given a lifetime supply. In fact, as long as you attend to the body's basic requirements for food, water, sleep and shelter, there's really very little you need to do to maintain it. The body already knows how to breathe and transport oxygen to all the cells and tissues; it knows how to circulate blood and nutrients, and how to digest food and excrete waste.

You don't need to worry about operating your senses and managing the faculties of sight, sound, taste, touch and smell. Your eyes automatically connect to visual objects; your ears automatically hear sound, and so on.

In fact, your body is the ultimate in user friendly instruments. It doesn't come with an instruction manual because it's all pretty much taken care of for you.

Sometimes it pays to stop and marvel at the sheer wondrousness of creation. Our very being here is a miracle! If the conditions on

Earth were even the slightest bit different—if its orbit happened to be a fraction closer to or farther from the sun—this planet would be nothing but a barren, inhospitable hunk of rock floating through space.

Yet here we are; gifted with an incredible body and mind and all the resources and tools we need in order to live and appreciate the wonder of being alive.

The human mind, alas, often assumes that this isn't enough in itself.

We delude ourselves into believing that life somehow owes us something.

Nothing could be further from the truth. Life has already given us everything; everything that we have and everything that we are.

The first step of karma yoga is learning to recognise that.

We each owe the world, life, and the Intelligence behind it, an enormous debt for our very existence.

To live a miserly, grasping life, desperately trying to hoard resources and scavenge whatever we can, regardless of the cost to others and the environment, is an insult to both oneself and God. It leads to an unhappy life of entitlement and dissatisfaction; because no matter how much such a person gets, it's never enough.

The wise person lives with an attitude of gratitude. They seek to give at least as much as they take from life. To live with a contributory mindset, to offer something back to the world in some way, leads to a far healthier and happier state of mind.

It also forms the basis of karma yoga.

Life is a gift and when somebody gives you a gift, it's natural to want to repay it. That doesn't mean that you have to live up to some saintly ideal and deny your basic needs and desires. It does, however, mean that you live from a sense of gratitude, humility and generosity. These are healthy, dharmic values as opposed to dissatisfaction, conceit and selfishness.

Alas, life won't always deliver all that we might want and desire. It can't. The universe is not set up to satisfy all of our personal desires and whims. It's unreasonable to expect circumstances and events to always align with our personal preferences.

Life experiences can also be painful and traumatic. Many of us must navigate extremely difficult and challenging circumstances. This is, after all, a field of duality, and there is no good without bad, no up without down and no pleasure without pain.

In dealing with the play of the opposites, we must each seek to develop as much dispassion and equanimity as we can. Working to acquire the fourfold qualifications is an excellent way to fortify the mind, insulating us from life's many pains and challenges.

Without these qualities, many people lose themselves in self-pity and despair, lamenting all that "could" and "should" have been. This is a trap that must be avoided at all costs. Resentfulness is a disempowering and destructive mindset; one that brings little but misery to ourselves and others.

The first step of karma yoga is to consciously shift to a mindset of gratitude and appreciation for all the good you've been given in life.

That includes the simple, everyday miracles many take for granted, such as the ability to see, hear, taste, smell and touch; to look up in wonder at the stars at night; to enjoy the embrace of a loved one; to feel the warmth of the sun on your skin; to live, experience, love and dream.

Life has given us all of this freely and generously, asking for little in return. Karma yoga is our way of expressing gratitude in action and looking for ways to repay the gift of life.

2. Offer Your Actions to God

As noted in the previous chapter, some seekers have difficulty with the word God due to its misuse at the hands of religion.

The problem lies not with the word itself but the many misconceptions that exist around it. Chapter Eleven tackles the subject head-on, unfolding the topic of God in a clear, concise and logical way. You are, of course, free to substitute the word God for whatever term you feel most comfortable with: the Universe, the Source, the Divine and so on.

As the Infinite Creative Intelligence behind all life, and the very substance of which the universe is made, everything actually belongs to God.

God is everything, everywhere; and is all around us in both form and essence. That's why you needn't go to a temple, church or mosque in order to worship the Divine; wherever you stand is holy ground.

God has given you everything, all of which is on temporary loan. Recognising the enormity of this gift naturally kindles a gracious and devotional attitude. You come to realise the necessity of "paying the rent", so to speak; of giving something back in return for the gift of life.

That's where we come to the second principle of karma yoga.

You pay your rent by offering your daily actions as a gift to God.

It doesn't matter what you're doing. Whether it's some great and noble endeavour to benefit the world or simply brushing your teeth in the morning, you can sanctify the action and offer it up in gratitude to God. That way, any action, no matter how small, becomes an act of worship.

By adopting a contributory mindset, you no longer do things for your own sake, or for a desired end, but as a way or repaying the debt you owe life. Your work becomes your worship.

This is especially rewarding when doing things for other people, whether it's cooking a meal for your family, taking care of a child or doing a favour for a friend. All interactions and transactions become holy when you consciously honour the Divinity within that person; the God shining within as their innermost being. By serving others, you are serving God. By serving yourself, such as feeding, bathing and taking care of your body, you are also serving God, for your body belongs to and is a part of God.

Karma yoga converts your entire life to a field of service and devotion. Every action, no matter how small, becomes sacred when you do it not for its own sake, but as an offering to the Divine.

This is a wonderfully rich and fulfilling way to live your life. You'll find that you only want to offer actions that are noble, dharmic and worthy of God. As a result, you naturally refrain from actions that are self-debasing or which might be harmful to yourself and others.

By recognising your body as a sacred temple, you find yourself inclined to treat it with the appropriate love, respect and care. You might be compelled to quit smoking, stop drinking as much alcohol or avoid junk food. After all, filling your body with toxins is hardly a fit way of offering thanks for its existence.

Everything you do becomes an offering of love; a way of contributing something to the Divine force that created the stars, the galaxies, the Earth and you.

Krishna summarises karma yoga in the Bhagavad Gita's third chapter:

> Selfless action, without thought of personal gain, liberates. The wise perform action not for themselves, but as an offering to the Divine. All beings have been created and had their needs provided for by the Creative Intelligence of life. Honour life and repay this gift by sanctifying your actions. By fulfilling your duty to life, you will thrive, as promised by the scriptures.

He also goes on to say that:

> Anyone who enjoys the fruits of life without offering anything in return is a thief.

A miserly approach to life brings sorrow. Living with generosity, however, purifies the mind, neutralising one's entrenched desires and aversions, leading to a peaceful and contented heart.

The Five Offerings of Karma Yoga

The scriptures offer five essential ways in which you can implement karma yoga in your life.

1. **Worship God in any form.** In order to purify the mind and render it fit for Self-Knowledge, it's important to live a God-centred life, however you choose to perceive God; whether as a personal deity, the totality of creation, or the unmanifest essence and foundation of all that is. Worship of the Divine might take the form of prayer, contemplation, meditation, the reciting of a mantra, or performing a daily ritual, as is the tradition in India. These will all be explored in Chapter Twelve in the topic of devotion.

2. **Honour and serve your parents and elders.** Another aspect of karma yoga is honouring and respecting your parents, who brought you into the world and raised you, providing you with all that you needed in your formative years. This respect and reverence should be extended to all your elders. As your elders age, be there for them, providing support and care as they did for you as a child. Of course, while this easy if you enjoy a positive and healthy relationship with your parents, it can be difficult if your relationship was challenging. Unfortunately, some people have dysfunctional and even abusive parents who were unable to provide the love, stability and support they needed and deserved. If this happens to be the case, the best you can do spiritually is to work on healing this wound and finding forgiveness in your heart. The power of forgiveness should never be underestimated. It doesn't mean sanctioning what another

person did to you. It means making your own healing and psychological and spiritual growth a priority, turning pain into a springboard for liberation.

3. **Worship the scriptures.** This means having the appropriate respect and reverence for the teachings, which are your bridge to Self-Realisation. This worship might take the form of regular study and contemplation of the Vedantic scriptures. The more diligently you immerse yourself in the teaching, the more it will transform your life, purifying both mind and heart and, in time, leading to enlightenment and liberation from lack, limitation and the worldly sorrows of samsara.

4. **Serve humanity.** Living a dharmic life means being willing to help others as and when appropriate. By keeping love in your heart and living with kindness, compassion and generosity, you are serving God in human form. This not only benefits others but also purifies the mind like nothing else. It doesn't mean you need to become a compulsive do-gooder, which can potentially be a trap for the ego. All you need do is respond appropriately to each situation in life with generosity, kindness and a willingness to reach out and help those who need it. Our goal should always be to give more to the world than we take from it and to leave it a better place for our having been here.

5. **Serve nature and all living beings.** Our service should not be restricted to our fellow human beings. We all live and depend upon this planet for our very existence and survival. Caring for nature, the environment and animals is a key aspect of dharma and something we should all be committed to. At present, humanity is exploiting and plundering the natural world, creating tremendously bad karma that succeeding generations will have to deal with. So, make it your duty to help the environment where you can. Reduce your consumption, minimise your carbon footprint and recycle. If you haven't

already, adopt a vegetarian or vegan diet which not only dramatically helps the environment but also prevents the needless suffering of animals.

3. Relinquish the Outcome

The final step of karma yoga, relinquishing our attachment to the outcome and accepting what comes with equanimity, effectively neutralises the agitation inherent in taking action.

Every day, we undertake a succession of actions, each with a specific goal in mind. Because we tend to become emotionally invested in the desired outcome, our actions are often accompanied by stress, insecurity and agitation.

The Bhagavad Gita states:

> You have the choice to act, but no choice over the results of that action. The results of action are never under your control. Desire for the fruits of your labour should never be your motivating factor.

This statement emphasises three key points. First of all, life consists of action. We can choose which actions we undertake; hopefully guided by dharma. The second point is that we have no choice over the results of that action. It's not up to us how things turn out. Once we perform an action, the result will be determined by countless factors outside our direct control. Finally, our actions shouldn't be motivated solely by the desire for certain results.

A Shift in Mindset

Let's start with the third point, which ties in with the second step of karma yoga. Krishna says that a person's actions should never be motivated solely by the desire to achieve certain ends.

Obviously, you will have certain goals in mind, otherwise you wouldn't have been compelled to take the action in the first place.

This becomes secondary, however. As a seeker of liberation, your primary goal is always to achieve a pure mind; a mind capable of attaining Self-Knowledge.

You do this by converting your work to your worship; by sanctifying your actions and offering them up to God in gratitude for the gift of life.

This subtle but vital shift in mindset helps neutralise the binding desires and aversions which otherwise dominate the psyche.

These desires and aversions lie at the root of all emotional disturbance. A life driven entirely by one's conditioned likes and dislikes will be a relentless rollercoaster of ups and downs; alternating highs of triumph and lows of frustration, anger and sorrow.

Another problem with attachment to the results of your actions is you remain dependent upon objects for your happiness. Because you have no control over the results of your actions, each time you don't get the outcome you want, you suffer. Indeed, the Bhagavad Gita warns that, "Action prompted by desire and anxiety over results will always cause misery."

Even when fulfilled, unchecked desire leads to dependence on objects; and desire, when thwarted, leads to anger or depression.

Both disturb the psychological equilibrium, distorting one's perception and deluding the mind. A deluded mind is incapable of seeing and responding to life with the necessary clarity and objectivity. Such a mind easily loses touch with dharma, leading to all kinds of problems both internal and external.

Self-destructive behaviour rapidly spirals into spiritual suicide. After all, a disturbed mind is incapable of effectively practising self-enquiry. This keeps the individual immersed in samsara and the cycle of desire, frustration and sorrow.

Accepting the Results of Action

Karma yoga neutralises these dangers by changing the way you approach action; and, just as importantly, the way you receive the results of action.

Krishna tells us to:

> Perform every action without attachment to the outcome, and accept what comes with grace, whether it be success or failure. Thus, you will find inner peace in the midst of action. This evenness of mind is the essence of karma yoga.

The key phrase here is, "Accept what comes with grace, whether it be success or failure."

Whether your action yields the desired result or not, what happens is a product of the law of karma; of cause and effect. It's a law to which all beings are subject. It cannot be controlled or circumvented, no matter how hard a person might try.

That's why, as a karma yogi, you take whatever results come with as much grace and equanimity as you can.

It may not be what you initially wanted, but, in order to maintain a still and peaceful mind, you accept it without resistance. That doesn't mean, of course, that you won't necessarily take more action to attain a different result. As children, it's drilled into us that "if at first you don't succeed, try, try again."

So, we're not talking about passive fatalism. You won't simply roll over, give up and never attempt anything again.

What you will do is consciously adopt a calm, stoic and pragmatic mindset. You recognise that what happened has happened, what is is, and there's no point throwing a tantrum over it.

A certain degree of emotional reactivity may be inevitable, for it's built into the human design. It's important, however, that you not hold onto bitterness and resentment. Instead, you respond with maturity and restraint, in the knowledge that sometimes you win in life and sometimes you lose. That's simply the nature of duality. Very often, our suffering doesn't come so much from what's happened as it comes from our reaction to what's happened.

Nothing Happens Arbitrarily

Life isn't a game of random chance. In spite of what some people claim, this isn't a chaotic, lawless universe. Quite the contrary, it's an ordered, lawful universe governed by inviolable natural laws.

As we'll explore in Chapter Eleven, these laws of creation, and the creation itself, are the product of Ishvara or God; the eternal Creative Intelligence pervading all things. The results of all actions are, therefore, dispensed by God.

This is not a personal God sitting on some throne, looking down upon the creation and arbitrarily deciding who wins and who loses. We're talking about the impersonal, macrocosmic Intelligence responsible for the creation and governing of the entire cosmos, including the laws of dharma and karma.

Whether you're pleased or displeased by a certain outcome, by recognising that the results of your actions are dispensed by the Creative force responsible for the entire phenomenon world, you come to realise that there's not a single atom in the universe that's out of place.

The karma yoga attitude enables you to accept both the good and the bad in life by recognising that, ultimately, there are always other factors at play and a higher principle governing all that happens.

Some readers may struggle with such a notion. If that's the case for you, please come back to this chapter after you've worked through the middle section of this book. You may find you have a vastly different perspective.

The results of any action come with both a seen and an unseen component. The immediate, seen and experienced result will be readily known to us. But there's also invariably an unseen, unknown result that will manifest in the fullness of time.

Human beings only ever see things from a limited vantage point. Because there are usually hidden downsides to every upside and upsides to every downside, we're not always the best judge of what is good and bad, or what is desirable and undesirable when it comes to results.

That's why it's wise not to succumb to blind emotional reactivity upon not getting what you want. Instead, you can look for the hidden upside and the opportunity to transform the seemingly unfavourable result into something more fortuitous.

As the macrocosmic Intelligence responsible for the creation, God, which is all-power and all-knowledge, sees, knows and is the entire picture. Because dharma is essentially the Divine law made manifest, we can be assured that this Creative Intelligence is benign and wants the best for all creatures and beings.

Human beings, of course, abusing the faculty of free will, constantly violate dharma and must suffer the consequences. This is not the fault of God, but rather the fault of our ignorance of God and the importance of dharma.

A Pragmatic Approach to Life

The true alchemy of living is knowing that there's a greater force at work, dispensing the results of all actions according to the laws of dharma and karma. Even when you don't get what you want, you're able to use it as a springboard for spiritual growth and strengthening your muscle of dispassion.

Karma yoga doesn't remove the duality of life and the fact that all beings are subject to both gain and loss, pleasure and pain, happiness and sorrow.

What it does is neutralise the mind's attachment and agitation by cultivating a mature, holistic and pragmatic outlook.

As karma yogi, you are clear about what you can and cannot control. You naturally focus on what you can control; your own actions. While you obviously still undertake action in order to attain specific results, you're no longer doing it solely for yourself, but as an act of service, devotion and gratitude for all the good you've been given in life.

This, in time, frees the mind from attachment, grasping and the crippling expectations and demands you've placed upon life—not to mention the fruitless emotional tantrums you might otherwise experience when you don't get what you want.

You know there's little point squandering your precious life energy worrying over outcomes you cannot control. You surrender those to the all-pervading Intelligence that creates and guides the stars, the galaxies and you, too.

You live simply and humbly, grateful for life's blessings and committed to following dharma at all levels. To live in such a way is to live in alignment with God; and, regardless of circumstances, such a life brings peace, happiness and satisfaction.

There's no better summary of karma yoga than Krishna's words in the Gita's second chapter:

> Living with the karma yoga attitude creates a tranquil heart and dispels the delusions of the mind. One becomes dispassionate toward the things of this world, all of which come and go of their own accord. No longer fixated on the various objects of the senses, the mind becomes serene and steady, and it comes to rest in contemplation of one's own Self. Becoming established in Self-Knowledge is the gateway to liberation.

The 3 Steps of
Karma Yoga

1   Cultivate **Gratitude**

2   **Offer** Your Actions to God

3   **Relinquish** the Results

Summary

- Traditionally, only renunciants with no worldly ties devoted themselves to liberation. However, it's wholly possible for people with worldly karma, including jobs and families, to attain enlightenment.
- The mind must be adequately prepared, however, and karma yoga is the primary means of doing that. That's why the practice of karma yoga is essential for all seekers of liberation.
- The three stages of karma yoga are cultivating gratitude, contributing back to life and relinquishing the outcome.
- Gratitude means appreciation for all that we have, all that we are, and all that we've been given in life.
- To repay this debt, we offer up our actions to Ishvara, or God, in a spirit of devotion and worship. Everything we do in life, from the profound to the mundane, can be sanctified as an offering to the Divine.

- The five prescribed offerings of karma yoga are worship of God in any form, unconditional respect for your parents, worship of the scriptures, service to humanity and service to nature and all living beings.
- The final stage of karma yoga is to accept whatever result comes, whether desirable or undesirable, as being the will of God.
- This creates the peace and evenness of mind necessary to prepare the mind for Self-Knowledge.

8.
The Entry Point

Arise! Awake! Stop not until the goal is reached.
Katha Upanishad

Congratulations on completing the first section of this book. We've now laid out the necessary foundations for understanding Vedanta and enlightenment. Before moving on, let's summarise what we've learned.

What causes us to be "unenlightened"?

The fundamental human problem is a deep rooted self-identity crisis. At our core, we don't feel like happy and complete beings. In fact, we feel fundamentally incomplete and subject to a terrible sense of lack, limitation and insufficiency.

How does this sense of lack manifest?

This self-dissatisfaction compels us to seek happiness and wholeness in the world around us, whether through money, possessions, love, sex, food, fast cars or an endless number of other fleeting pleasures. Although the objects of our desire vary greatly from person to person, it all amounts to the same thing: we are seeking happiness and wholeness outside of ourselves.

What's the problem with that?

The problem is that when we don't get what we want we suffer—and when we do get what we want we also suffer! Our attachment to the object of our desire inevitably brings sorrow. Everything in the phenomenal world is subject to change and eventual loss. Object-based happiness is, therefore, temporary at best. When it again turns to dissatisfaction and grief, we again find ourselves rummaging through the scrapheap of samsara looking for morsels of object-based happiness. So we keep spiralling in an endless cycle of desire, action and attachment; the whirlpool of samsara.

How do we get out of samsara?

The only way out of this predicament is to get to the root of the problem and deal with that. Vedanta reveals our real problem to be a sense of self-lack and self-insufficiency. We don't feel whole and complete in ourselves.

Why?

Ignorance has clouded our view of who and what we are. We have taken ourselves to be what we are not, as the next chapter on self-enquiry shall demonstrate.

What's the solution?

There's only one solution to ignorance and that's knowledge. In this case, our self-ignorance can only be remedied through Self-Knowledge. Self-Knowledge alone leads to enlightenment or liberation; which the scriptures unanimously declare to be life's highest goal.

What exactly is enlightenment?

The Bhagavad Gita describes the enlightened person as follows:

Those who realise the Self, and are satisfied with the Self alone, enjoy eternal contentment. Such people, having found the source of joy and fulfilment within, no longer seek happiness or gain in the external world. Secure in themselves and dependent upon no objects whatsoever, they have nothing to gain or lose by action.

The ultimate fruit of liberation is a simple but deep-rooted satisfaction with one's own Self and the world. Instead of being bound by frustrated desires and ceaseless craving, the enlightened feel utterly whole and complete in themselves, are free of binding desire, free of fear and free of the need to manipulate the objects of the world in order to attain happiness. In the words of Swami Paramarthananda: Prior to enlightenment, life is a burden. After enlightenment, life is a blessing.

How can Vedanta help me attain enlightenment?

Vedanta is an ancient body of knowledge designed to remove the false notions we've superimposed onto the Self. It promises an end to self-ignorance and the world of suffering this ignorance causes.

Is there a catch?

There's no catch, but in order for the teaching to be effective, the student must have certain mental qualifications: primarily, the ability the discriminate, as well as a degree of dispassion, mental discipline and the genuine desire to be free.

What next?

The student requires a teacher from the Shankaracharya lineage capable of unfolding the three stage teaching process of Vedanta. These three stages are listening, reasoning and deep contemplation. The student will sit down and listen as the teacher unfolds a radical new understanding of Reality—which will, in time, remove one's existential suffering and grief.

That doesn't sound so hard!

It's not. Vedanta is pretty easy if you're ready for it and have the ability to open your mind and at least temporarily set aside what you think you already know about yourself and the nature of Reality. Approach things with openness, good faith and a beginner's mind.

I can do that!

Good! If you're truly committed to liberation and are willing to do what is necessary to attain it, you're set to go.

The next section shall systematically unfold the heart of Vedantic teaching. So, when you're ready, let's get started.

Part Two

The Power of Self-Knowledge

9.
Self-Enquiry

> When your false perception is corrected, your suffering ends also.
>
> *Adi Shankara*

Who are you?

That's the primary question we're concerned with in Vedanta. It's also, as it happens, the doorway to liberation.

We all know that we exist. That much is self-evident. After all, you don't need anyone to tell you that you exist, because that's probably the one ironclad certainty in life. That you exist is never in question. The real question is who and what you exist as.

If I ask you to tell me who you are, you might say something along the lines of, "My name is Madeline. I'm thirty-five years old and was born and live in London. I have a husband and two young children. I'm an artist and I love musical theatre, freshly brewed coffee and reading crime novels."

That all may be true.

But does it *really* answer the question of who you are?

Or is it simply a list of incidental characteristics; a set of circumstances and facts woven into a story about who you think you are; who you assume yourself to be?

Would you still be *you* if you had a different name; if you were called Jane rather than Madeline? What if you were three decades older, or younger? Would you still be you if you were the opposite gender or from a different country on the other side of the world? What if you had no kids and had a completely different career, or no career at all? If you preferred tea to coffee and hated crime novels?

If such characteristics were altered, how would that affect you; the real you?

And what exactly is that "you", anyway?

Let's think of this chapter as a treasure hunt. The treasure we're seeking? Nothing other than your own true Self!

A catalogue of false identification

You Are Not Who You Think You Are

In common with all human beings, you've basically derived a sense of identity, a persona, by identifying with your biographical story; with the circumstances and events of your life. That might include your birth place, parents and family, immediate environment, your age, sex, conditioned beliefs and ingrained likes and dislikes. These have all shaped your "personhood".

Psychologists call this the self-concept; the mental idea you have about who you are. Your self-concept is far from solid. In fact, it's constantly changing and evolving; modifying to each new experience and the way you process and interpret those experiences. The person you think you are today is almost certainly different from the person you thought you were twenty years ago.

So, here's an interesting question. If your self-concept is subject to change, can that really be who you are? Can something so changeable actually be real?

Vedanta has a very specific and exacting definition of what constitutes "realness". In short, that which is real doesn't change. For example, a dog cannot be a dog in the morning and a cat in the evening. Its essential qualities of dog-ness are immutable; they don't change from moment to moment. That's how we know that a dog is really a dog.

The same logic applies to the question of who you are at the most essential level. The real part of you doesn't, and cannot change, even if the rest of you appears to undergo constant modification.

Over the course of a single day, a human being can assume a succession of different roles and identities: you can be a parent, a son or daughter, a teacher or student, employer or employee, and so on. These roles change depending on the context of the situation. When you're with your parents, you're a son or daughter, yet when you're with your own child, you're the parent. You might be a teacher by day, yet you're also going to night school, in which case you then become the student.

These roles build the framework of your "story", along with your biographical data, memories, experiences, beliefs and opinions.

But what do such roles *really* say about you; the reality of you?

They cannot be you, because they change frequently; even over the course of a single day.

As, of course, do your body, mind, thoughts, mood and sense of identification. One moment you identify with your body as you lament, "I'm fat!" The next moment you identify with your emotions by saying, "I'm sad". One moment, during an experience of triumph, you feel confident and good about yourself and then, five minutes, later something happens to shatter your confidence and you suddenly feel lowly and inadequate.

The idea that you are a fixed entity with inherent, set characteristics is false. The person you think you are is subject to perpetual change and modification. Your story of "you" is always changing. Even the subtlest shift in your mood can drastically alter your self-concept.

Something so fickle and changeable cannot be real, according to our definition.

To put it simply, you are not who you think you are. After all, who you think you are is always changing from moment to moment.

The Three Bodies

We're still left with the million dollar question: *who are you?*

At this point in our process of self-enquiry, it would be helpful to consider some of Vedanta's teaching models for understanding what constitutes an individual being. What I'm about to share is not something I've invented myself. It's ancient knowledge from the Vedas. This knowledge has remained unchanged over the millennia—because, again, that which is real does not change.

First and foremost, Vedanta states that we don't actually have one body, but three bodies.

Of course, we're all familiar with the physical body, which is comprised of physical matter. We're also blessed, however, with a subtle body and a causal body. It's the combination of these three bodies that constitute a living, conscious being.

The Three Bodies

Gross Body
Composed of physical matter/ the five elements.

Causal Body
Composed of causal matter. Repository of unconscious, karma, vasanas (conditioned tendencies).

Subtle Body
Composed of subtle matter. Consists of mind, ego, intellect, sense organs, organs of action and physiological functions.

1. The Gross Body

The gross body is another term for the physical body and, therefore, needs little introduction. In Tattva Bodha, Shankara explains:

> The gross body is that which is made up of the five elements. It is born of the good actions (karma) of the past, is the vehicle by which one gains experience in the world, both pleasurable and painful, and is subject to the six modifications: to exist, to be born, to grow, mature, decay and die.

Funnily enough, another term for the physical body in Vedanta is "the food body", for the body is literally made of and sustained by the food that we eat.

This body is our primary vehicle for transacting with the world. Believe it or not, it's considered good karma to have been born in a human body. The reason is simple. Human beings are blessed with the faculty of refined intellect. That enables us to attain liberation from the cycle of birth and death, something we will explore in subsequent chapters.

The gross body, which is obviously finite and has a limited lifespan, tends to be most people's primary centre of identification. It is, after all, clearly visible to you via the senses—and, wherever you go in life, there it is.

Because of ignorance, you assume that the body and its various components and attributes not only belong to you, but are you. "I'm tall," you might say, or "I'm thin", "I'm old" or "I'm young."

What you are doing when making such statements is mutually superimposing the qualities of the body onto yourself and your sense of Self onto the body.

Fortunately, the idea that you are the body is easily negated. As we shall see when we delve deeper into self-enquiry, the body is not you, but is an object known to you. As such, it cannot *be* you.

The gross vehicle provides a temporary abode for Consciousness and is subject to all kinds of limitation, from various illnesses and injuries to eventual death.

We think of the body as being alive; and it is, but it possesses no inherent life of its own. It is, after all, comprised of physical matter—which is, by itself, is as inert as a rock.

In order to be granted life and sentience, the gross body requires the presence of two other bodies: the subtle body and the causal body.

2. The Subtle Body

Our second vehicle, the subtle body, interfaces the physical body. But, as its name implies, it is not visible to the outer senses, for it is composed of subtle rather than gross matter. Tattva Bodha states:

> [The subtle body] is also born of the good actions (karma) of the past and is an instrument for subtle experience. It consists of seventeen components: five sense organs, five organs of action, the five physiological functions, the mind and the intellect.

By itself, the gross body is just a lump of inert matter. When associated with the subtle body, however, the physical body is illumined by Consciousness and granted life and sentience.

Both bodies work in unison, allowing us to experience the world of the senses and to take action in that world.

Of the subtle body's seventeen components, outlined above, we're most likely to identify with the mind, intellect and ego. These give rise to our own private inner world of thought, emotion, memory, belief and imagination.

Let's take a look at the subtle body in a little more detail.

1. *The Sense Organs*

The sense organs are a vital component of the subtle body and are divided into two categories.

First of all, we have the five senses of knowledge, or the perceptive senses, which provide us with information about our environment.

Then we have the five senses of action, which, as their name implies, allow us to take action in the world.

So, the senses of knowledge allow us to *know*, and the senses of action allow us to *do*.

The five senses of knowledge and their respective sense instruments are:

1. The faculty of seeing (eyes).
2. The faculty of hearing (ears).
3. The faculty of smell (nose).
4. The faculty of taste (tongue).
5. The faculty of touch (skin).

While the sense *instruments*, the eyes, ears, nose, and so on, are part of the gross body, the actual sense *organs* belong to the subtle body.

That explains how you are able to see, hear, touch, feel and move in a dream, when the sense instruments, such as the eyes, ears, etc., are dormant and unavailable. The sense organs are capable of functioning without the physical body. That's why they are considered part of the subtle body.

These sense organs all relate to our ability to perceive. But what good is perception if we cannot respond to our experience?

Accordingly, we also have five sense organs of action. These are, along with their sense instruments:

1. The faculty of speech (mouth).
2. The faculty of moving objects (hands).
3. The faculty of locomotion; moving from place to place (feet).
4. The faculty of reproduction (genitals).
5. The faculty of excretion and removing waste (anus).

If the first five sense organs, the organs of knowledge, are like entry gates, enabling us to take in information about the world, the five organs of action are the exit gates, enabling us to respond to the stimulus and transact meaningfully with the world.

When we mistakenly identify ourselves with the senses, we're liable to make such statements as "I see", "I hear", "I taste", and so on.

2. The Physiological Functions

Another component of the subtle body are what we call the *pranas*, or the physiological functions. These are what provide the physical body with life, energy and vitality. Once again, there are five key functions at work:

1. Respiration, by which we take in oxygen and expel carbon dioxide.
2. Circulation, allowing the necessary oxygen and nutrients to be transported to the body's cells and organs.
3. Digestion, by which essential nutrients are extracted from food.
4. Excretion, by which waste is processed and removed from the body.
5. Expulsion, which relates to the removal of foreign bodies or harmful substances from the body. This may, for example, take the form of sneezing or vomiting.

To reiterate, the physical body is composed of physical matter, which is itself inert. It's the interfacing subtle body with its senses and the key physiological processes that bless it with life, energy, vitality and health. The moment the physiological functions cease, the physical body dies.

When ignorance causes a person to identify with this aspect of the subtle body, they'll make statements such as "I'm hungry", "I'm thirsty", "I'm breathing", "I'm digesting my food" or "I'm sneezing or coughing".

3. *The Mind and Intellect (Plus Memory and Ego)*

There are four more vital components of the subtle body, although Tattva Bodha chunks it down to two.

The first, the mind, needs little introduction. Along with the physical body, the average person's sense of identification will tend to align with the mind and its various thoughts, feelings, emotions and desires.

In the Vedantic model, mind is the seat of emotion, desire and doubt; in short, our capacity to feel, experience and to question that experience, as we invariably do.

When we identify with the mind, we essentially *become* our feelings, as evidenced by statements such as "I am happy", "I am sad", or "I am angry."

The subtle body works as follows. The senses of knowledge relay data to the mind. The mind takes this sensory input and arranges these streams of information (sight, sound, touch, smell and taste) into one, coherent experience.

The mind then responds by emoting; by reacting to what we are experiencing. This reaction will be coloured by past experience and by our operant conditioning. We either tend to like what we're experiencing, or we don't.

We also have a tendency to doubt or question what we're experiencing. This is because, as we all learn, often the hard way, we cannot always trust the senses alone. We need to interpret and evaluate what we're experiencing and determine whether something is safe or unsafe; desirable or undesirable.

That's where the intellect comes in. The intellect deals with higher reasoning and our ability to make informed decisions. Incidentally, when Awareness identifies with the intellect, we find ourselves making statements such as "I know", "I believe" or "I am certain".

The intellect judges and evaluates our experience using memory (another faculty of the subtle body) and past experience. We ideally respond to situations in a way that will get us what we want and avoid getting what we don't want.

Intellect, therefore, is the decider. It determines the action we should take in response to a given situation.

Animals have both a mind and an intellect, but human beings have a far more developed intellectual capacity. It's this faculty of intellect that has, for better or worse, enabled us to become the dominant species on the planet.

So, what happens next? Once the intellect has decided exactly how we should respond to a situation, we then take action, courtesy of the ego.

The ego is the final component of the subtle body and accounts for our sense of doership. We become a "doer" when the ego marshals the senses of action in order to take the appropriate action, whatever that might be.

This sense of being a doer is tremendously powerful. Indeed, it has to be, in order to grant us the sense of being an autonomous agent of action in the world.

It's easy to see how, through ignorance, we can identify ourselves with the doer/ego function, as evidenced by statements such as "I act" and "I did this or that". For most people, this sense of being an ego, a doer and enjoyer of action and its results, is an almost impossible identification to break.

3. *The Causal Body*

Lo and behold, we're not done yet. There's one final body we must consider, which we call the causal body. Somewhat equating with the Western notion of the unconscious, the causal body is, as its name suggests, the cause of the other two bodies. Tattva Bodha describes it as follows:

> The causal body is inexplicable, beginningless and of the nature of ignorance. It is that which causes the gross and subtle bodies to come into being, is the source of self-ignorance and is free from duality.

It's helpful to think of this body as the unmanifest seed state and the repository of all our past karma. (Please note, karma will be the topic of Chapter Sixteen.)

Unlike the first two bodies, which can be experienced—the gross body is perceived via the senses as physical matter and the subtle body is known via the subtle processes of thought, emotion and so on—the causal body cannot be experienced directly.

We can infer its existence, however, because it's the seed state out of which the other two bodies arise, are sustained and have their being.

During deep, dreamless sleep, the gross body is asleep and unavailable to us and the subtle body (including the senses, mind, intellect and ego) recedes into the causal body like a wave merging back into the ocean.

We can no longer transact with either the physical world or even the subtle world of our thoughts, dreams and imagination. All differentiation between subject and object is negated.

That's why, in deep sleep, we no longer experience a sense of duality and are ignorant of everything, hence the causal body's association with ignorance.

As the saying goes, ignorance is bliss, and we experience this dreamless sleep as an immense and all-encompassing bliss. That's why everybody wants a good night's sleep and why we object most vehemently to being awoken from it.

We also taste the bliss of the causal body in the waking state, too, when the mind is sufficiently stilled, such as through the attainment of a desire, the absence of fears or doubt and in the quietude of meditation.

The Five Sheaths

Another model for understanding the nature and constitution of the individual being is called the five sheaths (or *koshas* in Sanskrit).

Rather like the layers of an onion, we each possess five "sheaths", each of which represents a certain aspect of the gross, subtle and causal bodies. We have the food sheath, the vital air sheath, the mental sheath, the intellect sheath and the bliss sheath.

THE FIVE SHEATHS

1. **The Food Sheath** might sound peculiar, but is actually another term for the gross or physical body. As noted, our physical body is literally composed of and sustained by the food that we eat (and, indeed, prior to our birth, the food consumed by our parents; our mother in particular). It is created from the five elements and, upon reaching the end of its lifespan, this vessel again returns to the five elements.

2. **The Vital Air Sheath** corresponds to the physiological functions of the subtle body. This includes respiration, the circulation of blood and other vital fluids and essences, digestion,

excretion of waste and the ability to expel foreign bodies and unwanted substances. The vital air sheath also includes the five organs of action: our capacity for speech, moving objects, propelling the body, procreation and elimination of waste. Once food is consumed by the gross body, or food sheath, this is converted to energy by the vital air sheath, which allows for the smooth functioning of all bodily processes and the ability to take action in the world via the senses of action.

3. The Mind Sheath relates to, you guessed it, the mind. This sheath is associated with both the mind itself and the five organs of knowledge (the capacity for seeing, hearing, touching, tasting and smelling). These senses automatically relay their respective streams of information and the mind arranges it all into one combined experience. In response to the stimulus, the mind emotes, generating either desire or fear; attraction or repulsion.

4. The Intellect Sheath. Once the mind has processed the sensory data and generated an emotional response, the faculty of intellect will evaluate, judge and make a decision with regard to the appropriate action. Together, the vital air, mind and intellect sheaths constitute the subtle body and its functioning.

5. The Bliss Sheath is last, and by no means, least. This sheath is associated with the causal body and the deep sleep state. It's a common misassumption that we somehow aren't present in the state of deep sleep. In actuality, we are, for we know whether or not we've had a good sleep and will most certainly have been aware of the subtle passage of time. The senses are simply inactive. Because there are no objects to cognise, the mind merges into the causal body like a wave folding back into the ocean. In this causal state, we experience a sense of expansive bliss, free of objects, thought, division and duality. Just as ignorance is bliss, so is sleep; something that we all enjoy and are extremely unhappy to have disturbed.

The All-Important Discrimination

We've now explored the constitution of the human being in terms of the three bodies and the five sheaths; two unique models for understanding what comprises an individual entity.

So, here's the important question: just where are *you* in all of this?

We've seen how easily we slip into identification with each component of the three bodies. We are all naturally inclined to identify with the physical body. "Don't touch me", you might say; implying that you are, in fact, your physical form and something that can be touched.

We also readily identify with the subtle body. Try to notice that the next time you find yourself identifying with your thoughts and feelings, or with being hungry, thirsty or tired. You certainly experience such things, but are they, in fact, the essence and totality of what you are? Are *you* really tired, or hungry, or are you simply experiencing tiredness or hunger?

After introducing the three bodies and the five sheaths, Tattva Bodha delivers a crucial discrimination. Shankara states:

> My possessions, whether my house, my bracelet, or my clothing, may belong to me; but, clearly, that which belongs to me must be other than myself, who am the knower of these things. In the same way, while the three bodies and the five sheaths may seemingly belong to me—"my body", "my mind", "my intellect" and "my ignorance"—they must clearly be other than myself, who am the knower. Therefore, the Self must be other than the aggregates of the three bodies and five sheaths.

In other words, you are not that which is known.

Because these bodies and sheaths are objects known to you, they cannot be you—the knower. They cannot be the Self.

Obviously, you can own any number of material objects, but these possessions are easily distinguished from *you*, for you are that which owns them. The same is true of all objects, whether gross or subtle—and that includes your own body and mind.

The knower is always distinct from that which is known. The subject cannot be known as an object. So, what you truly are must be *other* than the components of the three bodies and the five sheaths. They are a part of you, just as your hand and your foot is part of you, but they are not *you*.

Guided Exercise 1
Where Are You?

Let's continue our self-enquiry by trying a little experiment.

1. If I were to ask you to point to yourself, where would you point? Actually do it right now and see what happens. *Where are you?* Point yourself out to me.
2. I'm almost a hundred percent certain you will point to your body. Let's get more specific, however. Which part of your body did you point to? Did you point to the top half of your body or the bottom half? This will reveal where you intuitively locate your basic sense of "I am-ness".
3. If I were a betting man, I'd wager you pointed to the top half of your body. So, here's the next question. When I ask you to point yourself out to me again, will you point above or below your neckline?
4. Most people will probably point to the head but some people may point to their heart or chest. If you point to your head, are you above or below the nose? Many people tend to get the sense that "they" exist in the area around or between the eyes. If you pointed to your heart, are you the right or the left side of your chest? See if you can get really specific as you zero in on the

location of this sense of existing; of being you.
5. Our enquiry doesn't end there. You get the sense that "you", as a person, are somehow located inside the head or the heart area. That's fine. But here's the next, all important question: *How are you aware of existing at this point in your head or heart?* What is it that's *aware* of this point of "am-ness"?
6. Take a moment to really consider this question. You have a sense that, as a person, you're somehow located in your body—but how do you know that? What is it that enables you to be aware of this sensation?
7. The answer is, of course, Awareness.
8. Where is this Awareness located? Where does it begin and where does it end?

Where, indeed!

Awareness is impossible to pinpoint. It has no particular location. It pervades the mind and senses. It also pervades all perceptions, all thoughts, images, sounds and experiences. Like space, Awareness encompasses everything and cannot be pinned down whatsoever.

Not only that, but it never changes. It's the very same Awareness that has experienced the outer world of objects and the inner world of your thoughts from the moment your body was born until this present moment.

So much has passed through your Awareness in all that time.

You've experienced an infinitude of sensory perceptions, thoughts, feelings and ideas about yourself and the world. You've seen your body grow from a little child to, presumably, a mature adult.

It's the very same Awareness all this time, however.

The Awareness looking out of your eyes right now is no different to the Awareness that looked out of your eyes as a newborn baby.

As we saw in our example with Madeline, the characteristics that comprise our personhood, our sense of who we think we are, are not only arbitrary but also subject to change and modification.

The Awareness pervading them, however, never changes and never modifies to experience. It's always just *there*.

This Awareness is what we might term an essential factor, because it's always present and it never changes. Recall that our definition of what is real is that which never changes.

We'll come back to this realisation repeatedly because its importance cannot be overstated. It is, in fact, the key to shattering the chains of samsara and ending our misplaced emotional suffering.

The Three States of Consciousness

Before we go on to explore the nature of Awareness in greater detail, there's another key Vedantic teaching which may help tie this all together. It comes from the shortest but one of the most important Upanishads, the Mandukya Upanishad.

Did you know that you don't actually experience the same state of consciousness throughout the day?

In fact, each and every twenty four hours, we go through three distinct and separate states of consciousness. These are the waking state, the dreaming state and the deep sleep state.

Let's briefly explore each state before seeing why the implications of this are so profound.

1. *The Waking State*

During the waking state, the mind and senses are conscious and focused outward. The eyes relay images, the ears relay sound, and so on. The gross body, subtle body and causal body and all their components function in synchronised harmony, allowing us to interface and transact with the external world and to accomplish various goals and ends. When Awareness is associated with the

The Three States of Consciousness

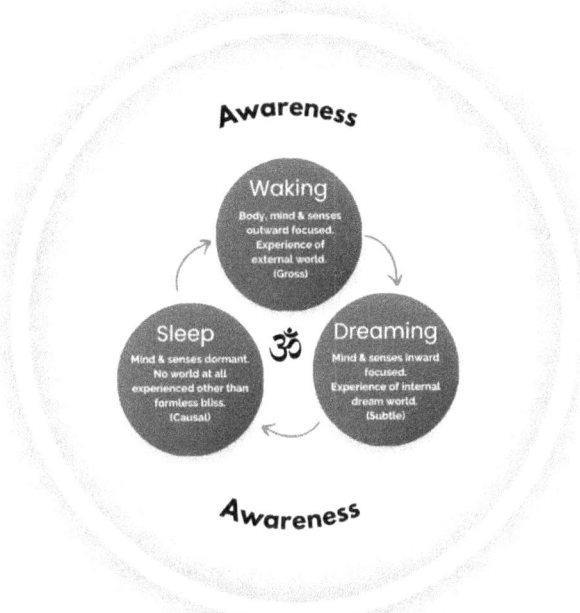

waking state, we become the waker or the waking state entity; in other words, the person who goes about life doing and achieving various ends.

2. *The Dream State*

The Dream State occurs when the gross body is asleep and the senses turn inward. While the gross body is dormant, the subtle body is still very much awake and projects an inner world based upon the various impressions and conditioning accumulated in the waking state. No longer experiencing the external world, we instead become immersed in an inner, subjective world of various subtle forms and experiences. Awareness associated with this state of consciousness is called the dreamer or dreaming state entity. Incidentally, the dream world we experience is just as real to us as the waking world until we happen to wake up and again become the waking state entity.

3. The Deep Sleep State

The Deep Sleep State is a state in which both the gross and subtle bodies are both dormant. We experience neither the objective outer world nor the subjective inner world. Instead, consciousness is at rest in a state of non-dual blankness which happens to be highly blissful and refreshing to both body and mind. Essentially, the subtle body has merged into the causal body in a state of restful ignorance, devoid of knowledge or cognition. In this state, Awareness is associated with and seemingly "becomes" the deep sleeper. As stated earlier, contrary to what people may assume, we very much experience this state because, upon waking, we are very clear whether or not we slept well. We are also aware of the passage of time. Sleep is not experienced as simply the instantaneous closing and opening of the eyes. Awareness remains throughout. In deep sleep, however, there are no objects to cognise and no mind or subtle body to produce impressions. So, while Awareness is there, there is nothing to be aware of.

The Essence of Self-Enquiry

The implication of this teaching is simple yet profound. It reveals that the person you think you are, the waking state entity, is, in fact, only present in one of the three states of consciousness you experience in any given day.

Remember, what is real is unchanging. If the waking state entity was real, it would be present at all times in *all* states of consciousness.

The experiencer, however, is constantly changing.

The person you assume yourself to be, whatever your name and biographical detail, is just one facet of your identity and is far from permanent. Indeed, because you are constantly shifting from waker to dreamer to deep sleeper, you cannot be any one of those entities.

So what, then, *are* you?

The real you, must, by definition, be that which is always present and which pervades all three states.

So, there has to be another, more fundamental, aspect of your being; something present in all states of consciousness which is not subject to change.

This, the Upanishad reveals, is simply Awareness (or Consciousness with a big "C"); the knower of these three states. Awareness is present in the waking state, in the dream state, and also in the deep sleep state when both the gross and subtle bodies are dormant. Awareness is the one factor that pervades all three states.

Awareness, then, has to be your Self; the true essence of what you are.

Bingo!

Here we have the essence of self-enquiry.

Are you the body?

No, for the body is an object known to you and is only present in one of the three states of consciousness (the waking state). Because the body isn't permanent and is an object known to you, it cannot be the subject; it cannot be you. The knower is always distinct from the known.

Are you the mind, intellect, ego or senses?

Again no, because, again, these are objects known to you. The subtle body is experienceable through the functioning of the mind and senses, as well as the capacity for memory and the physiological processes. It's also present in only two of the three states of consciousness (the waking and dream states). It only appears to be "you" when you superimpose your sense of Self, your sense of "I am-ness", onto it. We'll discuss the nature of this superimposition in greater detail later on.

Are you the causal body or the unconscious?

Again, no. The causal body cannot be experienced directly. But its existence can be inferred because it's the repository of all our karma [explained in Chapter Sixteen] and is that by which the gross and subtle bodies manifest and function. Subsequent chapters will make this clearer to you.

In conclusion, we've seen that the individual person is made of various components, including the three bodies and five sheaths. It also continually shifts between the three states of consciousness.

These are all elements of your being, but they are not you. They cannot be you because they can be objectified and are subject to change and impermanence.

When all the inessentials are negated, only one essential factor remains: Awareness.

You are the pure Awareness in which your body, mind, ego and all your thoughts, memories and beliefs appear; and the light by which all things are known. You are that which is unchanging, intangible and formless, yet always present.

This Awareness is the one, eternal Self; the topic of our next chapter.

Summary

- The primary question Vedanta is concerned with is: who are you?
- We all know that we exist, but our identity hinges upon numerous incidental characteristics, from our name, biographical details, to our occupation, age, beliefs and the various roles we play in life. These are constantly changing from moment to moment.
- Vedanta's definition of real is that which never changes.
- The three body teaching states that we each have three bodies: a gross (physical) body, a subtle body and the causal body. We're already intimately familiar with the gross body, made of physical matter.

- The subtle body, made of subtle matter, consists of seventeen components. These are the five sense organs of knowledge (seeing, hearing, smell, touch and taste), the five sense organs of action (mouth, hands, legs, genitals and anus), the five physiological functions (respiration, circulation, digestion, excretion and expulsion), plus the mind and intellect (and, by extension, the memory and ego).
- The causal body, made of causal matter, is not experienced directly but can be known by inference. It is the unconscious, unmanifest seed state containing all our karma and from which the subtle and gross bodies arise.
- The five sheaths is another model for understanding the composition of the individual being. These sheaths are the food sheath (physical body), the vital air (or physiological function) sheath, the mind sheath, the intellect sheath and the bliss sheath (corresponding to the causal body).
- Each day all beings undergo three successive states of consciousness: the waking state, the dream state and the deep sleep state. Awareness, or Consciousness, pervades each of these states and is the one common and continuous factor; the one thing that never changes.
- Self-enquiry reveals that you cannot be the three bodies, the five sheaths or any of the three states of consciousness. These are all known to you as objects. They are also subject to change and are impermanent. You are the knower, not that which is known; the subject and not the object.
- You can only be the pure Awareness in which the body, mind, ego and all thoughts and forms appear; the light by which all things are known. All things phenomenal are subject to change, but Awareness is changeless and eternal

10.
The Self

> When you hear about the Self, meditate upon the Self, and finally realise the Self, you come to understand everything in life.
> *Brihadaranyaka Upanishad*

The subject matter of Vedanta is the Self—you! By breaking the shackles of self-ignorance and knowing the Self as it truly is, you attain life's highest goal, ending suffering and revealing the essence of all things.

Of course, you already actually know the Self.

After all, we all instinctively know that we exist. The fact that you exist, that you are, is self-evident. So, you do know that you *are*; you just perhaps don't know *what* you are.

Our fundamental problem in life is rarely what we assume it is. In spite of whatever our circumstantial issues might be, the true problem hinges upon the "I", on the self—or, rather, the self that we assume ourselves to be.

Under the spell of ignorance, we go through life blighted by the curse of the inadequate self; the notion that we are a lacking, limited little person subject to pain, struggle, loss and eventual death.

How can you be happy when saddled with such a self?

There's no escaping what we are. So if you are dissatisfied with who you are, and most human beings are to a greater or lesser degree, how can you ever experience true happiness; a happiness that isn't dependent on always getting what you want?

Fortunately, as our foray into self-enquiry revealed, you are not actually the lacking, limited self you may have long assumed yourself to be. That is a case of mistaken identity. It comes from taking the apparent to be real; from making the assumption that because you experience a body and mind you are that body and mind.

The last chapter examined our tendency to identify with the components of the three bodies and the five sheaths (or, to put it simply, identifying ourselves as the body, mind and ego). Each, however, is impermanent, subject to change and is available to you as an object of perception, whether gross or subtle. In short, they are factors known to you. The known will always be distinct from the knower.

The underlying constant, the factor pervading each of these variables, is Awareness. What you actually are, therefore, is Awareness.

You might recall that Vedanta's definition of real is that which never changes. Awareness is the one thing that never changes; the one thing that never comes and goes and can never be lost. A person can radically change over the course of a lifetime, physically and psychologically, but Awareness never changes whatsoever. It's the one unchanging factor amid a sea of ever shifting variables.

You might be wondering why, however, if Awareness is always present and is the core of who and what we are, it's something we generally overlook? I mean, just how often are you even aware of your Awareness? Why is it relegated to the periphery of our attention despite being the core of our being?

The Tenth Man

Once upon a time, ten young monks made their way through the forest on their way to a nearby town. Recent floods had burst the banks of the river and the men had no option but to swim across to the other side.

Upon reaching the other side, the eldest of the monks, who'd promised his Master that he would keep watch over everyone, decided to make sure that everybody had safely crossed the river. He lined up the men and counted each of them in turn. "One, two, three, four, five, six, seven, eight, nine..."

Nine! There were only *nine* of them.

Where was the tenth?

Overcome by despair, he counted again and again and each time he could count only nine men. One of them must surely have been swept away by the current? Was it possible he had drowned?

Just as they were about to begin a search, they were approached by a wise old man who happened to witness the entire commotion. "Excuse me," the old man said. "I couldn't help but notice your trouble. If you allow me, I can produce the tenth man for you."

Sceptical yet desperate for help, the monk agreed to let him help.

The old man asked the monks to again stand in line. He touched each on the shoulder as he counted slowly, "One, two, three, four, five, six, seven, eight, nine, ten!" He smiled as he touched the leader of the group on the shoulder. "You, my friend, are the tenth man. You forgot to count yourself!"

What an unspeakable relief! The tenth man hadn't drowned in the river, after all. He'd been there all along hidden in plain sight.

This story is a metaphor for our own desperate search to find our true Self. It's crazy the lengths we'll go to in order to find the Self; whether by engaging in various practises, rituals or techniques and hopping from teaching to teaching.

This Self that you're so eager to find?

It's already present and available to you, as it has been *all along*.

The Self, Awareness, is right here, right now, as close to you as your own breath and as clear as the morning sun.

The only reason you've not been aware of it is that, like the counting monk, you've been looking for it outside of yourself. You've counted absolutely everything but the most obvious thing of all—your own Self!

It's been obscured by ignorance and the only way to reveal it is to remove that ignorance. That's precisely what Vedanta does, for Vedanta is a tool for removing self-ignorance.

The Mystery of Awareness

Like the tenth man, Awareness is already present and plainly obvious.

Without it, you wouldn't be able to perceive or experience a single thing. Awareness is our carrier of reality; the light that reveals all things. The only reason we fail to apprehend it is ignorance.

What can we say of this Awareness?

We can say with certainty that Awareness is always present and is self-revealing. We don't need a second Awareness in order to reveal it, for, like the shining sun, it reveals itself.

Whatever experience you're having, whether in the waking state, the dream state, or even the void of deep sleep, Awareness is always there. Like the light illuminating the objects of a room, Awareness pervades all perceivable objects and underlies your experience of absolutely everything. It's an omnipresent light with no beginning, no end and which relies upon nothing else for its existence.

Incidentally, "Awareness" is capitalised here to distinguish it from the act of simply being aware *of* something; for example, I can say I am aware of the fact it is daytime; I have awareness of daytime. Awareness is not awareness of this or that. It doesn't come into existence only when we become aware *of* something. On the contrary, it's always there as the very ground of our being.

Equally, don't think that it's a different, special or "exalted" Awareness because of the capitalisation; something that you need to seek, find and add to yourself. It's already fully present, right now, as the simple, ordinary, everyday Awareness by which you've experienced your entire life.

Another important note. In Vedanta, the words Awareness and Consciousness are used interchangeably. They point to the same thing. So, sometimes the Self is described as Awareness and sometimes it is described as Consciousness. Neither word is entirely quite right, because both can be misleading unless properly understood. They are, however, the best terms that we have in English.

The nature of Awareness or Consciousness has always been a source of mystery to scientists. In resignation, many have dismissed it as an irrelevant epiphenomenon. They concede that it's there but dismiss it as nothing but a byproduct of the brain's functioning. That assertion is neither satisfactory nor even, ironically, scientific.

Because the physical sciences pertain only to the material world, scientists will naturally assume that Awareness/Consciousness is somehow a product of the body and mind.

However, this assumption makes little sense when you consider that the body and mind are, by themselves, insentient.

The body is composed of physical matter and the subtle body is composed of subtle matter. Matter is inert. Just take a look around at the various elements: rocks, metals, liquids, wood and so on. By itself, matter lacks life; it lacks sentience.

It is only granted sentience when associated with a subtle body, as in the case of human beings, animals and, to a lesser extent, plants. That's the difference between a rock and an animal or a human. The rock only has a gross body and not a subtle body, whereas a sentient being necessarily possesses both.

The sentience, however, does not come from the subtle body itself. The subtle body acts as a reflecting medium. It reflects the light of pure Awareness, which is the Self. (We will discuss the reflection teaching in greater detail in the Chapter Fifteen.)

Awareness, then, is not generated by the body and mind and it does not depend upon them. Quite the contrary, the body and mind, in order to function and operate, depend upon Awareness.

Just as electricity brings life to electrical appliances, Awareness is the sentience that brings life to all living beings. It is not a part, product or property of the body or mind. It pervades and enlivens both.

While the body is time-bound and subject to death, Awareness is deathless and eternal. It existed before these bodies came into being and will exist eternally after they are gone.

Guided Exercise 2:
A Meditation on Awareness

Before we continue our discussion on Awareness, here's an opportunity for you to explore this for yourself with the following guided exercise. Find a place where you can sit quietly and remain undisturbed for a few minutes. (Because it requires you to close your eyes at a certain point, it would be helpful to get somebody to read it to you, or you can find recordings of the guided meditations from this book on the author's website, unbrokenself.com.)

1. Take a moment to notice the objects in the room around you, whatever they happen to be.
2. Now, be aware of the fact that you are aware of these things.
3. Your attention is now split. You are aware of the objects—and you are aware of the fact that you're aware of them.
4. Close your eyes. Notice how the objects are now gone and yet Awareness remains.

5. Keeping your attention fixed upon your Awareness, answer the following questions as best you can. You will do this by exploring your own direct and immediate experience; by seeing and intuiting the answer with your own inwardly focused attention. Take as long as you need to answer each question.

6. *Does this Awareness have a location?* Can you pinpoint where it is? Does it have a particular location or is it all around? Is it restricted to a certain spot or is it all-pervading?

7. *Does this Awareness have a shape?* A form? Does it have a colour or is it formless and without attribute?

8. *Can you find a beginning or an end to this Awareness?* Or is it beginningless and endless?

9. *Does it have an age?* Is it a young or old Awareness, or is it neither?

10. *Does it have a gender?* Is it a male or female Awareness, or is it neither?

11. *Does this Awareness have any lack or limitation to it?* Or is it, in fact, whole and complete in itself?

12. *Is there any separation or distance between you and this Awareness?* Or are you, in fact, one?

13. Take as long as you like to "hang out" in Awareness, contemplating its nature in your own direct and immediate experience.

14. If any thoughts or feelings arise, simply notice them as objects arising in Awareness and allow them simply to pass by like clouds drifting across the sky. Don't let them carry you away. Notice to whom they arise. Remain centred as Awareness; as that which pervades all mental formations.

15. As you bring your attention back to your body and the room, take note of your answers and notice any changes to how you feel.

The Universal Ground of Existence

You might wonder where this Awareness comes from.

As noted, under the paradigm of materialism, many scientists assume it to be a property of the body and mind. That's an understandable assumption when you consider that the physical sciences generally operate from a "bottom-up" analysis of the world.

They see the universe as starting from the microscopic, constituent parts of matter, which combine to form the elements, objects and, over the course of a long evolution, the stars, galaxies, planets and the living beings that populate our world.

This bottom-up principle is a helpful way of understanding the world of objects. With the right know-how, you can generally take something apart and, by analysing its various parts, figure out how it was put together and how it works.

This does not, however, help us understand the principle of Awareness/Consciousness or how and where the universe originates.

You can take the most powerful magnifying device in the world and reduce matter and sub-atomic particles right down to their smallest components and still have no idea where it all originates. What you'll end up with is just—nothing.

The physical sciences are a means of knowledge for the physical world. They are not a means of knowledge for the non-physical. That's where they reach the limits of their usefulness to us.

To understand things from a more cosmological perspective, we must adopt a "top-down" approach. That's precisely what Vedanta does with its own powerful and unique methodology.

The unifying theme of the Upanishads is the principle of a universal ground of Existence; a singular, Non-dual, all-pervading, Absolute Reality.

The Upanishads call this *Brahman*.

The word Brahman is derived from the Sanskrit root *brih*, which means "expansive".

The name itself doesn't matter, however. We can substitute the word Brahman for "the Self", because Brahman is the Absolute, Universal Self; that which is the very essence and totality of all beings and all existence.

The Upanishads contain countless meditations upon the nature of this Self. The Mundaka Upanishad declares:

> [Brahman] is not the object of sense perception, is unborn, lacks any kind of attributes, is eternal and all-pervading and is the cause of all beings.

The Chandogya Upanishad says:

> Smaller than a mustard seed, this Self, dwelling in the hearts of all, is greater than the earth, greater than the sky, greater than all the worlds. This Self, giving rise to all works, all desires, all odours, all tastes, who pervades the universe, who is beyond words, who is joy abiding, who is ever present in my heart, is Brahman indeed.

The Isha Upanishad declares this Self to be "the Supreme Reality, enshrined in the hearts of all." Eternal and changeless, "the Self is subtler than thoughts and subtler than the senses" and "without the Self, life could not exist."

The thirteenth chapter of the Bhagavad Gita states:

> The Self has no beginning, is limitless, and is neither existent as an object nor non-existent. Pervading everything, it dwells in all beings. Everywhere are its hands and feet; everywhere are its eyes and faces. Though free of the senses, it shines through the functioning of the senses. [...] That which is both within and without all beings, it is immovable, yet is the cause of motion.

Both near and far, its nature is so subtle that most beings fail to perceive it. Though indivisible, it appears divided into separate beings and objects.

One of the key understandings is that the Self, the nature of which is pure Awareness or Consciousness, is not personal, but universal. The Awareness illuminating, animating and sustaining your body and mind is the very same Awareness shared by me, and every other being in the universe.

This Awareness, this Self, is definitely not a product of any individual body-mind-sense complex. Rather, each body-mind-sense complex is a reflecting medium for this one, singular Awareness, much as all the windows, lakes and mirrors in the world reflect the light of the same sun; a multitude of reflections of a singular light.

According to the Vedantic scriptures, this light is the Self, Brahman, and it underlies and pervades everything in the universe of form and multiplicity.

It is both transcendent, in that it exists beyond all things, and immanent, in that it exists as the immediate, ever-present *beingness* of all things.

It is not something you have to search to find. As one of the great sayings of Vedanta proclaims: You Are That! You can never not be the Self.

What is it that prevents us from realising this most fundamental aspect of our nature? The answer, again, is ignorance. Just as the tenth man was blinded by his own ignorance and temporarily oblivious to his own presence, so, too, are we blinded by our inability to turn within and realise the incredible truth of our own being.

Our minds and senses are instead hooked to the outer world of name and form and, driven by our relentless sense of self-lack and incompleteness, we pursue wholeness through the acquisition of various material ends and experiences.

Our birthright is Divine and yet, through self-ignorance, we live as paupers.

It's only by removing this ignorance of the nature of our Self and coming to realise what we truly are—the light of all lights, forever shining through and beyond the mind and senses—that we finally break the spell of samsara and come to know the unspeakable Wholeness of our own nature.

The Limitless Self

In the Bhagavad Gita, Krishna defines the Self as:

> [...] That which is limitless, imperishable and unchanging. It is That which gives all beings existence and resides within them as their innermost essence.

The first line alone bears careful contemplation.

The scriptures describe the Self as being limitless—and limitless is an extremely strict definition.

Objects of any kind are always, by their very nature, limited. They occupy a position in space and time and have certain boundaries. They are also subject to change, division and destruction.

As the Self is limitless, it cannot, therefore, be an object of any kind.

It has no form as such, because form necessitates limitation. Rather, it must be without boundary, without shape, mass or definition.

By implication, it must be omnipresent; existing at all places at all times.

That which is limitless cannot be time-bound because anything that exists in time will inevitably have a beginning and end. Indeed, as the Gita states, the Self is "imperishable and unchanging". Unlike anything in the world of phenomenal objects, it was not born at a certain point in time and space; and, therefore, it can never die or change in any way.

How can the human mind even begin to conceive of such a thing (or, rather, "non-thing")?

How, indeed. The Self cannot be objectified. It cannot be experienced as an object in the way you experience and know your body and mind.

This universal ground of Being is subtler than the mind, senses and thought and so cannot be grasped by them.

As human beings, we are all too familiar with limitation. Our lives are beset with limitation in every way. We have limited time, limited energy, limited perception and limited knowledge. The mere notion of limitlessness is foreign to us.

Attempting to describe the Self is a futile endeavour, for how do you describe the indescribable?

You may notice that Vedanta generally talks of the Self in terms of negation. That's because it's easier to say what it isn't than what it is.

Therefore, we can say that the Self is without limit, without form, without birth or death. It is also not subject to time, change or modification and is without boundaries of any kind. You might say it is, to borrow the title of a recent fantasy film, *Everything Everywhere All At Once*.

Some may be perplexed by what I'm describing and wonder how on earth we can ever experience it if it is indescribable and beyond the mind and senses.

The fact is, however, that we are never not experiencing the Self.

Recall that it is limitless! If it is without limit, then it must always be present and we must, therefore, be experiencing it everywhere all the time.

One of the few positive statements we can make is that the Self is self-shining and self-revealing. It doesn't need another source of light to reveal it. It reveals itself and all things by its own eternally present light.

You're experiencing it right now as the very Awareness in which you perceive your body, mind, sense perceptions and thoughts.

It's the same Awareness that's been aware of everything that has ever happened to you or ever will happen to you.

You know it as the very light of your own being; your innermost Existence and Consciousness.

You don't need anybody else to tell you that it exists because it's the one thing you can be absolutely certain *does* exist. It is *you!*

This Awareness is always present, whether you are experiencing the state of waking, dreaming or deep sleep.

Without it, you'd be unable to experience a single thing. It's the most intimate aspect of your being, the core of what you are and it has been present for the entirety of your lifetime and beyond.

The key understanding of Vedanta is that the individual self is non-different from the Universal Self.

The analogy is often used of the relationship between the waves and the ocean. Each wave might seem to possess an independent existence of its own, but they are actually non-different from the vast ocean containing them. The waves and the ocean are one.

If there's nowhere and nothing this universal Self, Brahman, is not, then it must be the core of what you are, what I am and what everybody else in existence is.

The Mundaka Upanishad states, "The Self is the one life shining forth from every creature."

It exists as a singular light shining throughout eternity, manifesting as an entire universe of forms; including all our different bodies and minds. One Self with an infinite number of faces. (The relationship between this Self and the universe of forms will be unfolded in the next chapter.)

Existence, Consciousness and Bliss

While the Self is ultimately impossible to describe, the Vedantic scriptures state that it is of the nature of *Sat Chit Ananda*, meaning Existence, Consciousness and Bliss. Let's see what that means.

1. Existence

Tattva Bodha defines Existence as "That which remains unchanged in the three periods of time [past, present and future]."

Existence is the very basis of reality.

Because we are conditioned to relate to objects, we tend to assume that existence is a property belonging to the objects themselves.

"This pen exists," you might say, "or my dog exists," or "my neighbour exists." But do these various objects each possess their own, unique existence? That would mean that there are trillions of different existences belonging to each and every object.

Contrary to popular assumption, existence is not a product or property of the various objects we encounter.

Consider this. If I hold up a gold ring as ask you if the ring exists, you will naturally say, "yes, of course it exists!"

We can't argue that the ring isn't there. It's an empirical fact. I'm holding it in my hand!

However, does the ring actually have an existence of its own?

If you think about it, what I'm actually holding is just gold; gold fashioned into a particular shape called a "ring". The ring doesn't have its own existence. *It borrows its existence from the gold.* No gold, no ring!

If I were to melt it down, the ring would cease to exist but the gold would remain. The ring, therefore, never exists apart from the gold. It is simply *gold plus a certain name and form*.

In the same way, all beings borrow their existence from the Self.

We'll explore the mechanics of this in the next chapter and beyond. Recall that the Self is the universal ground of Existence—appearing as an entire universe of forms and objects, including, as it happens, you and me.

Existence belongs not to the constituent parts, all the names and forms, but to the underlying substratum of Existence, which is pure Awareness/Consciousness. That's why the Self is described as Existence or Beingness. Everything in creation owes its existence to this Self, just as the ring owes its existence to the gold.

2. *Consciousness*

The Self is said to be of the nature of Consciousness. Once again, the words Consciousness and Awareness are synonymous and can be used interchangeably.

Tattva Bodha briefly explains that, "Consciousness is of the nature of pure Knowledge." This means that Consciousness is that by which all things are known.

Existence and Consciousness are not separate principles; they are but two facets of the Self. Because there's only one Self, there's only one Consciousness in existence. This Consciousness is shared by all beings; much as the same sun is reflected by a world of different mirrors. One light, many reflections.

Contrary to the assumption of the materialist, Consciousness is not a part, product or property of the body or mind. Rather, the body and mind are adjuncts, temporarily endowed with Consciousness. They borrow Consciousness much as the moon borrows the light of the sun in order to shine itself.

The Self existed before the universe came to be. In fact, owing to its limitless nature, it has never *not* existed. Unlike the things of the phenomenal world, it is uniquely independent in that it relies upon nothing else for its existence.

The Self pervades all the bodies and minds, granting them temporary sentience, much as electricity pervades a house and is capable of powering all electrical appliances.

Although seemingly "inhabiting" all bodies and minds, Consciousness is never limited or affected by those bodies and minds. The Self is, after all, limitless and impervious to change.

While the death of a body means that Consciousness can no longer function through that particular form, Consciousness does not and cannot die. The material forms of the world rise and fall like ocean waves, but there is no death. Consciousness not only pervades the world of form; it transcends it.

In its second chapter, the Bhagavad Gita states:

> While bodies are subject to change and death, the eternal Self, reflected as man's indwelling Consciousness, is impervious to destruction. Anyone who thinks that the Self can kill or be killed is ignorant of their own essential nature. This Self is never born, so it can never die. Ever present and changeless, it is without beginning and end. When the body dies, the Self remains. Just as worn out old clothes are cast aside, this indwelling Consciousness discards worn out bodies, replacing them with new ones. The Self cannot be pierced by weapons, nor burned by fire. Water cannot wet it and wind cannot dry it. Untouchable by anything in this world, the Self is all-pervading, immovable and eternal.

Bodies come and go, but the Self endures throughout eternity. Consciousness has no opposite and no "off switch". It's a self-revealing light, enlivening all bodies and minds, shining eternally without beginning or end.

3. Bliss

The scriptures describe the Self as being of the nature of not just Existence and Consciousness, but also Bliss.

Tattva Bodha explains, "Bliss is of the nature of limitless Wholeness."

Unlike emotions such as happiness, desire, anger or fear, this Bliss is not a passing emotional state. In fact, it's not a state at all. It is best understood as the freedom of being without limitation of any kind; without desire or fear and being completely whole and satisfied in your own Self.

This deep and abiding contentment is one of the fruits of Self-Realisation and enlightenment. It's the realisation that you don't need anything in order to feel whole and complete, because Wholeness is the very nature of your Self.

Even the unenlightened will taste this sense of Bliss and Wholeness—perhaps in deep meditation or upon the fulfilment of a cherished goal or desire. Contrary to what you might assume, the joy you experience isn't coming from the act of meditation or from attaining the object of your desire.

The Bliss comes not from outside you, but from within you and can be experienced when the mind and heart and are particularly still and reflective. It comes from within because bliss is actually the nature of the Self. Unlike the body, mind and ego, the Self is free of limitation; and freedom from limitation is experienced as a deep and lasting bliss and contentment.

It's this Bliss that all beings are seeking, whether they know it or not. Alas, try though you might, and I imagine you have, this Bliss is nowhere to be found in the world of objects. It can only be found within, for it's the very essence of your being.

Light and Water

Vedanta offers a range of analogies and metaphors for helping us to understand the Self; at least as far as it can be understood by the mind.

Shankara provides a number of them in his text, Atma Bodha. He says:

> Just as all beings live in the light of the sun, the body, mind and intellect exist and function in the light of the Self.

Light is a particularly helpful analogy.

Just as no physical objects can be perceived without light, nothing at all, either in the material world or the subtle world of thought, dream and imagination, can be perceived without the illuminating light of pure Consciousness or Awareness.

This Consciousness is always present, yet, astonishingly, despite its constant, unchanging presence in our lives, most people are barely aware of it.

If I asked you to describe the room you're sitting in, you'd probably tell me its size and dimensions, the colour of the carpet, the walls and ceiling, and also the various objects decorating the room. You're unlikely to describe the light in the room; the light by which all these objects are visible and known to you. This light is clearly evident and pervades the entire room—and yet almost everybody takes it for granted (until it's not there perhaps!).

Similarly, Consciousness pervades everything that you will ever see, experience and encounter. It's the very medium by which such things are known and experienced; the canvas upon which the painting of your life appears.

Like the light in the room, the Self pervades and reveals all the objects, yet is independent of those objects. It existed prior to the objects and will exist long after they are gone.

Consciousness, like the sun, shines equally upon all; the good and bad, the beautiful and ugly, the sublime and mundane, without a hint of favouritism and without being modified or changed by any of it.

Of course, the phenomenal world is a duality and, when the sun sinks below the horizon, physical light is replaced by darkness.

The light of the Self, on the other hand, has no opposite, no particular location and is without boundary; beginningless and endless. It contains our entire experience of reality and is utterly inseparable from us; for it is the Self of all beings.

We've already mentioned the analogy of the waves and the ocean. Shankara speaks of this in Atma Bodha:

> Like waves in the ocean, the worlds arise, live and dissolve in the Supreme Self; the substance and cause of everything.

When you gaze at the ocean, your attention will likely be drawn to the waves. On a Summer's day, the waves may be smooth and glacial with barely a ripple, whereas, on a Wintery day, the waves are whipped into a turbulent tempest of foam and frenzy.

These waves might seem to have an independent life and momentum all their own. But they are, of course, inseparable from the ocean and possess no independent existence in and of themselves. Both wave and ocean are united by the fact they are nothing but water. Water pervades the ocean and is both the cause and very form of the waves dancing upon its surface.

Similarly, at a grand, cosmic scale, all the worlds, galaxies and universes arise in the Self like waves upon the ocean. Although all the forms therein appear to have an inherent existence of their own, they are all but waves upon the great ocean of Consciousness. Just as water pervades and unites the entire ocean, the cosmos is pervaded and united by the Self; the ultimate and only Reality; the cause and substance of everything in existence.

The Highest Truth

The essence of Vedantic teaching can be found in what we call the Great Statements or proclamations. These statements encapsulate the entire Truth of Reality in just two or three short words. Perhaps the most famous is *Tat Tvam Asi*, meaning "I Am That", or "You Are That". It comes from the Chandogya Upanishad's sixth chapter; where guru Uddalaka tells his student Shvetaketu:

> All creatures have their root in the one Being, although they know it not. That Being, the subtle essence pervading all of creation, is the inmost Self of all. That is the Truth; the Self Supreme. You are That, Shvetaketu, you are That!

This statement will only hit home if you have a clear definition of the meaning of both "You" and "That".

We explored the "You" part of the statement in the previous chapter. It refers to the individual entity; the soul functioning in the world of form via the three bodies. This is the person you have always taken yourself to be; the individual self (with a small "s").

"That" refers, of course, to the subject matter of this chapter: the Absolute Reality that is Brahman, or the Self with a capital "S".

While the individual self is associated with form and with the three bodies, Brahman is free of form and is the universal ground of Reality. Formless, divisionless, limitless and not subject to time, modification or death, the Self pervades the entire universe.

The statement "You are That" affirms that the individual self, the person, is, in fact, identical with the Absolute Self, and is, therefore, of the nature of Existence, Consciousness and Bliss.

This may be hard to reconcile at first. After all, as a human being, you clearly experience all kinds of limitation, so how can you possibly be one with the Self, which is forever free of limitation?

Returning to the ocean allegory, the realisation that the individual self is non-different from the Universal Self is akin to the wave realising that it doesn't exist in isolation from the ocean.

If the wave could think, it might presume itself to be a separate form with a finite lifespan and a clear beginning and end. After all, there's a point where the wave arises and a point where it disappears.

The realisation that it is non-separate from the ocean destroys the idea that it can somehow cease to exist. The form of the wave may cease to exist, but its essence is water and the water was there before, during and after the appearance of wave.

Enlightenment is the realisation that you're not a separate wave—you are one with the ocean!

There's only Self in existence—pure Consciousness/Awareness; deathless, untouchable and ever free—assuming the appearance of a universe of objects and forms, including all the people, animals and plants.

Just as the wave gains freedom from mortality by knowing that it is nothing but the ocean, your freedom comes from the realisation that you, the individual self, are non-separate from the deathless Eternal Self.

But for a case of mistaken identity, caused by false identification with the body and mind, you were never *not* free.

You are the essence of freedom itself—unchanging, eternal and pure.

That's the ultimate Truth of Vedanta.

The remainder of this book shall prove it to you.

Summary

- The Self is the primary subject matter of Vedanta.
- We all know that we exist, so we're aware of the Self, but most of us are subject to self-ignorance and, identifying with body and mind, we perceive the Self as limited rather than limitless.
- Awareness is universal in nature. It pervades all things and is the inmost sentience and life of all beings.
- Awareness, the Self, is not a part or product of the body and mind. The body and mind depend upon Awareness for sentience and life, not the other way around.
- The Upanishads call the Self Brahman; which means the Universal, Non-dual ground of all Existence.
- The individual self is non-separate and non-different from the Universal Self, just as the waves are non-separate and non-different from the ocean.
- The Self is of the nature of Existence, Consciousness and Bliss.
- Awareness and Consciousness are used interchangeably and are synonymous with the Self.
- This isn't some kind of special, exalted Awareness or Consciousness. It's the ordinary, everyday Awareness by which you experience all things, gross and subtle.
- Bliss is the recognition of the absolute Wholeness of your nature as the Self; having no division, no limit, no sense of incompleteness whatsoever.
- The Great Statement "I Am That"/"You Are That" affirms the essential oneness of the perceived individual and the Self.
- Just as the same sun can be mirrored countless times, the same, singular Self appears as countless beings.
- Freedom from suffering comes by breaking the spell of self-ignorance and knowing your true identity as the Self; unchanging, eternal and pure.

11.
God, Maya and the Creation of the Universe

> Everything in the cosmos—energy and space, fire and water, name and form, birth and death, mind and will, word and deed, mantra and meditation—all come from the Self. The Self is one, though it appears to be many. Those who realise the Self go beyond decay and death, beyond separateness and sorrow. They see the Self in everyone and obtain all things.
> *Chandogya Upanishad*

The previous chapter explored the nature of the Self as pure Awareness or Consciousness. This Self, we learned, is universal, meaning the same in all, limitless, Non-dual, formless and not subject to birth, death or change.

This does leave us with an apparent contradiction, however. For how do we explain the world of matter that we all so readily experience with our senses; not to mention the countless trillions of seemingly separate beings living in it?

In short, how do we reconcile Non-duality with duality?

The process of creation usually entails a change in the substance of which it is made. In order to make butter, for instance, we need to churn milk. Once the milk becomes butter, it'll never be milk again.

If the Self somehow becomes and inhabits the entire universe, wouldn't that suggest a transformation of some kind—and contradict the assertion that the Self is changeless? How can the limitless at the same time appear to be limited?

These are pertinent questions.

In answering them, this chapter will unfold the concept of *maya*, the creative potential inherent in the Self, and examine the nature of God and the manifest universe; the world of name and form that needs no introduction to us,

The Two Factors of Creation

Two factors are necessary for any creation. First of all, you need an efficient cause, meaning the intelligence to create a thing. Then you need a material cause; a substance out of which to fashion it.

Let's say I show you my wristwatch. It's nothing fancy, I assure you, but suppose I ask you, "Did somebody create this?" You'll probably give me a funny look and say, "Well, of course somebody created it."

That's basic logic. It's here, so it had to be created. Something cannot appear out of nothing. If you think about it, an effect automatically presupposes a cause.

My watch obviously required material components in order to exist. That includes a steel casing, a glass covering, a crystal and other compounds, wiring and, of course, hands to tell the time.

Of course, these objects by themselves do not constitute a watch. They must be assembled correctly. For that, we need a watch-maker; somebody with the necessary knowledge and experience to take these components and fashion them into a functioning timepiece. Hence, with a bit of time and effort, a watch is created.

These two factors, the material cause (the raw components) and the intelligent cause (the watch-maker) combine to create the object.

The same principle of creation applies to most things, including the universe itself. The very fact the universe exists demonstrates that a creative principle was involved; something with both the necessary intelligence and power to create it.

So, how did the universe come about? Who or what could possibly possess the unfathomable intelligence needed to create the stars, galaxies, planets and people? And where would the necessary components and materials to create them come from?

The Creation Equation

Let's step back and recall that, as the all-pervading, Non-dual ground of Existence, Brahman—the Self—is all that exists. Eternal, unchanging and beyond time, the Self is the sole Reality and sum total of everything.

It's hard to grasp with the finite human mind, but the Self is limitless in nature. There is, therefore, nothing that it is not; including me, you, your neighbours, your cat, and any being that has ever been born, or ever will be born, in the entire history of the universe.

If you think about it, if there things that the Self was not, then it wouldn't be limitless, would it?

So, once again, how does the Self *become* this universe of seemingly different and diverse forms and beings?

If the Self really is unchanging, eternal and without form, then how do we explain the universe of multiplicity? How do we resolve this seeming contradiction?

At the Absolute level, the Self is Unmanifest. It has no form, division or differentiation. It's simply one, eternal Consciousness; without boundaries, without change and without limitation of any kind. The technical term for it is *Nirguna Brahman*, which means "the Self without form."

Now, here's the secret to the creation of the universe.

Inherent in the Self is a creative power called *maya*.

Maya is difficult to define. It has no direct equivalent in English, although it is taken to mean "magic" or "illusion"; that which makes something appear to be other than it is.

Maya makes the impossible possible. Like a magician's sleight of hand, it allows the formless, unchanging, Non-dual Self to appear as an entire universe of form, differentiation and duality—without actually changing at all!

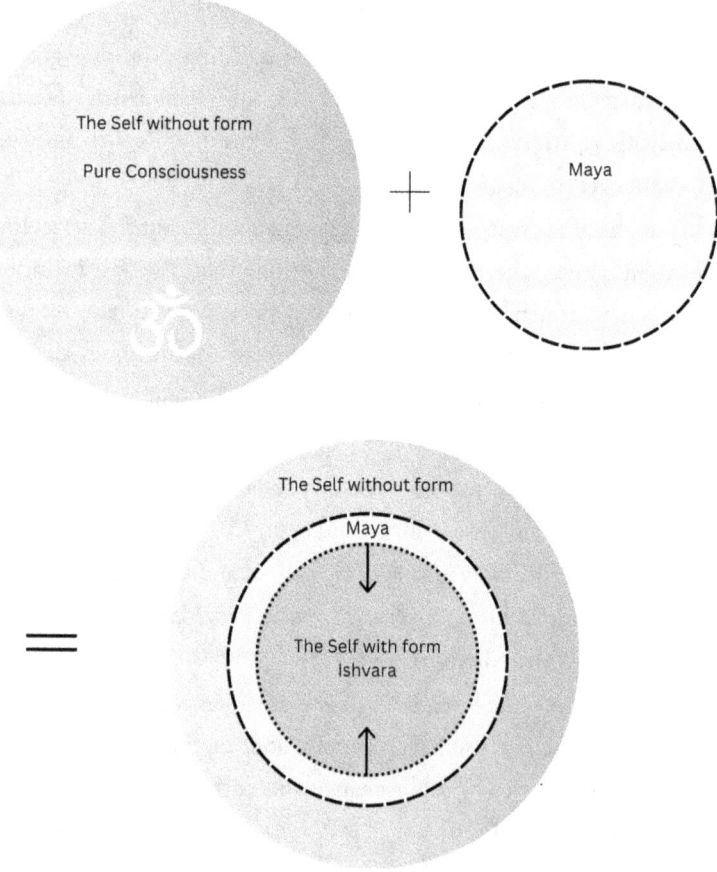

The two (non-separate) factors involved in the creation of the universe

It's the power of maya, which exists within the Self, which allows for the entire cosmos to manifest; the world that we all experience with our mind and senses.

Of course, it's all still Brahman; all still the Self. If the world of creation existed independently of the Self, then the Self would be limited and dual. That's why, for the purpose of understanding, we can divide the Self into two "portions": the Self without form (Nirguna Brahman) and the Self with form (called *Saguna Brahman*).

Therefore, the creation equation is as follows:

The Absolute/Unmanifest (The Self without form)
+ Maya
= The Relative/Manifest Universe (The Self with form)

Maya itself isn't the creation. It's the unmanifest potential for creation which exists within the Self as a latent power. So, it doesn't exist independently of the Self.

It's the alchemical combination of maya and the Self that gives rise the world of creation. It's that by which the manifest arises from the Unmanifest rather like a wave appears from the ocean.

Again, it's important to understand that the relative/manifest world does not exist separately or independently of the Self. It exists within the Self, much as your thoughts, dreams and every sense perception you've ever experienced exist within you; within your mind.

Just Like a Dream

A helpful analogy is to think of dreaming.

When you sleep each night, entire worlds are magically conjured in your mind, each containing an infinite number of potential objects, people, scenarios and experiences. When you're dreaming, of course, you take it all to be entirely real.

Your dreams aren't real, however. They exist within you and are created by you. In actuality, you are both the efficient and material cause of your dreamworld. Your mind is both the intelligence which fashions the dream and the substance of which the dream is made.

While you may become immersed in your dreamworld, you, the real you, is never actually affected or altered by your dreams. No matter what you dream, and what you do, become or experience in the dream, you wake up the very same person the next morning.

That's because you exist apart from the dream. You existed before, during and after the dream. Your consciousness pervades and lends life to the dreamworld, yet is not changed or contaminated by it in any way. Despite being both the creator and very substance out of which the dream is made, you are of a different order of reality to the dream.

In the same way, the Self pervades and lends life to the manifest universe, but is not ultimately contained by it or affected by it in any way.

The contradiction between Non-duality and duality is only a seeming contradiction. The world of duality exists within Non-duality, rather like the dream of Consciousness at a vast, macrocosmic scale.

Maya is what makes this "dream" possible, allowing duality to appear within Non-duality and the one Self to seemingly become an entire universe of names and forms. Maya is the bridge, as it were, between Consciousness and matter.

The Power of Maya

The scriptures describe maya as beginningless and inscrutable. Inscrutable means that it cannot easily be understood. It doesn't adhere to logic any more than the mind's ability to dream adheres to logic. It is beginningless because it is a power inherent in the Self and the Self is beginningless.

Maya is synonymous with ignorance because it prevents us from perceiving Reality as it actually is.

With its twin powers of concealment and projection, maya basically hides the Self from us. Rather than perceiving the Self as the totality of all that is, under the spell of maya, we see only a distorted reality.

We see the myriad forms of the world, including our own body and mind, with which we identify, but we cannot perceive the underlying Reality beneath and within those forms: the pure, Non-dual Consciousness that is the very foundation and essence of all things.

In short, because of maya, we mistake appearance for Reality. We get caught up in the dream.

Maya has three specific powers:

1. The power to know.
2. The power to do.
3. The power to rest.

When maya is operant, these powers manifest as three specific qualities or "energies", which we call the *gunas* (another Sanskrit word without a clear English equivalent). These three qualities are basically the constituent forces out of which the universe is made. Think of them as maya in hard form.

The three gunas each correspond to one of maya's powers. They are as follows:

1. *Sattva:* reflective in quality, expressing the power of knowledge.
2. *Rajas:* dynamic in quality, expressing the power of action.
3. *Tamas:* inert in quality, expressing the power of rest.

These three qualities come together in infinite combination, serving as the three primary "colours" by which the entire world of form is "painted".

We'll explore this in more detail in Chapter Thirteen. For now, it's enough to understand that the power of Maya, combined with the Self, Consciousness, creates the universe of names and forms; the world inhabited by you and I.

Ishvara

Let's recap. Vedanta involves a fair bit of repetition because the best way to understand something is to go over it again and again, each time from a slightly different angle.

Everything begins and ends with the Self. As we learned in the previous chapter, the Self is one, limitless and indivisible. It never changes and can never change, because change necessitates limitation. It's subtler than the mind and senses, so is technically indescribable.

That said, the scriptures state that it is of the nature of Existence, Consciousness and Bliss. It is the very ground of being; the substratum of all that exists.

If you want its technical term, Vedanta refers to it as Nirguna Brahman; the Unmanifest Absolute; the Self without form.

While the Self remains formless and without differentiation, maya is a creative principle within the Self, which makes it appear to take on form—and, boom, an entire world of duality is conjured into being, much as your dreamworld appears in your mind at night, only on a vast, macrocosmic scale.

This does not negate the Self as previously described.

In actuality, you might think of the Self as having two simultaneous modes or orders of reality: the Unmanifest and the manifest; the Self without form and the Self with form. One does not negate the other.

The Self plus maya creates a different, yet simultaneously existent, order of reality which we call Saguna Brahman, meaning the Self with form and attribute.

Another word for Saguna Brahman is *Ishvara* (pronounced Eesh-wara).

Ishvara means God. If, like many, you struggle with the word God, please don't stop reading just yet! We shall unfold this topic bit by bit with unassailable logic.

Ishvara is the Self plus the power of maya. It's the alchemical combination by which the universe is created; both the gross matter of our bodies and and the subtle matter of our minds, thoughts, memories and imagination.

You might think of Ishvara as the cosmic equivalent of our watchmaker. Only Ishvara doesn't just create watches. It creates the entire universe and all the forms therein. Ishvara is, therefore, both the efficient and the material cause of the creation: the Intelligence inherent in all forms and and the very substance of which they are made.

The latter point is an important one. The Upanishads liken the process of Ishvara creating the universe to a spider creating its web. The spider is the intelligence that creates the web and it also provides the very substance of the web, which is a part and product of its own body.

What's more, the spider creates the web out of itself without changing or ceasing to be a spider. In the same way, Ishvara, the Self associated with maya, moulds its very body (comprised of the three gunas) into the manifest universe without losing itself in the process of creation.

Everything is Ishvara

We live in an intelligent, lawful creation; an orderly matrix governed by certain physical, psychological and spiritual laws. An inner intelligence pervades all things right down to the tiniest of subatomic particles.

Let's consider the human body. Every cell in your body is programmed to function in precisely the right way in order to maintain the health and functionality of the body. It's just as well, too, because imagine if you had to consciously direct and instruct all your cells and organs to do what they're meant to do. That would be a stressful endeavour to say the least!

Fortunately, Ishvara has already programmed every cell of your body to function exactly as it should according to its respective nature. A skin cell will behave as a skin cell and a stomach cell will behave as a stomach cell. The functioning of all your body's systems, from the various organs to the circulation of blood, respiration, digestion, and so on, are all programmed and governed by the Intelligence that is Ishvara.

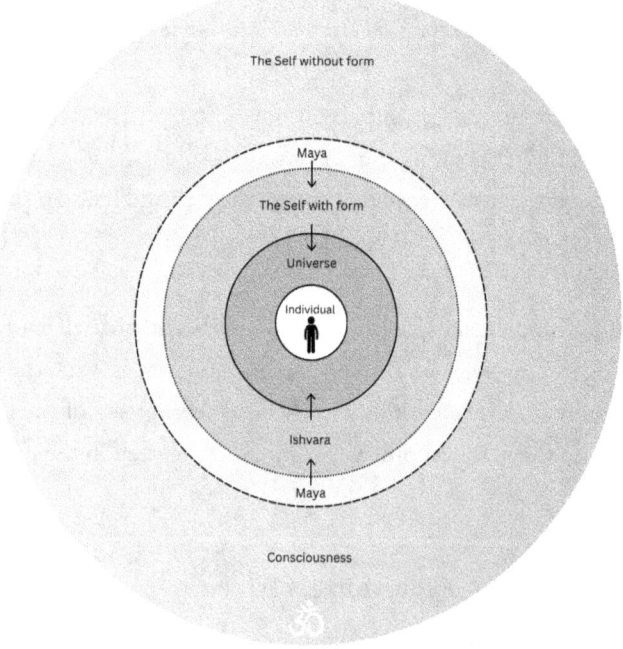

One creation in Consciousness

The same goes for everything in the natural world. Flowers, plants and trees know exactly how to grow and develop owing to this inbuilt Intelligence. Nature is a wondrous, intelligent ecosystem in which all the constituent parts work together, nothing is wasted and everything contributes to the totality.

Ishvara maintains not only the physical laws, but also the law of dharma, by which all beings are inclined to follow their respective natures and so contribute to the totality of creation. In addition, Ishvara governs karma and is that which dispenses the results of all our actions, something we've touched upon in Chapter Seven and will explore further in an upcoming chapter on karma.

Again, Ishvara does not stand apart from the creation. Ishvara is the creation; both its very substance and the intelligence supporting, sustaining and directing it.

The implications are profound. God is not an external factor; something separate from the creation. Needless to say, the Lord is not a bearded old man sitting on a throne in the clouds looking down upon the world. If God was indeed separate from the creation, that would mean there was something God was not, rendering God finite rather than Infinite.

In actuality, God *is* the creation itself—not only the Intelligence inherent in each living thing, but also the very material of which it is made.

If you want to find God, you needn't go on a pilgrimage to some church, temple or mosque. All you need do is take a look around you. God is everything everywhere, pervading the entire universe, even if Its Divinity doesn't manifest in all forms.

The Self is, therefore, both duality and Non-duality. It is both what you see with your eyes and your capacity to see. It is everything known and knowable and the very power of knowledge itself; the sentience and innermost Existence and Consciousness by which you live, breathe and have your being.

This is what the great mystics have proclaimed across the ages. In heightened states of consciousness, such seers have pierced the illusion of maya and discovered the unity of all things, seeing all forms and beings as different expressions of the same Divine source.

It could be argued that our modern day epidemic of depression and anxiety is caused by a sense of disconnection from God. Materialism robs us of our ability to appreciate the Divinity of life. We look around and see only the elements comprising an object; mountains are just piles of stone and dirt, the sun is nothing but a sphere of hot gas, and rivers and oceans are but H_2O.

Whereas the ancients saw and revered the Divinity of nature, our culture is lost under the spell of materialism, and we fail to understand the root of all material form. The ability to perceive the Divinity in all forms brings about a sense of wonder, awe, reverence and connectedness with God—which is, whether we know it or not, what we seek above all else.

The Creation of the Universe

The scriptures describe the universe as cyclic in nature, something with which many scientists concur. It exists in a manifest state for a certain duration of time, before resolving back into the Unmanifest.

As any physicist will attest, matter can neither be created nor destroyed. It can, however, change form, just as liquid changes into vapour when heated to a certain temperature, transforming from visible to invisible.

When dormant, the universe exists in seed state in the causal body. The causal body is the all-pervading and relatively eternal repository of karma. Much as our mind and senses merge into the causal body when we fall asleep at night, the entire creation resolves into the causal body when unmanifest. The three energies of creation, the gunas, are completely dormant in this state.

After a certain duration "asleep", the universe eventually comes back into manifestation as the gunas stir back to life. This re-awakening is initiated by fructifying karma. Rajas, the quality of projection and activity, breaks the equilibrium of perfect rest. This results in what scientists call "the big bang". The cosmos explodes into existence, emerging once again from the causal body and eventually coalescing from subtle matter into gross, physical matter.

This is a gradual evolution, not dissimilar to the way a dormant seed, in the right conditions, will sprout and evolve from a seed into a seedling and then eventually into a tree. How does the seed know to become a tree? The knowledge is pre-encoded into the seed in potential form; until such time as the conditions are right for it to manifest.

All of creation is pre-encoded with the innate Intelligence of Ishvara. That's how all forms automatically possess the knowledge to develop, grow and function according to their respective natures. Life is not an arbitrary chaos, but an intelligent matrix of self-replicating fractals.

The quality of sattva, knowledge, contains everything needed for the subtle and gross elements to combine in order to create the necessary forms. Rajas bestows the required energy, power and momentum to catalyse this evolution. Tamas, the densest of the three qualities, is responsible for the eventual solidification of the causal and subtle elements into physical matter.

Tattva Bodha goes into some detail on the grossification of the subtle elements into matter, stating:

From maya, space is born. From space, air. From air, fire. From fire, water. From water, earth.

It's unnecessary to dive into too much detail here. The key understanding is that creation is a top-down process. Causal matter, which is to say the karma stored in the causal body, evolves into subtle matter, which then evolves into physical matter.

Things don't, therefore, evolve *from* matter. They evolve *into* matter. That's how we go from the Unmanifest, the formless and indivisible Consciousness that is the Self, to the manifest universe, from the tiniest of subatomic particles all the way to the vastest of stars and galaxies.

The Self: Both With and Without Form

All creation borrows its existence from the formless and indivisible Self; Brahman.

Matter itself, a product of maya, is inert. It's the Self, the principle of Consciousness, which animates and enlivens all of creation, much as the sun enables all life to exist and flourish upon the Earth.

This is not an act of "doing" on the part of the Self. Like the sun, the Self is actionless. It is, however, by virtue of its mere existence in combination with maya, that which brings life to the world of form.

The Self plus maya is Ishvara; the creator, sustainer and destroyer of all form.

Ordinarily, the intelligence which creates an object and the materials used to fashion it are different. The potter, for example, is clearly different from the clay used to make the pots.

That is not so with Ishvara, which is both the intelligent and material cause of the universe. Like the aforementioned spider, Ishvara creates the entire universe out of Itself while remaining unchanged. The very material substance of the universe is Ishvara's body; Consciousness plus maya, which goes through a gradual process of grossification from the causal to the subtle to physical matter.

If you think about it, what else could the universe be made of? If Ishvara used some other material, something separate from itself, then who or what made that? That would mean there was something other than Ishvara—and, if the Self is limitless and Non-dual, and Ishvara is the Self made manifest, that wouldn't compute.

There's nothing that is not the Self, including our own bodies and minds. The Self, Nirguna Brahman, is the "base reality", much as the clay is the base reality of the pot (after all, what is a pot but clay in a certain shape?). Nirguna Brahman, Consciousness without form, is always existent and completely independent.

Saguna Brahman, Consciousness with form, is always existent but not always manifest. It also depends entirely upon Nirguna Brahman for its existence, just as the pot depends upon the clay for its existence and waves depend upon the water. The universe is the relative reality; the Self, Consciousness, is the Absolute Reality.

The Macrocosm and Microcosm

When it comes to the creation, there are two basic levels to get our head around: the macrocosm and the microcosm.

The macrocosm means the universe as a whole, while the microcosm is one small part of it, usually in reference to you or I; the individual person. The former is the whole and the latter is a part of the whole. In this case, the macrocosmic creation is Ishvara, the total creation, while the microcosm is the individual being; each of which is like a cell comprising a larger organism.

1. The Macrocosmic Creation

As already noted, the process of creation is top-down in nature. It all begins at the macrocosmic level.

The power of maya allows the Self, Consciousness, to illuminate and stir the causal body into motion; thus birthing the entire cosmos.

The causal body, the storehouse of karma, is, as its name suggests, the cause of the macrocosmic subtle body and the macrocosmic gross body.

The macrocosmic gross body is the sum total of all the individual bodies; and the macrocosmic subtle body the sum total of all the minds.

The Self associated with maya at the macrocosmic level is Ishvara. Ishvara is both the Intelligence shaping and controlling the laws of creation and the very substance of that creation in the form of the gunas; the constituent forces of the material world.

Therefore, Ishvara is not some distant God sitting apart from the creation, casting judgement down upon the world. Ishvara is intimately involved in the creation as a dynamic, inherent, all-pervading Intelligence; all-knowledge and all-power. The implication, then, is that God is everything everywhere; the inmost essence and very substance of all things.

2. *The Microcosmic Creation*

Of course, it's the microcosmic level we're all readily familiar with: the individual, everyday level of "you" and "me".

Just as each cloud is made up of uncountable trillions of water droplets, Ishvara's universe contains countless gross and subtle bodies, each of which serve as a reflecting medium for the light of Consciousness.

The very same qualities that make up the universe—sattva, rajas and tamas—combine to form every individual. Physical forms are what we term gross bodies. This includes inanimate objects such as rocks, wood and metal. Such objects lack a subtle body, so are not capable of reflecting and expressing Consciousness.

When a gross body is associated with a subtle body, however, this becomes an instrument capable of reflecting Consciousness and we thus have what we call a living being.

Just as electricity powers an appliance, Consciousness functions through the three bodies, the gross, subtle and causal bodies, and

Chapter 11: God, Maya and the Creation of the Universe   187

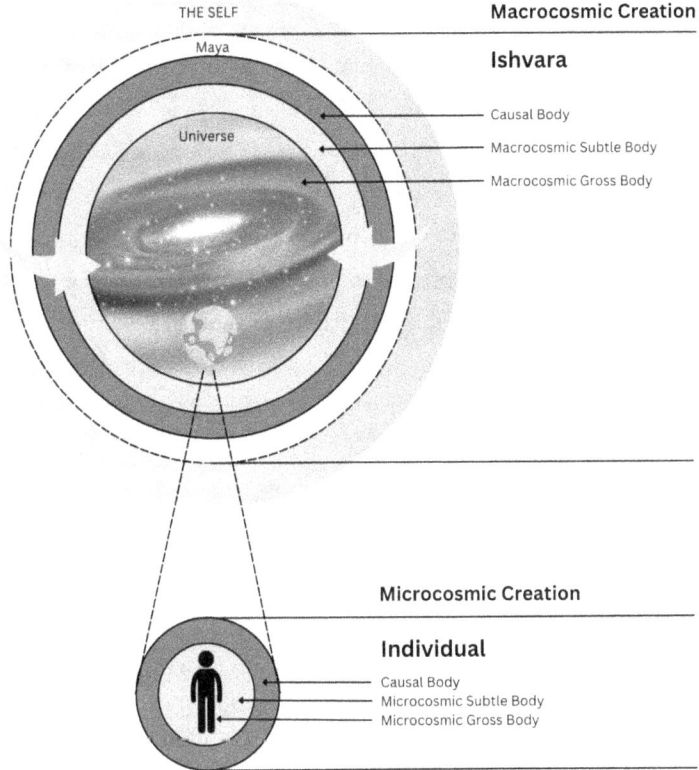

The Macrocosmic and Microcosmic levels of creation

moves between the three states of consciousness: waking, dreaming and sleeping.

Because Ishvara is the entire universe, our bodies and minds aren't actually separate from the Totality any more than a cell is separate from the body of which it is part.

We only perceive ourselves as separate due to maya and our ingrained sense of duality and "personhood". This is a product of ignorance, which distorts our true understanding of ourselves and reality.

In actuality, everything is connected and intrinsically one. Like the cloud made of water droplets, the universe is actually just one big gross body (comprised of all the individual gross bodies), intertwined with one vast subtle body (comprised of all the individual subtle bodes) and an endless and unmanifest causal body.

Individual beings, conditioned by ignorance, live a dream of separation based upon the testimony of the senses alone. We can only see a tiny part of the overall picture, which we take to be "reality". We may seem to exist independently as separate beings, but in actuality we're each cells in a larger organism, which is Ishvara.

The senses are only primed to process data relating to the field of matter; that which is visible and readily experienceable by the eyes, ears, mouth, nose and touch. Evolutionarily, we have evolved to see and process only a fraction of what is actually there; specifically the things necessary for our immediate survival. That means we're only ever seeing a fraction of the overall picture.

Human beings generally have no appreciation or understanding of the principle of Consciousness; which is essentially the "electricity" present everywhere and which grants life to all beings.

Here lies the root of our suffering. Maya is so immersive and its power of concealment so immense that we don't see reality as it is. Seeing only a tiny sliver of what's actually there, we are blinded to our own essential nature. We think we are small, weak, disconnected and subject to damage and loss, when, in fact, we are non-separate from God.

Just as the wave and the ocean are united by the fact they are both nothing but water, the individual and Ishvara are united by the fact they are nothing but pure Consciousness.

In Conclusion

This is a complex topic, undoubtedly the most difficult to comprehend in Vedanta. Hopefully, this chapter has shed light on the nature of the creation and its relationship to the Self. We'll continue exploring things from different angles throughout the rest of this book, using different teachings, analogies and ideas to help develop and refine your understanding.

Summary

- The Self is ultimately formless and without division or differentiation. The term for this is Nirguna Brahman (which translates as "the Self without form or qualities").
- Inherent in the Self, however, is maya: a creative power which enables the Self to appear as an entire universe of objects and forms.
- The term for the Self associated with maya is Saguna Brahman (meaning "the Self with form and qualities").
- Saguna Brahman is also known as Ishvara; Controller of the laws of the creation and the very intelligence and substance of the creation.
- Maya manifests as the three gunas, or qualities, which serve as the building blocks of creation.
- The three gunas are sattva, rajas and tamas; which represent the powers of knowledge, action and inertia.
- Creation evolves from the top down. From the causal body, subtle matter is created and this subtle matter eventually grossifies into physical matter.
- At the macrocosmic level, the gross, subtle and causal bodies belong to Ishvara, which pervades and sustains the entire universe.
- At the microcosmic level, each individual possesses their own gross subtle bodies, plus the causal body; instruments which are capable of reflecting Consciousness, making us living, sentient beings.
- We see ourselves as separate from others, the rest of the universe and God because maya distorts our vision, creating self-ignorance and the inability to perceive reality as it actually is.

- Just as the wave and the ocean are united by the fact they are water alone, the individual person and Ishvara, God, are united by the fact they are Consciousness alone.

12.

Devotion

Love itself is the actual form of God.
Ramana Maharshi

Devotion is a topic that naturally appeals to a certain type of seeker; often the more emotionally-driven person; the type of person who loves to love. Others, perhaps more intellectually inclined, may at first find it harder to grasp the power and necessity of a devotional mindset.

In actuality, the lives of all human beings are governed by devotion. Whether spiritual or secular, intellectual or sensual, each person worships at the altar of their own particular god.

Worldly people, by and large, channel their devotion into the pursuit of money, possessions and attainments, fame and reputation, pleasure and sense gratification. The more mature express their devotion to family and friends, to animals and nature, creative endeavours, charity and otherwise making a difference in the world. And, of course, we have the spiritual seeker, who devotes his or her attention to the worship of a higher principle—God, or the Divine essence at the heart of creation.

While the object of our worship varies wildly, devotion remains the nucleus of all our lives; an expression of that which we hold dearest to our heart and value above all else.

What Are You Really Seeking?

Contrary to what you might assume, whatever your focus of devotion, it's rarely the object itself that you're most interested it. You don't want the object for the object's sake, but because that object can provide a certain desirable end.

Take money, for instance. Nobody loves money for the money itself. What's so desirable about a stash of dirty old coins, gnarled slips of paper or digits on a bank balance? You love money because it is a means of attaining certain ends, invariably pertaining to security, pleasure and enjoyment.

If the ends weren't of sufficient value to you, you'd almost certainly channel your devotion elsewhere.

Although it may not be the easiest thing to admit, this also extends to our love of others. Generally, you love another person not for that person's sake, but because it pleases you to love them.

Perhaps that person brings you pleasure, joyful feelings, companionship, security or validation of some kind. Perhaps they simply make you laugh.

Whatever the reason, when a person or object ceases to deliver the desired ends—when they end up causing pain, stress and heartache—it won't be long before the love itself dries up.

The Brihadaranyaka Upanishad, one of the oldest Upanishads, addressed this by boldly asserting:

> A wife loves her husband not for the sake of the husband, but for the sake of the Self.
> A husband loves his wife not for the sake of the wife, but for the sake of the Self.
> Children are loved not for the sake of the child, but for the sake of the Self.
> Wealth is loved not for the sake of wealth, but for the sake of the Self.
> The universe is not loved for the sake of the universe, but for the sake of the Self.

At first glance, that verse might be taken as an admission of tremendous selfishness. In a sense, we're all selfish, although not perhaps in the way you might think. We're selfish in that what we're all ultimately looking for is nothing but our own Self—which is Divine.

We've established that the Self is of the nature of Existence, Consciousness and Bliss. That means that the wholeness, joy and freedom we've been seeking from others and the world of objects was right under our nose the entire time. It's always present and always available to us, because it's our very nature; the essence of who and what we are.

That's something the materialist, lost under the spell of ignorance, simply cannot understand. As a result, they continue seeking the Bliss of the Self by proxy alone; through objects, experiences and worldly acquisition.

The joy they experience when attaining the object of their desire is simply a taste of their own Consciousness, free from the taint of desire. The happiness is only temporary, of course, because all objects are subject to change; and it's rarely long before the fickle mind switches its focus to something different, better and more tantalising.

The seeker of liberation, on the other hand, has already pierced the murky veil of materialism. They know that object-based devotion leads only to attachment, frustration and dismay. With luck, they've come to learn that the only way to lasting freedom and fulfilment is through Self-Realisation; the recognition of our own Divinity.

That's why the highest form of devotion is devotion to God or the Self (God being the Self manifest). Why seek fleeting bursts of happiness in an impermanent world when you can have lasting happiness by laying claim to your own limitless and eternally whole nature—something that's always available to you?

The samsari is devoted to worldly ends alone. As a seeker of liberation, your job is to channel your devotion to a higher end; to the Infinity of your own nature. Whatever form it takes, the expression of Divine devotion and worship rallies the mind and heart, providing the necessary fire and resolve to attain the ultimate goal: freedom from suffering and limitation.

In the Bhagavad Gita's twelfth chapter, Krishna says:

> The path can be difficult for those whose identification with body and mind is strong. However, those who worship Me and to whom I am the supreme goal—who have relinquished all actions to Me and fixed their minds on Me with a devotion that knows no otherness—I will liberate from the ocean of samsara. Keep your mind and thoughts on Me, and there is no doubt you will abide in Me alone.

In Vedanta, the technical term for devotional practice is upasana yoga. Along with dharma and karma yoga, it's a key method for purifying and readying the mind for Self-Knowledge.

The word upasana literally means "sitting near". To practice upasana yoga is to focus the mind upon God through meditation, contemplation and worship. The form the upasana takes will depend upon the student's level of understanding God, as we shall see below.

The Problem of the Atheist

Unfortunately, the staunch atheist is disqualified at the outset. Ignorance prevents materialists from recognising that the material universe, itself an effect, must necessarily have a cause.

With uncompromising words, Krishna addresses this topic in the Bhagavad Gita's ninth chapter:

> The deluded fail to recognise My presence; never realising My limitless nature as the Lord of all creation. Devoid of wisdom, of vain hopes and fruitless action, their lives are fraught with calamity and suffering.

What worse suffering can you imagine than continually believing yourself to be a limited, lacking wretch, subject to pain, disease and death—when, in fact, you have a far deeper, vaster, transcendent nature untouched by worldly sorrow?

One of India's Puranic texts tells the tale of Indra, the king of the gods, who was once cursed to live a lifetime on Earth as a pig.

Perhaps not unexpectedly, once he became a pig, the mighty Indra completely forgot his Divine stature and became fully immersed in the illusion of maya; this world of name and form.

He greatly enjoyed rolling about in the mud and snorting happily for buckets of slop. He even fell in love with a lovely female pig and together they had several litters of piglets.

The gods in heaven were not amused. Indra had important duties that he wasn't attending to. He was too busy rolling about in filth in a way quite unbefitting a deity.

The problem was Indra had become so deeply ensconced in the illusion of being a pig that he'd completely forgotten who he truly was. Totally content indulging his animal passions and revelling in the appetites of his pig-body, he was unwilling to give it up—even for all the glories of heaven!

Of course, he did eventually return to heaven, but this story illustrates the power of maya, of ignorance. Like Indra, our attachment to the world of form can leave us rolling around in the dirt, content with meagre scraps and completely oblivious to our Divine inheritance.

All beings born into the world fall under the spell of maya. The senses are directed outward and, subject to ignorance, we take appearance to be real. Because we appear bound to a particular body and mind, that's where we superimpose our sense of identity; our "I am-ness".

Few ever question this gross misassumption, much less practice self-enquiry. This means, sadly, that they never come to know the Divinity of their birthright. Such souls are gods living as pigs, rolling around in the mud of samsara, completely ignorant of their true glory.

It's often the case that fervent atheists have endured negative experiences at the hands of corrupted religion. It's easy to understand their disillusionment and disdain when it comes to spiritual matters. Throwing the baby out with the bathwater, however, is neither a rational nor healthy reaction.

To deny God is to deny one's own existence! For without a transcendent, noumenal principle, the phenomenal world, and all of us in it, simply couldn't exist.

The Benefits of Devotion

Devotion to God has been demonstrated, time and again, to have a positive, healing effect on the human psyche.

Numerous studies conclude that a devotional mindset leads to significantly better psychological health and well-being than those with atheistic or agnostic beliefs. Having some form of relationship with God has been shown to reduce depression, anxiety and a wide spectrum of other mental health problems, including reducing suicide rates and resolving addiction issues.

In the Bhagavad Gita, Krishna says:

> Those of noble heart, gifted with a spiritual disposition, know the Self as the imperishable cause of all creation and seek Me with one-pointed devotion.

Devotional practice, or upasana yoga, includes the use of mantra, devotional rituals and deep meditation and contemplation. This practice sharpens, disciplines and refines the mind; all prerequisites for effective self-enquiry.

A worshipful mind is also the perfect weapon for loosening the bonds of ego-identification. Conducted in the right spirit, upasana yoga helps to open and expand the mind, moving the seeker from fixation with the body-mind-sense complex to a greater understanding and appreciation of one's unity with a higher principle.

Upasana yoga is actually an aspect of karma yoga, because devotion is expressed in worship; in action.

It prepares the student for the Knowledge that the wholeness they seek is not outside of them, but exists inwardly as the core and essence of their being. In summary, Shankara stated that:

Seeking after one's own real nature is the essence of devotion; the enquiry into the Truth of one's Self is devotion.

The Three Levels of Understanding God

In order for something to exist, there must be a creative intelligence responsible for its creation. Something cannot arise out of nothing. That's why the phenomenal universe must necessarily come from an unseen noumenal factor; the unseen cause responsible for producing the visible effect.

We can, therefore, infer the existence of Ishvara or God; the creative force responsible for manifesting this unimaginably vast, intricate, innately intelligent and impeccably designed universe.

The way we see, understand and worship God is largely determined by the level and depth of our understanding.

According to Vedanta, there are three levels of understanding God. These are:

1. A Personal God
2. A Universal God
3. The All-Pervading Absolute

Each successive level does not contradict the previous, but simply expands our vision and perspective.

Devotion can be either dualistic or Non-dual in nature. The first two levels of understanding God fall into the category of dualistic devotion, while the latter is Non-dual, as we shall see.

Dualistic devotion relates to the worship of God as Saguna Brahman; the Self with form and qualities. The dualistic devotee finds a form of Ishvara/God that serves as a symbol and focus for their love, prayers and offerings.

A higher aspect of dualistic devotion is learning to see the Divine in all things around you, for the entire creation is both the manifestation of God and the very substance of God.

This, with time and grace, will culminate in Non-dual devotion.

Non-dual devotion relates to the worship of Nirguna Brahman; the Self without form and qualities, sometimes called the Absolute; the limitless, all-pervading Consciousness that you, and all beings, ultimately are. This worship takes the form not of mantras and prostrations, but the practice of Self-Knowledge; specifically, claiming your oneness and unity with this universal Consciousness.

In order to understand this evolution from dualistic to Non-dual devotion, let's take a look at each of these three definitions of God.

1. A Personal God

The first way of understanding God is as a personal deity; an anthropomorphised form in possession of Divine characteristics, such as omnipotence and omnipresence.

Some students may struggle with the idea of a personal God. They balk at the retrograde cliché of God as an old man with a long white beard sitting on a throne in the clouds. After all, if we know that Brahman is the formless, all-pervading essence of Existence, why on earth would we worship a personal deity?

The fact of the matter is the mind finds it difficult to grasp the abstract and conceive anything outside its own limited, direct experience. It will naturally, therefore, seek something more concrete.

For example, if I ask you to think of gold—just *gold*, without being in any particular form—you might find it rather difficult. On the other hand, if I ask you to imagine a gold ring or a gold coin, you have something concrete for the mind to imagine and sustain its focus upon.

Deep contemplation of Brahman, the Self, or pure Consciousness, is the key to liberating the mind. Yet, because Consciousness is subtler than the mind and has no form, no boundaries and no parameters, it's impossible for the mind to grasp.

That's why, at least initially, it's far easier for the mind to relate to God in the form of a symbol; a personal deity; a concrete manifestation of the Divine.

The particular form of God you chose is entirely up to you. It should be one that you feel an affinity with; one you have some reverence for. The Indian pantheon of gods and goddesses offers a wealth of deities to choose from, including Shiva, Krishna, Durga, Kali, Ganesha, and so on.

God is, of course, non-denominational. You might also feel inclined to channel your devotion to Jesus, Mary, Buddha, Lao-Tzu, or any other form of the Divine that resonates with you.

If that really doesn't work for you, you might want to use the symbol of an angel, some other cosmic being, or something from nature; a big tree or some kind of animal, as an embodiment of God.

Unfortunately, some religious devotees get so attached to their deity that they seek to disavow all others. They fail to realise that God has more than just one form. All the many and varied forms of God are but different faces of the one, Eternal Self.

The worship of God can take many forms. In India, devotees perform various offerings, rites and ceremonies, which often involve lighting fire and offering flowers, incense, reciting mantras and singing devotional hymns.

Krishna states in the Bhagavad Gita:

> Whatever is offered to Me with devotion—whether a leaf, a flower, fruit, or even a drop of water—I gladly accept. Whatever you do, make it an offering to Me.

The focus of devotional ceremonies is always giving. Giving of yourself with love, care and devotion helps tame the ego and neutralise the entrenched and agitating desires and attachments at the root of the human psyche. That's why Vedanta places such importance on devotion.

A Daily Devotional Ceremony

Performing sacred rituals has a way of nourishing and healing the mind, reorienting our attention from the mundane to the Divine, and cultivating a sense of calm, focus and devotion.

Unfortunately, modern secular society has little value for ritual and most people, including spiritual seekers, rarely make the time for it in their busy lives.

It is an effort, however, that's well worth making. Traditionally, followers of Sanatana Dharma (or Hinduism) perform a *puja*, or devotional, ceremony at least once a day in honour of their deity.

Some such ceremonies take place at the local temple but others are conducted in one's own home. These rituals can be quite exacting and elaborate, adhering to every letter of the ritualistic portion of the Vedas.

The puja ceremony is an opportunity for the devotee to offer praise and thanks for all they've been blessed with in life.

The benefit of such ceremonies is immense; particularly for the seeker of liberation. Even the simplest of rituals redirect one's attention from the body-mind-sense complex and its many cares and woes to the Divine ground of Existence that is the Self or Brahman.

As karma yoga in action, this purifies the mind and cultivates the positive values and mental qualifications necessary for Vedanta to work.

Here's a suggestion for a simple, streamlined puja ceremony. It can be carried out in your home in as little as two to three minutes per day.

1. Create a scared altar in your home. If you don't already have one, a sacred altar is a place where you can gather some items that are sacred and cherished to you and which reflect or represent God. All that you need is a small table or shelf. You might include a picture or statue or some other representation of your chosen

personal deity.

2. Approach the altar with reverence. Seeing it as an embodiment and symbol of the Eternal Self, bow to your chosen deity and invoke its love, light and presence.
3. Light a candle or lamp. In cultures throughout the world and across the ages, fire and light symbolise Divinity; light being synonymous with seeing, understanding and knowledge. Fire is also the element that burns away the past and cleanses all impurity from the mind and heart. By lighting a candle or lamp, you are symbolically kindling the fire of your own love, devotion and God-nature. Mentally say something along the lines of, "I offer this light to you with love and gratitude, O Lord."
4. Light some incense. As you do so, with reverence, again offer it to your deity; "I offer this incense to you with love and gratitude, O Lord." Incense has been used since ancient times as a spiritual offering representing purification, sanctification and beauty. The type of incense is a matter of personal choice, but sandalwood is frequently used in devotional ceremonies.
5. Present an offering. Lovingly and reverently offer a flower or a piece of fruit to the deity; "I offer this flower or fruit to you with love and gratitude, O Lord." The offering is sanctified by presenting it to the deity.
6. If you feel so moved, offer a prayer. Pray from the heart. It may be a prayer of gratitude or blessing or a prayer to invoke help and grace. Always offer thanks.
7. (Optional) Chant a mantra. See below.
8. Closing. When you are finished, blow out the candle and make a dedication from your heart. Then, with an attitude of peacefulness, presence and care, go about your day.

This simple ceremony combines most of the key elements of a puja. Commit to doing it daily at least for several weeks. You'll probably find that you look forward to this little ritual, which is the perfect way to start your day and you will surely notice the healing, fortifying and calming effect it has upon the mind and emotions.

A Simple Mantra

You may already be familiar with certain Sanskrit devotional mantras, such as *Om Namah Shivaya, Om Nam Bhagavate Vasudevaya, Hare Krishna Hare Rama,* and so on.

If you feel compelled to incorporate mantra meditation into your practice, and it's something I highly suggest, it makes sense to use a mantras associated with your chosen personal deity. Or you might simply chant Om three, seven or eleven times. The syllable of Om, which we call the pranava, represents the Eternal Self.

Mantras are composed of seed syllables which are spiritually charged and which harmonise the nervous system, purifying the mind and heart, and awakening us to the inner recognition of the Self.

An easy and powerful mantra I recommend is Om Namah Shivaya.

Om, which is a potent mantra in itself, represents the Self as pure Consciousness. It generally prefaces all mantras, because the Self is that which exists before all else.

Namah has two meanings. Firstly, it is used in many mantras as a salutation to God. Its two syllables, *na* and *mah*, literally mean "not me"; so it is also a negation of the false self, our misidentification with the body/mind/ego.

Shivaya refers to Shiva, one of the names given to Brahman, or the Self. Therefore, the meaning of Om Namah Shivaya is a recognition that I am not this limited ego-self, but am the Eternal Self; pure, all-pervading Consciousness. This mantra is, therefore, a perfect encapsulation of the highest truth of all the Vedas; the knowledge "I Am That".

The mantra is pronounced "Aum Nah-muh Shiv-Aye-uh."

Use mala beads and perform at least one full mala (108 repetitions). Begin chanting quickly and then gradually lengthen the gap between each chant, basking in the stillness and bliss of the silence; a reflection of your own Consciousness. Contemplate the meaning as you chant; the unity between you and the Divine.

Guided Exercise 3:
Meditation on God As a Personal Deity

Upasana yoga is meditation upon God, both in the form of the personal deity and the universal form. This first meditation incorporates a personal deity of your choice and is adapted from a Puranic text called the Srimad Bhagavatam.

1. Find a comfortable place to sit where you won't be disturbed. Sit upright, yet not rigid, and let your hands gently rest upon your lap.
2. Become aware of your breath as it moves in and out of your body. Allow your attention to settle where you're most aware of the movement of your breath, whether that's the inflow and outflow of air at your nose or the gentle rise and fall of your belly.
3. For a few minutes, practice breathing in, holding for a couple of seconds and then extending your out-breath. Breathe in as normal, hold, then allow your exhale to lengthen. This has a tremendously calming affect on the body, mind and nervous system.
4. While continuing to be aware of your breath, mentally chant the syllable Om on both the in-breath and out-breath. Breathe in and chant Om, then breathe out and chant Om.
5. As you breathe in and out, while maintaining the same gentle rhythm of breathing, gradually increase the number of times you

mentally chant Om on each breath. The aim is to hear it "chanted within like the continuous peal of a bell". All the recitations of Om merge into a single, continuous, all resounding OM. Gently attune yourself to this sound vibration.

6. Turn your attention to either your heart or the space between your eyes; wherever you feel drawn. Imagine a beautiful lotus within the space there. Its petals are closed. As you focus upon it, imagine the petals opening, like a flower awakening to the light of the sun. Notice that within the heart of the lotus you can see the sun, the moon and the element of fire, one within the other.
7. Mentally call forth and envisage the benign form of your personal deity seated at the heart of this lotus. Feel yourself enveloped by luminous rays of Divine light.
8. Meditate upon this form of God, extending your love and devotion and opening your heart, mind and being to the radiation of its Divine grace. Be open to their presence, feeling their light, love and radiance surround and encompass you, filling and nourishing you with Divine Bliss.
9. If, at any point, your attention wavers, simply bring it back to the deity seated within the lotus of your heart or mind.
10. At some point, you may find your attention become so absorbed that you can feel your identity merging with God. All mental barriers dissolve and you are simply aware of Divine unity, oneness and non-separation. Feel your mind and heart merging into the light and love of God, until not a trace of separation remains. Feel yourself enveloped, cradled, immersed in the Divine Unity and Bliss.
11. Remain in meditation as long as you like.
12. When you are ready to return, extend your love and gratitude and slowly, gently return your attention back to the physical body.

2. A Universal God

There's a higher, more advanced understanding of God for those capable of expanding their mind to accommodate a higher vision.

The Upanishads make it clear that God is not just that which created the cosmos. God is also the very substance and material of the cosmos. Much as the spider creates a web out of its own body, Ishvara creates the entire universe out of its own being.

The creation, therefore, does not stand apart from God. The creation is God. So, in order to see God, all you need do is open your eyes and take a look around you. This very world is the form of Ishvara.

It can be hard thinking in such terms. That's why this understanding of Ishvara requires a slightly more refined mind.

Consider this. When you see a person, you don't see them as an assemblage of separate parts (ie., a conglomeration of eyes, nose, face, hair, arms, legs, chest and so on). You see them as a whole.

Because of its unfathomable vastness, we tend to view the universe in terms of separate parts; an endless assortment of objects; of "this" and "that". With spiritual knowledge, however, we come to view the entire universe as one all-pervading *whole*. We cease viewing the universe as a collection of parts and are able to understand the universal form of Ishvara—as one, unfathomably vast, cosmic being.

The middle chapters of the Bhagavad Gita unfold this magnificent cosmic vision of God:

> It is from Me that the entire creation has arisen; it is in Me that it is sustained, and in Me that it is resolved again. I am the eternal and imperishable womb of creation; That in whom all people and all things have their being.

In the eleventh chapter, Arjuna relates his incredible vision of God as the totality of all beings and all creation:

O, Krishna, in your body I see all the gods and every living creature in existence. In your magnificence, you have infinite eyes, arms, mouths and stomachs and you are embodied in every form. I can see no beginning, middle or end to you, O Lord of creation. The cosmos itself is your body.

The universe is one—and that one is God. Ishvara's macrocosmic gross body is the sum total of all physical bodies, objects and forms. Similarly, Ishvara's macrocosmic subtle body is the sum total of the subtle realms, including all the minds and the thoughts, dreams and imagination of all living beings.

The conclusion is inescapable: God is everything, everywhere. There is nothing and nowhere God is not. At this level of understanding, you're relating not just to a personal God, but a universal God.

When you understand that God is everywhere, your relationship with the world changes. You become more accepting of life's seeming imperfections, including the imperfections of others.

Knowing God as always present in every form, the entire world becomes the temple of your worship. By recognising and honouring Ishvara as the beauty of nature, as the animals, the rivers, the sun and stars, you sanctify the whole of life and life becomes a joy to experience. When you deeply realise that God is ever present and all around you, you experience fulfilment, reverence and love no matter where you are.

The Scottish-born mountaineer and environmentalist John Muir was describing just this when he wrote the following words:

> He said, "The sun shines not on us but in us. The rivers flow not past, but through us. Thrilling, tingling, vibrating every fibre and cell of the substance of our bodies, making them glide and sing. The trees wave and the flowers bloom in our bodies as well as our

souls, and every bird song, wind song, and tremendous storm song of the rocks in the heart of the mountain is our song, our very own, and sings our love."

When your eyes and heart are open, it's easy to see the splendour of God in all things that are wonderful and brimming with beauty; in the warm light of sunrise, the glistening morning dew, the beauty of flowers and trees, the singing of birds and the rhythmic roll of waves upon the ocean. God shines as that which is great in all great things.

In the Bhagavad Gita, however, Arjuna learns, much to his shock, that being universal, Ishvara also encompasses life's less pleasing aspects, such as time, ageing, illness and death.

Indeed, creation cannot exist without destruction. It takes a mature mind to understand that, if Ishvara is all that exists, that must necessarily include the less pleasing aspects of life. After all, in the world of duality, up cannot exist without down, day cannot exist without night, and birth cannot exist without death.

We have no option but to accept this as the nature of the phenomenal universe.

The play of opposites, the dance of duality, can only be transcended through Self-Knowledge. You must simply accept that, as long as you are in possession of a body and mind, duality inevitably presents a measure of both pleasure and pain.

At this point, some students bring up the question of evil. Did God create evil, and if so why?

Evil is a product of human beings, not God. It is born of the misuse of free will and the wilful violation of dharma.

The law of dharma, of right action, is the law of Ishvara running the creation. To follow dharma is to live in alignment with Ishvara which obviously brings good karma.

To transgress dharma is to go against Ishvara and this always invites misfortune and bad karma. Evil, then, is a product of mankind violating the law of God; ie., dharma, and then having to face the karmic consequences.

When Arjuna beholds the vast cosmic vision; seeing Krishna (Ishvara) as the entirety of the universe, his initial reaction is wonderment and awe. When he beholds the destructive component of Ishvara, such as time, decay and death, his reaction turns to fear. Upon realising that God must necessarily be every aspect of life, both the pleasure and the pain, his final reaction is one of reverence and devotion.

That's precisely the attitude one should have toward Ishvara: respect and reverence.

Guided Exercise 4:
Meditation on God's Universal Form

This second upasana meditation is a little more advanced and focuses on the universal form of Ishvara.

1. Find a comfortable place to sit where you won't be disturbed. Sit upright, yet not rigid, and allow your hands to rest gently upon your lap.
2. Become aware of your breath as it moves in and out of your body. Allow your attention to settle where you're most aware of the movement of your breath, whether it's the inflow and outflow of air at your nostrils or the gentle rise and fall of your belly.
3. For a few minutes, practice breathing in, holding for a couple of seconds and then extending your out-breath. Breathe in as normal, hold, then allow your exhale to lengthen. This has a tremendously calming affect on the body, mind and nervous system.
4. While continuing to be aware of your breath, mentally chant the syllable Om on both the in-breath and out-breath. Breathe in

and chant Om, then breathe out and chant Om.
5. Allow your focus to gravitate to either the space between your brow or your heart centre. Open yourself to the infinitude of the Self; pure, formless Consciousness. The Self plus maya gives rise to Ishvara; the Supreme Cause in whom the entire universe exists and from whom the entire creation evolves. Realise that Ishvara, God, created everything. So, everything is, therefore, God.
6. Become aware that the very world is the visible form of Ishvara; the very body of Ishvara. God is incarnate as the very universe and this incarnation is permanently available to us. This understanding will change our attitude toward life; toward the universe.
7. Contemplate the vision of the cosmic form of Ishvara from the Bhagavad Gita. Imagine the vast heavens are the Lord's head. The sun and moon are His eyes and the stars above are a celestial crown. The Earth is His feet and fire is His mouth. Dharma, the eternal law of moral order, is His back and very support. The grasses, plants and trees are His hair. The mountains are His bones. The sea is the Lord's lifeblood and the rivers and streams are His arteries and veins.
8. Become aware that this magnificent Divine form expands outward still farther, containing the entirety of creation, including all living beings. The entire cosmos is the body of Ishvara. Feel this Divine unity of all things; the Divine presence pervading all things and shining as the innermost being of everything.
9. Remain in contemplation as long as you like.
10. When you are ready, gently and gradually bring yourself back to full awareness of the body and the room in which you are sitting. Don't unconsciously throw away the object of your meditation, however. Allow yourself to reflect on it throughout your day. Remember that every time you take a drink of water you are in

contact with Ishvara. The sun, the moon, the rain, the clouds, the smell of the earth—it is all Ishvara. You are surrounded by Ishvara and always experiencing Ishvara. With this knowledge, your every experience is Divine.

Regular practice of upasana meditation, and the ability to comprehend God as the entire creation, both gross and subtle, will most certainly sharpen, hone and prepare the mind for the third and highest understanding of God. It's here that we make the jump from dualistic to Non-dual devotion.

3. The Formless Absolute

The first level of understanding God is as That which created the world. The logic of Vedanta then follows that God not only created the world but is the world. The entire universe is, therefore, the body of God.

It's easy for misunderstanding to creep in here. If God is the world, then surely that must mean there's no God beyond the world? For example, when you churn milk into butter, you'll never get the milk back in its original form. Does this mean that if God fashions the entire cosmos out of Itself, God is "lost" in the creation much as the milk is lost in the butter?

Here Vedanta emphasises an important point: God appears as the world, but does not *become* the world.

There are two aspects, as it were, to Brahman or the Self: a higher and a lower aspect.

The higher aspect is *the Self without form;* the Absolute; pure, undifferentiated Consciousness.

The lower aspect is *the Self with form;* in other words, the Self, Consciousness, plus maya. That's what we've just been speaking about.

Maya "conditions" the Self to appear as the world of matter and form; including Ishvara, the macrocosm, and the individual person, the microcosm.

The lower aspect, which manifests as the world of form, depends entirely upon the higher aspect, the formless Self, much as a wave depends upon the ocean for its existence.

Crucially, the creation of the world of form does not affect the higher aspect; the Absolute, Unmanifest Self. The form and formless exist simultaneously as two different orders of reality.

This third level of understanding God, as the Absolute, formless and indivisible Self, is extremely difficult for most people to grasp. After all, it cannot be objectified. It's infinitely subtler than the mind and senses, so there's nothing for the mind to grasp onto.

Knowledge of the Self as the Non-dual, all-pervading totality of Existence can only be be provided by the teaching of Vedanta.

It's only Knowledge of the Self as the eternal, formless, self-shining cause and foundation of Existence—and, crucially, the realisation of our oneness with that Self—that can free the mind from samsara. No other knowledge will do it.

This Absolute aspect of God is not worshiped through ritual, prayer and upasana meditation, but through the contemplation of the scriptures and the practise of Self-Knowledge.

That's considered the highest form of devotion; the full realisation of our essential oneness with God. All distinction between devotee and the object of devotion falls away when we integrate and actualise the essence of the teaching, "I Am That".

The Bhagavad Gita identifies three types of devotee:

1. Those who seek God as a way of attaining worldly gain.
2. Those who seek God as an end in itself.
3. Those who seek to realise their oneness with God.

Krishna states:

> Among these [types of devotee], the *jnani*, the one who knows their oneness with the Self, is most distinguished. Such souls are unwavering in their devotion and are always united with Me in mind and heart. All are exalted, but the jnani, being absorbed in Me, is non-separate from Me and has attained the highest goal in life, beyond which nothing more is to be gained.

Jnani is a term for the enlightened being; the one who has successfully penetrated the veil of ignorance and come to know the truth of their being as pure Consciousness/Awareness.

The entire spiritual path is rooted in devotion, for, according to the Bhagavad Gita, whatever you worship you eventually attain.

The first two stages of devotion, which are dualistic in nature—devotion to a personal God and devotion to God as the very form of the universe—should, in time, lead to the third and highest stage of devotion: Non-dual devotion; which is the realisation of one's own nature as the Self.

As our means of Self-Knowledge, Vedanta is essentially the practise of Non-dual devotion. The Non-dual devotee worships the Absolute by applying Vedanta's three-fold process of listening, reasoning and deep contemplation of the teaching.

In the Gita, Krishna promises that, "By knowing that Self-Realisation is the ultimate goal, and pursuing it with all your heart, you will be united with Me."

Non-dual devotion is to know and abide as your true Self; the Divinity that's within you, that is you, and all other beings.

The beauty is that you don't need to look anywhere to find the Self. It's already present and already attained. You already are the self. You have never been and can never be anything other than the Self.

All that's necessary is to keep the mind sufficiently qualified and allow the teaching of Vedanta to strip away the ignorance that has blinded you to the boundless beauty, peace and Wholeness of your own true nature.

This doesn't necessarily mean that you abandon the other two forms of devotion; the worship of Ishvara as a personal deity and as all the forms in the universe. Many liberated souls continue to do so long after gaining freedom from samsara.

Why not? To live with a worshipful mind and a devotional heart is highly purifying. It generates a great deal of joy, neutralises ego identification and enables Self-Knowledge to continue dissolving the shackles of ignorance.

"Those who worship Me will reach Me," Krishna promises.

Keep your mind, thoughts and heart upon the Self, the ultimate Reality, that which pervades all things as water pervades the ocean, and you will come to know, beyond all doubt, your oneness with it.

Summary

- All peoples' lives are driven by devotion. We are devoted to that which we value above all else.
- Whatever a person happens to be seeking in life, ultimately what they want is the wholeness, joy and freedom inherent in their own Self. This is something that materialists fail to see, however. They keep chasing happiness in samsara instead.
- The spiritual seeker knows that what they ultimately seek is freedom from samsara, attained by Self-Realisation.
- Upasana yoga means meditating upon God and cultivating a devotional, worshipful mind through contemplation and devotional practises.
- The benefits of devotion to God have been widely demonstrated in clinical studies. Having a relationship with God has a significant range of health and psychological benefits. For the

seeker of liberation, it also is a superb way of purifying and readying the mind for Self-Knowledge.
- The way a person worships God will depend on their level of understanding.
- The three levels of understanding God are as a personal deity, a universal God, and the all-pervading Absolute.
- Most find it easier to begin with dualistic devotion directed to a personal God or a universal God. This will, in time, hopefully progress to Non-dual devotion, which takes the form of Self-Knowledge, as delivered by the three stage process of Vedanta.
- The highest form of devotion is to realise your non-separation from and essential oneness with God. This is also the key to enlightenment and liberation from samsara.

13.
The Three Energies

By transcending the three qualities, which are the cause of the body, one is released from birth, death, old age and sorrow, and gains immortality.
Bhagavad Gita

Chapter Eleven described the material universe, a product of maya, as being comprised of three basic energies or qualities, which we call the gunas.

Not many Westerners will be familiar with the word guna. The term originates from ancient Sankhya philosophy and has no direct English equivalent. I've described it as "energy", but the word literally translates as "rope", "string" or "thread".

The word "thread" is a particularly apt translation. Just as cotton threads combine to form the substance and essence of a shirt or a dress, the gunas are the threads that combine to constitute the entire material creation.

As maya made manifest, these three qualities are present in all beings and all forms. It's the interplay of these gunas that determine the constitution, quality and behaviour of any given object, from the subatomic particles of your body to the planets, stars and galaxies.

They constitute, shape and influence not only the physical world, but also the subtler realms of mind, thought and emotion. In short, there's nothing in the phenomenal world, gross or subtle, that isn't a product of these three qualities in infinite combination.

THE THREE GUNAS OR QUALITIES

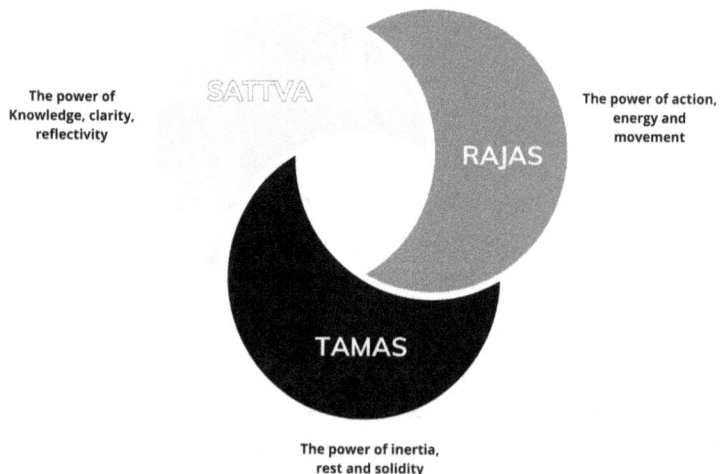

The Three Gunas

As you may recall, the gunas are called sattva, rajas and tamas. Let's briefly explore the nature of each, taking a look at how they influence the body and mind and how they can be leveraged in order to master your life and facilitate Self-Realisation.

1. Sattva — Clarity

The word sattva is derived from *sat*, which refers to the Self; the ground of pure Existence.

Sattva is reflective and revealing by nature. It allows us to perceive, understand and respond appropriately to things. As the very light that reveals objects, this guna is intimately associated with knowledge and truth.

Perhaps you can see why sattva is essential to the seeker of liberation. Only a sattvic mind is capable of gaining, understanding and retaining Self-Knowledge.

That's why all spiritual practice, including karma yoga, devotional practises, meditation and lifestyle management is geared at cultivating a predominantly sattvic mind.

A sattvic mind is a contemplative mind; a mind capable of seeing and understanding truth with clarity and freedom from distortion.

Sattva is also synonymous with happiness. That's why even those with no interest in Self-Knowledge would do well to cultivate a sattvic mind, which all but guarantees a happy, peaceful and successful life.

Reflective and revealing by nature, sattva brings peace and stillness, harmony and clarity.

When sattva predominates, your mind feels bright, clear and luminous. Emotional states associated with sattva include joy, love, friendliness, openness, creativity and inspiration.

People with a high degree of sattva tend to be peaceful, contemplative souls who delight in beauty and quietude. Spiritual growth is a priority for such people and, thanks to sattva, something that is easily attained.

Of course, as with anything in duality, each guna has its upside and downside. True to their name, each has the capacity to act like a "rope", causing a degree of bondage. That's why liberation isn't simply the cultivation of a sattvic mind. Liberation entails the complete transcendence of the gunas, as we shall see.

The downside to sattva is the tendency to become attached to peace and quiet. The sattvic person values solitude and silence, so the moment somebody or something happens to disturb that, they can become highly agitated and unhappy. Think of an otherwise mellow librarian who becomes a raging tyrant the moment somebody starts making noise and disturbance.

Sattvic people can almost become addicted to seclusion and quietude and feel the need to strictly control their environment. As a result, their own peace of mind is highly liable to be shattered when dealing with the next guna we'll discuss: rajas.

2. Rajas — Activity

Whereas sattva is reflective and revealing, rajas, the mode of energy and activity, has a projecting quality. It's rajas that enables us to function in the world by initiating and carrying out action.

We experience rajas as desire, passion, alertness and determination. Predominantly rajasic people are extroverts with boundless energy, excitement and ambition. They are very much driven by the desire for achievement and attainment and are highly focused on relationships, socialising and acquiring and amassing possessions, power and status.

As the quality of passion and activity, rajas is what gets us out of bed in the morning and motivates us to transact with the material world, doing what needs to be done and striving to attain various goals and ends.

As with all things, it comes with its downside. Too much rajas can lead lead to anger, greed, anxiety, stress and impatience. While sattvic types value peace and quiet, rajasic people can't stand silence and solitude.

Compulsively busy and prone to restlessness and anxiety, they are subject to endless and compulsive desires and are rarely satisfied with what they have. How can they be when the grass is always greener on the other side?

Forever uptight and perpetually stressed, with a tendency to annoyance and aggression, the rajasic person frequently flirts with burnout and exhaustion.

When wisely harnessed, the quality of rajas provides the necessary desire, determination and dynamism to pursue Self-Knowledge.

The rajasic mind, however, is fickle, wavering and prone to dissatisfaction. Very often, the rajasic have trouble sticking to any one thing for the required duration. This can make spiritual progress very difficult and is why, along with tamas, this quality must be kept in check.

3. Tamas — Inertia

Have you ever woken up to your alarm clock and had to drag yourself out of bed, bleary-eyed, sluggish and unable to even think until you've had a strong coffee?

Welcome to tamas! As the densest of the three qualities, tamas has an obscuring and veiling effect on the body and mind. This makes knowledge difficult because it leaves us prone to delusion and ignorance.

Tamas is responsible for both rest and sleep, so it certainly serves a necessary function. Too much tamas, however, and we experience inertia, laziness and apathy. Like a thick black cloud, it dulls the mind, making it difficult to think and act with clarity and objectivity. Even the simplest of actions can become an inordinate struggle when there's an imbalance of tamas guna.

On the emotional spectrum, this guna inclines a person to sadness, fear, boredom, melancholy, shame, apathy and ignorance. People with excess tamas invariably suffer from depression.

Those with primarily tamasic temperaments tend to revel in inertia. Their way of dealing with problems, or pretty much anything else for that matter, is through avoidance. The longer this goes on, the harder it can be to climb out of tamas' slippery pit of despair, indolence and apathy.

People with an extreme proportion of tamas guna may find it impossible holding down a job and honouring regular commitments. They'd rather lie in bed all day watching television, gaming or scrolling through endless social media feeds, envious of people with much better lives but lacking the motivation to improve their own. This becomes almost a kind of addiction. If sattva binds to quietude and rajas binds to activity, tamas binds to sloth.

The tamasic mind is spectacularly prone to ignorance and delusion. This invariably leads to misjudged actions and unremittingly bad karma of all kinds. Tamasic people often have no goal in life and see no purpose in anything. They not only fail to progress spiritually, but may actually regress spiritually, psychologically and physically.

Obviously, that's something the seeker of liberation must avoid at all costs. That's why it's so important to learn to manage and eventually transcend the gunas.

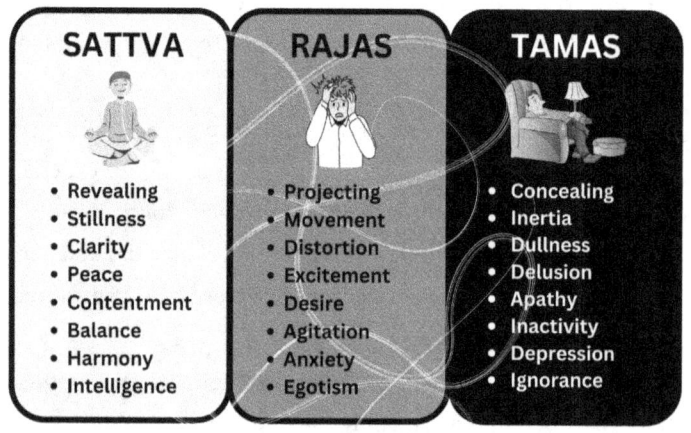

SATTVA	RAJAS	TAMAS
• Revealing	• Projecting	• Concealing
• Stillness	• Movement	• Inertia
• Clarity	• Distortion	• Dullness
• Peace	• Excitement	• Delusion
• Contentment	• Desire	• Apathy
• Balance	• Agitation	• Inactivity
• Harmony	• Anxiety	• Depression
• Intelligence	• Egotism	• Ignorance

The Dance of Rajas and Tamas

Try though you might, there's no escaping the gunas. They're constantly at play in our lives; their shifting proportions influencing and shaping our bodies and minds, our actions and behaviour and the very environment around us.

If you want to know which of the gunas is currently predominant, you need only take a look at the way you're feeling. Desire, craving, restlessness and anxiety point to rajas. Boredom, apathy and confusion suggest excess tamas. If, on the other hand, you happen to be feeling happy, peaceful and content, that's a sure sign that you're basking in the glow of sattva.

Unfortunately, although the essential nature of the mind is sattva, which enables us to be aware of and to know things, sattva is almost always contaminated by excess rajas and tamas. That's hardly surprising when you consider that modern day living subjects us to an unrelenting seesaw between rajas and tamas.

When you get up in the morning and reach for a cup of coffee, what you're doing is cultivating some rajas. You'll find rajas keeps you going throughout the day, providing the necessary energy and motivation to perform your daily tasks, jobs and obligations.

By the end of a busy day, however, you may find yourself collapsing on the sofa, physically and mentally exhausted. The rajas has burned itself out and collapsed into tamas. At this point, you're probably unable to even think. You might throw a pizza in the microwave, grab a beer and zone out to a few hours of mind-numbing television or doomscrolling on social media. Then the tamas eventually puts you to sleep altogether and the next day the cycle begins again.

Excessively rajasic people often find it hard to sleep. Constantly wired, they find it difficult to switch off and relax. Tamasic people, on the other hand, are subject to constant lethargy and may feel the urge to oversleep.

When not properly managed, both rajas and tamas can be a source of tremendous suffering.

The overly rajasic are subject to constant, almost unquenchable desire and compulsion. No matter what they do, have or achieve, they're never satisfied. The moment they get something, they immediately latch onto the next thing, which will always seem bigger, better and more appealing. The problem is, the allure of such desire can be so strong that the individual may be willing to cut corners and violate dharma; and this always generates problems in both the short and long term.

When tamas predominates, a person will find it difficult to think with clarity and to act with decisive intent. Virtually everything becomes a challenge and rather than facing their problems, they are inclined to simply ignore them and indulge their senses with food, alcohol, drugs and whatever else appeals to their various addictions.

All living beings are subject to the influence of the gunas. That's why it's essential, particularly for the seeker of liberation, to learn to recognise their effects and to consciously manage and master them. The key, as we shall see, is to always aim for a more sattvic mind and body.

The Gunas and Knowledge

Sattva is the root of calmness, purity, well-being and joy. Whenever you find yourself feeling happy, peaceful and calm, that's courtesy of sattva guna. Its revealing quality enables the subtle body to become like a calm and pristine lake, effortlessly reflecting the light of our own nature as Consciousness. When sattva predominates, you're able to see things as they are; hence, it has a revealing quality. Sattva makes knowledge possible.

A rajasic mind is like a fast-flowing river. When you look into a moving river, the light reflected upon the water surface appears in shifting, fractured glimmers. The motion of the water makes the reflected sunlight appear to be in motion. That's why rajas is said to have a projecting quality. Because a rajasic mind is agitated and in motion, it's not an accurate reflector of knowledge. When rajas is at play, we don't see things as they truly are; therefore, our knowledge becomes distorted.

Sticking with the water metaphor, a tamasic mind is like a muddy swamp. The water is dark, murky and incapable of reflecting any light at all. Even on a bright, sunny day, all you'll see, basically, is mud. That's why we consider tamas the obscuring guna. It prevents knowledge altogether because it's the opposite of sattva; it has no reflecting power.

Perhaps now you can see the importance of having a sattvic mind when it comes to gaining knowledge. Sattva enables us to see clearly. Rajas distorts what we see. Tamas, meanwhile, prevents us from seeing at all.

All Desires Are Desires For Sattva

Rajas, which tends to predominate in most people, compels us to pursue all kinds of goals, objects, acquisitions and sensory experiences. This is, of course, a necessary part of living. Life is karma; a succession of action after action. The cycle of human life generally works on a loop of desire-action-reaction repeated *ad infinitum*.

What is it that we're truly seeking, however?

The first few chapters analysed the zero-sum nature of object-based happiness. We came to see that what we really want is rarely the actual goal itself, but the sense of relief, satisfaction and peace we feel when we attain the goal. This happens when desire (rajas) gives way to contentment (sattva), and we're able to taste the Bliss of our own Consciousness in a mind temporarily freed from want and desire.

The problem is the mind becomes highly conditioned to rajasic mores. Our happiness, the experience of sattva, is usually short lived. In no time at all, the dissatisfied rajasic mind is again seeking more, different and better things to acquire and attain. Either that, or after the sattva wears off, the mind succumbs to tamas and we become discouraged, resentful or depressed.

All desires are ultimately desires for sattva: which, by its reflective nature, allows us to enjoy the Wholeness and Bliss inherent to Consciousness.

The good news is sattva isn't something that you need to seek and acquire. It's already there. The mind is sattvic by its very nature.

If the mind wasn't inherently sattvic, it wouldn't have the ability to reveal and know things.

So, given that the mind is sattvic by nature, what you actually need to do in order to enjoy this sattva is to neutralise excess rajas and tamas. That's the key to mind management. By learning to consciously manage the gunas, you're able to cultivate the peaceful and pure mind necessary for understanding and internalising Self-Knowledge.

To put it another way, a sattvic mind plus the teaching of Vedanta equals your ticket to freedom.

You Are the Choices You Make

As we've seen, each of the gunas has its upside and downside. The secret to successful and balanced living is the art of leverage. In other words, we learn to maximise the benefits of each guna and minimise its disadvantages.

To a large extent, success or failure in life comes down to self-mastery. Self-mastery means learning to effectively master your body-mind-sense complex; to wield this instrument with skill and effectiveness rather than being a slave to it. A large part of that comes down to guna management.

Your experience is, by and large, shaped by the choices you make. Everything in your life, from your lifestyle, line of work, home environment, the people you associate with and the media you consume, has a profound effect on the way you think and feel. This is basic cause and effect.

If you find yourself struggling with the seesaw of rajas and tamas, it's important to do two things. Firstly, you need to be aware of the choices and actions that are causing the imbalance. Secondly, you must be willing to make the appropriate changes.

A rajasic lifestyle, diet and environment will condition your body and mind to be restless, agitated and anxious. Similarly, tamasic life choices will leave you feeling lethargic, disengaged and depressed.

In order to address this, and in order to cultivate the sattvic mind necessary for liberation, all aspects of your life need to be consciously and judiciously managed. This is discussed in detail in the last four chapters of the Bhagavad Gita. Here are some tips for handy reference.

Gunas and Diet

Healthy eating isn't rocket science. We all know, more or less, which foods are good for us and which aren't. Whether or not we put this knowledge into practice is another story.

People can be incredibly stubborn when it comes to their dietary habits. They like what they like—generally, the food they're used to; the food they've always eaten—and are unwilling to change. I've seen people refuse to change their eating habits even when their life depended on it. That, in itself, is indicative of a tamasic mind.

It's essential to consider the effect the food that you eat is having on the quality of your body, mind and emotions.

Everyone is probably familiar with the saying, "you are what you eat." In actual fact, as we saw in Chapter Nine, one of the terms Vedanta has for the physical body is the "food body". The body is, after all, made of the food that you eat. The quality of food that you eat will obviously have an enormous effect on the quality of your body.

To enjoy a sattvic body and mind, it's important to minimise foods that have a rajasic and tamasic effect on the body and eat more sattvic foods. That's the essence of a yogic diet.

1. Sattvic Foods

Foods generally considered sattvic include fresh fruit, vegetables, nuts, seeds, legumes, wholegrain, certain oils and non-meat products. Some organic dairy is also traditionally considered sattvic. The sattvic diet, which places emphasis on fresh and unprocessed food, organic where possible, is designed to cultivate a healthy body and a calm mind.

2. Rajasic Food

Rajasic foods are known for their stimulating effect. This includes onions, garlic, spiced or salty food, chocolate, caffeinated beverages and soft drinks. If you are prone to excess rajas, it's best to steer clear of these foods. Rajasic foods aren't necessarily bad for the body, but that aren't as beneficial as sattvic foods and may cause disturbance to the body-mind equilibrium. This can clearly be seen in the case of caffeine and sugar, which invariably lead to a restless, unsettled mind and an overstimulated nervous system.

3. Tamasic Food

Tamasic food is a problem for many people, simply because there's so much of it around. The modern Western diet is highly tamasic. Whereas sattvic food is fresh and unprocessed, tamasic food is heavily processed and rarely fresh; therefore losing much, if not all, of its nutritional value.

Meat is heavily tamasic, as are eggs, pastries, bread, fermented foods, sugary foods and alcohol. Such foods are best minimised in one's diet as they have an inflammatory on the body and dulling effect on the mind.

The best way to find the diet that's appropriate for you is to take note of how you feel physically and mentally after eating certain foods. If you want a sattvic mind and body, you're unlikely to find a steady diet of pizza, kebab, sugary snacks and beer helpful in this regard.

Gunas and Lifestyle

It's always helpful to take stock of the way you're living your life and the effect this may be having on you.

Is your lifestyle one of balance and harmony, or is it causing stress, anxiety, boredom or apathy? The influence and effect of the gunas is pervasive, so everything in your life must be carefully examined in the light of this knowledge

1. Work

Life circumstances differ, but if you happen to be an average, working age person it's likely you spend a significant chunk of your time in the workplace. That's why it's important to, where possible, be in an environment that's healthy and conducive to your physical, mental and emotional wellbeing.

Some workplaces are exceptionally stressful, chaotic and high pressure. Spending your entire day in a wildly rajasic environment will obviously have a negative effect on both your body and mind. Too much rajas day in, day out, can lead to high blood pressure, anxiety, insomnia and various other stress related conditions.

Tamas can also be a problem in the workplace. This might manifest as an environment filled with conflict, gossip, paranoia, power games and backstabbing. This also has a correspondingly deleterious effect on both body and mind.

A sattvic environment is one where people come together to work for a common goal, treating each other with respect, cooperation, calmness and kindness.

If you find your workplace negatively affecting the quality of your life and other options are available, it may be worth trying to find a better and more harmonious environment in which to work, particularly if your goal is spiritual liberation.

Sometimes people are stuck with jobs they dislike out of sheer necessity and lack of other options. When that's the case, the application of karma yoga can help immensely in dealing with stressful situations. All you can do is your best, and then hand that, and the results of your actions, up to Ishvara to take care of. Even the littlest application of karma yoga can free the mind of immense emotional pressure. Remember that, with karma yoga, the objective is not to get what you want. The objective is simply a pure, sattvic, undisturbed mind.

2. Your Environment

Your immediate, everyday surroundings, such as your home and garden, can be rajasic, tamasic or sattvic in nature and this can, of course, have an enormous impact on your emotional state.

Noisy, chaotic and disorderly environments are rajasic in nature. Cluttered, dirty and squalid environments are tamasic. The ideal, sattvic environment is one that's clean, bright, orderly and calming. Create beauty and harmony wherever you can and strive to live in an environment that is nurturing to both mind and soul.

3. Leisure Time

The way you spend your leisure time should be carefully considered.

Rajasic activities, such as sports, dancing, running and working out are excellent when balanced with adequate rest and downtime.

Tamasic activities may be fine when winding down, but should be kept in moderation due to the negative effects of excess tamas. This might include drinking alcohol, smoking or vaping, and passive, mindless activity such as watching television and aimless online scrolling.

When it comes to entertainment, the gunas should certainly be taken into account. A lot of media entertainment can be highly tamasic and rajasic in nature. Extreme violence has become the norm in a lot of television, film and video games. Sensationalism, noise and fast editing can also trigger a rajasic response that will linger long afterward.

The effect of the gunas can be seen in music as well. Some music genres, such as metal, hard rock, dance music and chart pop can be highly rajasic in nature. This can, of course, be helpful at certain times of the day when you feel in need of a little rajas. Tamasic music includes the aggressive, violent lyrics often found in death metal and gangster rap.

As always, pay attention to how you feel after doing certain things. Often something may feel good at the time but comes with a hangover-like aftereffect. Do you feel rested or anxious after watching a gore-filled slasher movie? Do you feel physically comfortable after overeating and consuming heavy, tamasic foods? And just how good do you feel the morning after a night of binge drinking?

The cultivation of a peaceful, sattvic mind must be a priority for the spiritual seeker. Sattvic leisure pursuits are pleasurable, beneficial to mind and body and cause no negative aftereffects. Examples include moderate exercise, such as walking and hiking, time spent in nature, gardening and engaging in creative pursuits such as painting, singing, charity work and whatever else nurtures the soul and brings you joy.

4. Media Exposure

The effect of media has become an enormous problem for many people and, arguably, as a society. The mainstream media, ever hungry for clicks and sensationalist to its core, is unquestionably a hotbed of rajas and tamas. In the digital era, there's almost no escaping it either. Unless you exercise judicious restraint, it can generate a huge amount of mental and emotional agitation. Worse still is social media, a breeding ground for conflict, tribalism, misinformation and extremism.

Scientists have pointed out that human brain isn't designed to be constantly "switched on" to continuous media stimulus. The constant input and compulsive scrolling generates a lot of rajas, which inevitably leads to a corresponding tamasic crash.

The best way to navigate media is to exercise balance and restraint. This can be challenging given the omnipresent role media and connectivity now play in our society and daily lives. In order to protect your mind from unnecessary disturbance, it's advisable to limit and curate your usage of media, social media and smartphones or tablets. It may be helpful to experiment with regular media fasts and notice the effect this has on your mental and emotional well-being.

5. Other People

For better or worse, other people have an immense effect on our mental and emotional wellbeing. It's been shown that we tend to become like the people we spend our time with. That's why it's always a good idea to make sure that, insofar as you can, you only associate with people you'd happily be like yourself.

Obviously, there are many people in life, such as colleagues and family members, you have no choice but to be around. But beyond work and family, it's up to you who spend your time with.

People with highly rajasic temperaments can be exhausting to be around. Such people are always on the go, restless, agitated and driven by a potent combination of avarice and anxiety.

By comparison, tamasic people can seem more chilled out and easygoing. Tamas, however, unlike sattva, clouds the mind. Extremely tamasic people can often be reliant on alcohol and drugs, which create a narcoleptic stupor, making it hard to think clearly and function effectively.

Tamas can be initially enjoyable, particularly if you are subject to a lot of rajas in your daily life. It should never be overindulged, however. An excess of tamas can quickly lead to depression and a sense of apathy and pointlessness. It can cause a great deal of suffering for people; distorting the mind and opening people to all kinds of delusions and self-destructive ideas and mindsets. Once you've slipped into the pit of tamas it can be exceptionally difficult to claw your way back out again.

If you want to enjoy a sattvic mind, it's obviously preferable to spend your time with sattvic people. They're easy to spot. People with a sattvic temperament are balanced, happy, easy-going, caring, fun, adventurous, spiritual, creative and generally uplifting to be around. They have a way of making others feel good in their presence. Sattvic people bring out the best in others and tend to see the good in all things.

Of course, nobody is fully sattvic, rajasic or tamasic. Some of us are more inclined to a rajasic or tamasic disposition. If we're lucky, we may be largely sattvic in nature. The gunas function in each of us in varying proportions. For example, if you're lucky, you may be predominantly sattvic (say, around 50%) but have a streak of rajas (30%) and a little tamas thrown in (20%).

All three gunas are necessary, but with a little self-awareness and discipline, you can learn to manage their proportions in order to ensure a largely sattvic mind. It's always worth the effort, for a sattvic mind is not only a happy mind—it's a mind qualified for Self-Knowledge.

Final Tips on Guna Management

As we've learned, the gunas condition the body and mind and influence our thinking, reactions, behaviour and actions. The key is to recognise which guna is predominant and make any necessary adjustments. Here are some final tips.

Dealing With Tamas

If you find yourself overcome by tamas, you'll likely feel lethargic, fuzzy-headed and prone to fear, depression and demotivation. A tamasic mind is simply unable to attain and process Self-Knowledge, which requires clarity and refined, subtle thinking.

It's almost impossible to jump straight from a tamasic to a sattvic state. Instead, you need to burn off excess tamas by generating a little rajas. This can be done by, first and foremost, getting moving. Exercise, whether walking, running or working out at the gym is excellent for changing your physical and psycho-emotional state.

Cleaning up the diet is essential, and it's important to strictly manage your media input. Ruthlessly eliminate anything that might be fostering a tamasic mindset. Instead, expose yourself to positive input and be careful who you spend your time with. Make sure you're around people that lift you up rather than bring you down.

Dealing With Rajas

To counter tamas, you need a little rajas to get your energy moving. To deal with excess rajas, you have to calm it back down again. With a little practice, you can transmute tamas into rajas and then rajas into sattva.

Practices such as meditation, yoga, pranayama (breathing exercises) and qigong are highly recommended and wonderful for calming both mind and body. Mindfulness is also highly beneficial; the art of bringing your full attention to whatever you happen to be doing in the present moment. My favourite definition of mindfulness is, "The art of keeping your mind where your body is."

Be sure to spend some time in the beauty of nature, which has immense healing and restorative powers. Even a short walk outdoors beneath the sky and among trees and plants can shift your energy tremendously.

Watch your diet and avoid stimulants. Switch up your tea and coffee for decaf, herbal tea or water with a twist of lemon.

Steer clear of the news for a while (rest assured, it'll still be there when you come back to it). Limit your internet, television and social media usage and make sure that you're getting enough rest and sleep.

Avoid hanging out with rajasic people where possible and spend time with those whose energy makes you feel calmer, more peaceful and content.

Make spiritual devotion the centre-point of your entire life. Perform a daily devotional ritual such as the one suggested in the previous chapter. Convert all your actions to karma yoga by handing up everything you do to God, and learn to take it easy, enjoying the simplicity of the present moment.

By consciously taking charge of your life and managing the gunas as best you can, you steer yourself toward sattva, which manifests as harmony and balance; and is the key to a mind qualified for Self-Knowledge and eventual liberation.

Transcending the Gunas

Ultimately, the key to freeing yourself of the "ropes", the three gunas, is to transcend them. You transcend them by knowing that, while these three principles are an inescapable component of the world of maya, you, as Consciousness, are not bound by anything phenomenal.

The gunas affect the lower part of our nature, the body-mind-sense complex. They do not, however, affect Consciousness. Consciousness is beyond the material world. It is that which by which the material world is witnessed but cannot itself be witnessed.

This subject/object discrimination will be unfolded in the next chapter. It is one of Vedanta's primary methodologies for freeing the mind of suffering by removing our false identification with the material world, including the body and mind itself.

The gunas forever influence the body and mind, for they are the very forces constituting these instruments. Liberation is knowing, however, that you are free regardless of the current state of the body-mind-sense complex. Whatever the play of the gunas, true freedom is absolute and independent of all extraneous variables.

Now that we've analysed the constitution of the material world, the province of the gunas, the next chapter will delve right into the heart of Vedanta's primary topic: Self-Knowledge.

Summary

- The topic of this chapter is the material world and the three qualities of maya; sattva, rajas and tamas.
- These three qualities are present in all things. They constitute, shape and influence both our body-mind-sense complex and the world in which it lives.
- Sattva is the mode of clarity, knowledge, harmony and is revealing in nature. Rajas is the mode of action, motion, passion and is projecting in nature. Tamas is the mode of inertia, denseness, ignorance and is concealing in nature.
- You can know which guna is currently predominant by observing your thoughts, emotions and the condition of your physical body.
- A sattvic mind is required for knowledge, because sattva is revealing. Rajas obscures knowledge. Tamas prevents you from attaining knowledge at all.
- That's why it's necessary for the seeker of Self-Knowledge to cultivate a primarily sattvic mind. This is done by neutralising excess rajas and tamas.
- You are the choices you make in life. Discernment must be exercised in all areas of life from your diet and workplace to your leisure time, media exposure and the people you spend time with.

- Commit to eliminating rajasic and tamasic influences where necessary and hold sattva as your ideal. This will, in time, help you transcend the gunas altogether through the knowledge they affect only the material realm and not you, as Consciousness.

14.

Keys to Self-Knowledge

May the wise soul relinquish the pursuit of petty desires and take to the pursuit of Self-Knowledge, which alone leads to freedom from the bondage of birth and death!
Vivekachudamani

There's an ancient parable from India which perfectly demonstrates the difficulties inherent in gaining knowledge.

In the story, a group of blind men come across an elephant—something none of them have ever heard of or encountered before. They're each eager to learn what the creature is. Obviously, because they are blind they must rely on touch alone.

Each of the men is positioned at a different part of the elephant's body.

The man at the front of the elephant reaches out and takes hold of its trunk. "This 'elephant' is clearly long, narrow and wrinkled," he declares as he runs his hand along its trunk. "It's almost like a snake!"

The second man stands by the elephant's head. He reaches out and takes hold of the creature's ear. "No," he says. "This elephant is loose, large and floppy, almost like a piece of cloth!"

The third man happens to take hold of the tusk and shouts, "No, no, it's smooth, curved and sharp like a spear!"

Standing by the middle of the creature, the fourth man reaches out and all he can feel is the side of the elephant's body, so he proclaims, "It's large and flat, almost like a wall."

The final man happens to be at the elephant's rear, and he reaches out and takes hold of the tail. "You're all wrong," he states. "The elephant is slim and long, like a piece of rope!"

The moral of the story is clear. Each man was correct according to his subjective experience. What they were experiencing, however, was only a small part of the full picture.

What they should have done was confer and piece the information together, or perhaps get the help of somebody who could see the whole elephant and could describe it to them, helping them making sense of their experience.

The Big Picture

Without a clear and cohesive map of the terrain, spiritual knowledge can be a lot like that. Spiritual seekers may amass an assortment of experiences and knowledge. The ego likes to be right, so we tend to assume that we have a clear understanding of the whole truth even if we have but a single piece of the puzzle.

Vedanta is concerned with the big picture. That's why it offers a range of teaching methodologies to help build as clear, full and comprehensive a picture as possible. We don't just look at things from a single perspective. We consider them from multiple angles. That's the best way to develop a full and comprehensive understanding of Reality.

At this point, we've laid out the fundamentals on the nature of the Self, Ishvara and the creation. It's without doubt a multifaceted, nuanced and potentially confusing topic. You likely still have a number of questions and doubts. That's all part of the learning process. As we continue unfolding this vision of Reality from multiple angles, any confusion will hopefully be resolved.

This essential chapter delves into many of the key teachings at the heart of Vedanta, also known as *jnana yoga,* or the yoga of Self-Knowledge.

It's not a chapter to speed through. Instead, take your time to work through each section, making sure that you have a firm grasp of the logic before proceeding on to the next. As you do, you'll find that your understanding gradually grows, develops and refines—and everything begins to click. There will be a degree of repetition of certain key concepts; something to be embraced as a necessary part of the learning process.

Reflected Consciousness

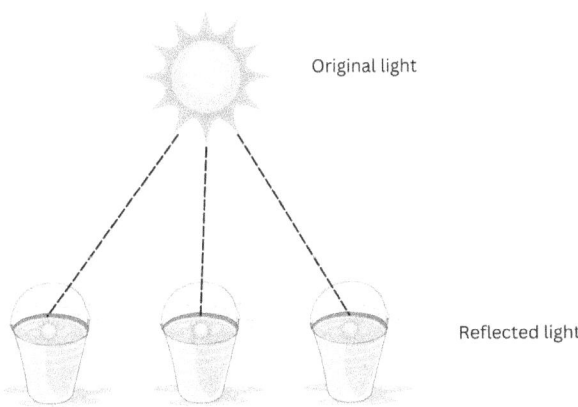

The idea of reflected Consciousness is best introduced using an analogy.

Let's say you're somewhere outdoors, and you come across several buckets of water sitting beneath the midday sun. You gaze into the water and see the sun reflected in each bucket.

Now, if you'd somehow never seen a bucket of water in your life, you might be forgiven for looking at the reflection and saying, "Oh, look, there's the sun in each bucket!"

Is it actually the sun that you're seeing in the water?

The answer is yes and no.

It is the sun, of course, but it's not the original sun, which is up in the sky. Having no light of its own, the water serves as a mirror or reflecting medium. Each of the buckets is reflecting the same sun. One sun, many reflections.

So, you might wonder, how does this relate to Consciousness?

Our tendency is to assume that our bodies and minds are themselves alive, possessing a distinct and inherent life and sentience of their own.

What if I was to tell you, however, that your body and mind have no life of their own?

Indeed, the gross and subtle bodies are made of matter, and matter is an inert property. Any life these vehicles possess is granted solely by the presence of the Self; Consciousness. Without this "mingling" of Consciousness and matter, the body and mind would be as inert as a brick.

What the subtle body has in common with the bucket of water is that both are reflecting mediums. The water in the bucket is a reflecting medium for the light of the sun, whereas the subtle body is a reflecting medium for the light of Consciousness.

When the subtle body is associated with a particular gross body, the gross body is granted life—and, thus, inert matter comes to life.

We have, therefore, the "Original Consciousness", which shines by itself and is limitless, all-pervading and without beginning or end. Then we have the "reflected Consciousness" which illumines and enlivens the subtle body, which, in turn, grants life to the gross body.

The actual life and sentience belongs not to these vehicles, but to the reflected light of Consciousness.

This can be hard to grasp. After all, you've likely spent an entire lifetime assuming that your body and mind possess their own innate, independent aliveness and sentience. In actuality, they're like the moon, which, having no light of its own, must "borrow" its luminescence from the sun. So, too, as individuals, do we "borrow" our consciousness from the Original Consciousness; the Self.

As the Mundaka Upanishad states, "[The Self] shines and everything shines after It."

Adi Shankara clarifies in his Brahma Sutra commentary:

> The individual soul is not directly the highest Self, because it is seen to be different on account of the adjuncts of body, mind and intellect [the Self, being formless, possesses no such adjuncts]. Nor is it different from the Self, because it is the same Self shining in all the bodies and minds. We might call the individual beings a mere reflection of the Self. Just as one image of the sun in water might tremble, the other reflections may not, depending on the nature of the reflecting medium.

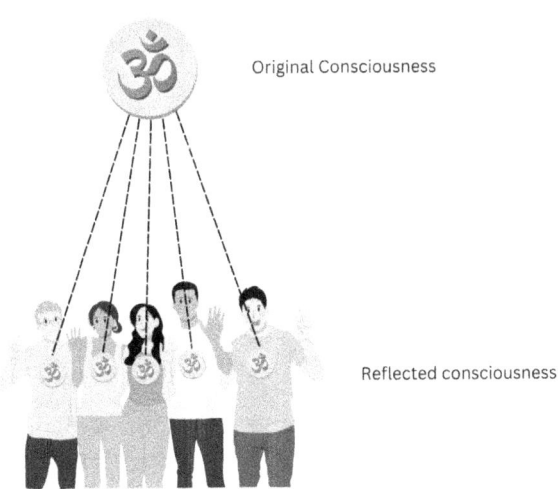

So, we have one Self, one light, with many reflections. The reflections differ according the quality of the reflecting medium.

Going back to the bucket analogy, if the water is still and clear, the sun will be reflected in perfect, pristine clarity. If the water is agitated, the reflected sun will appear agitated too. If the water is too muddy, there may barely be a reflection at all.

This is an important point. While all living beings are enlivened by the same reflected Consciousness, the quality of that reflection will depend upon the constitution of the reflecting medium.

That's why all beings express the same Self, the same Consciousness, in such astonishingly diverse ways.

The way Consciousness expresses differs according to an individual's state of mind, their temperament, mood and psychological conditioning—all of which are determined by the gunas; the three qualities of maya.

Both Ishvara and the individual serve as reflecting mediums for Consciousness. When Original Consciousness illumines the causal, subtle and gross bodies at a macrocosmic level, we get Ishvara or God; the totality of the field of creation. Original Consciousness illumining the causal, subtle and gross bodies at a microcosmic level creates an individual being; a person such as you or I.

Nothing in the world of form, from the tiniest ant all the way up to Ishvara, possesses any inherent life or sentience of its own. Our "aliveness" is not a property of the three bodies. It belongs to the Consciousness shining within. Once again, like the moon borrowing its light from the sun, all living beings borrow their life, light and sentience from a greater luminary—the Self; the one, eternal Consciousness.

The reflecting mediums are always limited and subject to defect and destruction, but the Self shines eternally without limit or blemish. What's more, this Original Consciousness is no more affected by its reflection than the sun is affected by its reflection in the bucket of water.

The Clay Pot Analogy

Learning to distinguish the real from the unreal is the key to liberating the mind.

Again, Vedanta's definition of "real" is that which never changes. Although something might appear to undergo modification, its true essence cannot change, or it was never real to begin with.

Krishna emphasises this in the Bhagavad Gita when he states, "The real never ceases to exist."

As for the unreal? The unreal never existed in the first place.

To illustrate the real and the unreal, Vedanta uses the example of a clay pot.

When we see a clay pot, we naturally assume that, yes, that is a pot.

Is it *really* a pot, though?

In actuality, the pot is just clay moulded into a certain name and form. The clay is what's real. It pervades the pot as both its form and essence. The pot is entirely dependent upon the clay for its existence.

The clay, on the other hand, exists independently of the pot. It was there before the pot existed, it's obviously there while the pot exists, and it'll be there when the pot crumbles to pieces. It lends its existence to the pot, which has no existence outside of the clay.

Another example we've already used is gold. You can take a piece of gold and fashion it into a variety of forms, such as a ring, a necklace, a coin or an ornament. Whatever form the gold happens to be in, however, all that's actually there, all that's actually real, is the gold.

Of course, you can't deny that you're holding a gold ring, but the ring has no independent existence of its own. It's simply gold plus a certain name and form.

That name and form is an incidental rather than an essential characteristic. You can melt the ring down again and turn it into a coin or paperweight. The name and form changes but the essence, gold, remains.

These analogies come directly from the Chandogya Upanishad:

By knowing one lump of clay, dear one,
We come to know all things made out of clay;
That they differ only in name and form,
While the stuff of which they are made is clay.
By knowing one gold nugget, dear one,
We come to know all things made of gold;
That they differ only in name and form,
While the stuff of which they are made is gold.

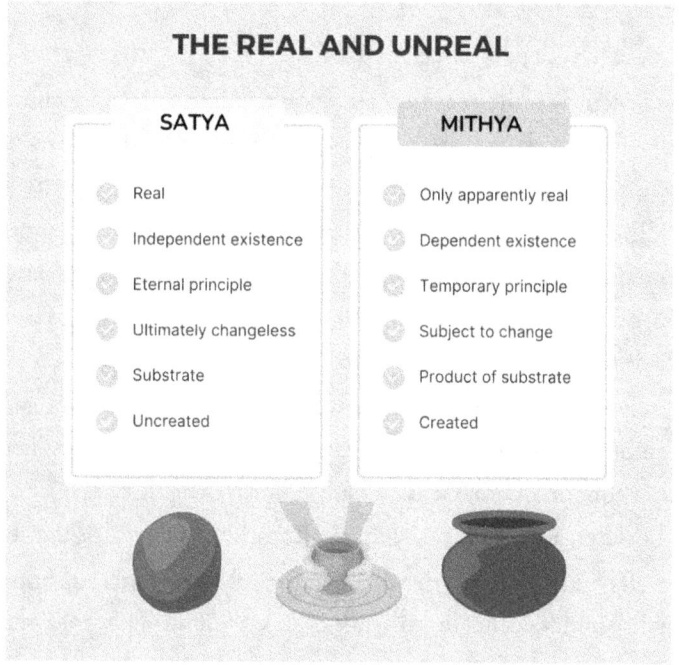

The Real and Unreal

Vedanta has two technical terms for helping us understand the nature of reality: *satya* and *mithya*.

Satya means that which is inherently real and which depends upon nothing else for its existence. Mithya means that which is unreal, or only apparently real. Mithya is unreal because it has no independent existence of its own. It depends entirely upon satya for its being.

To save you from getting mixed up with unfamiliar Sanskrit words, we'll refer to them simply as the Real (satya) and the only apparently real (mithya).

In our example above, the pot falls into the "only apparently real" category. That's not to say it doesn't exist. The pot clearly exists because you can see it, touch it and use it. It's only apparently real, however, because it borrows its existence from the clay. The clay, then, is real and lends its existence, its realness, to the pot.

The entire universe falls into the category of only apparently real. You can't deny that it exists. But it has only dependent existence because it cannot exist without the Self; the ultimate Reality; the ground of Existence itself.

As the only independently existent principle in existence, you might think of the Self as the independent Cause and the universe as the dependent effect.

The Self Alone is Real

This discrimination between the Real and the only apparently real is crucial. In Atma Bodha, Shankara says:

> Nothing whatsoever exists other than the Self, including the tangible universe of form. As all pots and jars are made of clay and cannot be said to be anything other than clay, so, too, do the enlightened see everything as the one Self.

The Self is the Reality underlying all objects and form; eternally existent and beyond time, limitation and defect.

The universe and everything in it exist only because of the Self. Like the clay pot, it has no tangible existence of its own. Its entire existence is borrowed from the Self; from Consciousness.

That's why the Upanishads declare that everything that exists is Brahman, the Self.

The higher aspect of Brahman (Nirguna Brahman) is completely Non-dual and unmanifest, while the lower aspect of Brahman (Saguna Brahman) combines with maya to create the universe of name and form. At the root of it all is Consciousness; the limitless and unchanging essence of all things.

You might still be confused as to how the Self can manifest the entire universe out of itself and yet still remain unchanging.

Surely, you might argue, in order to become the universe, the Self must undergo a process of change and transformation?

Vedanta again highlights the principle of maya. Maya allows the changeless Self to appear as an ever-changing universe of form without undergoing any change or modification whatsoever.

Maya can be likened to the power of your mind to dream at night. When you dream, you can become anything imaginable. You can be young or old, male or female, a bird, a cat, a pop star, an alien or President of the United States. Yet in spite of whatever you might dream, you, the real you, remain unchanged by it. No matter how wild and wacky your dreams, you always wake up the same person the next morning.

You know that if you dreamt you robbed a bank you don't need to hand yourself in to the police when you wake up. That's because the dream was only apparently real. It borrowed its existence from you, and was experienced in you, while you remained unchanged by it.

One of the most important statements in Vedanta is Shankara's assertion that, "Brahman alone is satya and the world is mithya." This means the Self alone is Real and the world is only apparently real.

Despite the incredible outward diversity of life, all the things of the world owe their very existence to the one, singular Self; Consciousness.

The materialist makes the assumption that Consciousness depends upon matter. Vedanta, however, reveals that it's quite the opposite. Consciousness is the substance and essence of everything, so matter actually depends upon Consciousness!

Consciousness alone enjoys an independent existence. It is uncreated, eternal and, unlike anything in the world of objects, is self-existent and reliant on nothing else. It existed before the universe came into being, it exists through the duration of its being, and will exist after its dissolution.

Consciousness, the Self, is primary. It is described as sat, meaning Existence. All other things are secondary, for they depend upon Consciousness in order to exist. Consciousness exists with or without the world, but the world cannot exist without Consciousness. That's our definition of Real.

Upadhi: The Limiting Adjunct

Another key teaching to help us understand the nature of the Self and creation is what we call the *upadhi*.

Upadhi is usually translated as "limiting adjunct".

You're probably still none the wiser, and I wouldn't blame you. So, what is an upadhi, or limiting adjunct?

An upadhi is something that makes another thing appear to be *other* than it is. Basically, one object superimposes its qualities onto another object, creating the illusion that it's different than it actually is.

Let's say you have a clear crystal and you place a red cloth behind it. The proximity of the cloth and the crystal will cause the crystal to take on the redness of the cloth. You now appear to have a red crystal. The red cloth is, therefore, an upadhi of the crystal. It superimposes its qualities onto the crystal, making the crystal appear to be other than it is.

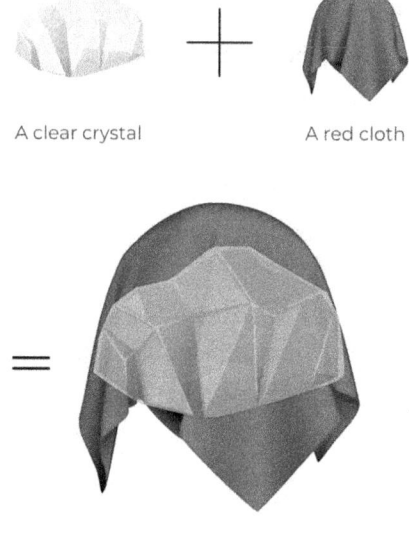

A "red" crystal

The implications are profound when you apply this understanding to the Self and the creation. Basically, the world of form, itself a product of maya, becomes an upadhi to the Self; pure, formless Consciousness.

At a macrocosmic level, the gross, subtle and causal bodies are an upadhi, making the Self appear as Ishvara. At the microcosmic level, the gross, subtle and casual bodies are also an upadhi, making Consciousness appear to be an individual person.

All along, the Self is formless, indivisible and without attribute. The upadhis of the three bodies, however, make the Self appear to possess form and attribute. Like a magician's illusion, the impossible becomes possible through maya's cosmic sleight of hand.

The Brahma Sutras reference this by stating:

> Just as light which has no form appears to be endowed with various forms because of the object which it illumines, Brahman, which has no attributes, appears as if endowed with attributes.

I was once sitting at a restaurant and the waitress brought a jug of water to the table. The glass jug was green in colour. This made it look like the water inside the jug was green. Of course, when I poured some water into a glass I could see the water itself wasn't green. The jug was simply acting as an upadhi, conditioning the water to appear green. Owing to their proximity, the greenness of the glass was superimposed onto the water.

In the same way, the world of maya, from Ishvara down to the individual body-mind-sense complex, superimposes its attributes onto the Self. *Et voila*—the Self appears to *become* the entire universe and everything in it.

In actual fact, however, the Self never becomes limited. It remains formless and changeless. The limitation belongs only to the adjuncts of maya; whether we look at it from the macrocosmic perspective of Ishvara (the universe) or the microcosmic perspective of the individual (the person).

Maya is the upadhi, making the Self appear to be endowed with form and limitation. It conditions the Self to appear other than it is, just as the red cloth conditions the crystal appear to appear to be red and the glass jug conditions the water to appear to be green. It's all a case of superimposition.

Superimposition

The idea of superimposition is fundamental to understanding Reality and the nature of ignorance.

Superimposition means wrongly ascribing certain qualities and characteristics to a given object. We've already used the example of the crystal in proximity to the red cloth, whereby we superimpose red onto the clear crystal.

Self-ignorance causes us to superimpose the limitations of the body and mind onto the Self; Consciousness. It's this act of superimposition, whereby we confuse the Real and the only apparently real, which causes us to feel incomplete, lacking and forever seeking happiness in the world of form.

This sense of limitation and sorrow is a product of ignorance; specifically, our failure to correctly understand the nature of Reality and our own Self. The only way out is to eradicate the ignorance altogether. That's what Vedanta, the science of Self-Knowledge, is uniquely tooled to do.

The Rope and the Snake

In order to illustrate the nature of ignorance and superimposition, Vedanta traditionally uses the metaphor of the rope and the snake.

One night, as dusk falls, a weary traveller reaches the outskirts of a village and is delighted to find a well. He moves toward it, eager to quench his thirst. He's about to reach for the bucket by the well, when he catches sight of something that makes him freeze in dread. Sitting by the bucket is a snake, its body coiled and head upraised, clearly ready to strike.

Just as you'd expect, the man experiences a potent and visceral reaction. His heart seizes in dread, the breath is knocked from his lungs and he begins trembling in fear. What should he do—how will he avoid being attacked by this enormous coiled serpent?

Fortunately, a villager with a lantern appears on the scene and asks if the man is alright. In that moment, the lantern light reveals that what's sitting by the bucket is not a snake after all. It's simply a length of coiled up rope!

The traveller lets out a sigh of relief. The "snake" disappears in an instant, because it was never really there.

Upon analysis, we can't say that the snake didn't exist, because it existed in the man's mind. He experienced the very same shock, anxiety and terror that he would have had he been face to face with an actual snake. He'd been living a false, yet nevertheless terrifying, reality of snake-ness.

So, while the snake existed in a sense, it wasn't real. The snake was entirely superimposed upon the rope.

This superimposition wouldn't have happened in broad daylight. It happened at dusk, when there was just enough light to see there was something there, but not enough for him to correctly perceive what it was.

It's not by chance that we refer to ignorance as being "in the dark". In this story, the darkness represents ignorance and the snake is the superimposition that happens as a product of that ignorance.

Ignorance and Projection

Again, the fundamental problem of human beings is that, subject to the ignorance of maya, which makes things appear to be other than they are, we unwittingly perform an act of mutual superimposition.

We superimpose the Consciousness that we are onto the body-mind-sense complex; and we, in turn, superimpose the body-mind-sense complex onto Consciousness. In other words, we falsely declare that "I am the body and mind" and "the body and mind is my Self".

Our superimposition doesn't actually affect the object onto which we're projecting false qualities. The rope remained rope even though the man in our story was convinced it was a snake. Similarly, the Self remains the Self—changeless, limitless and free of sorrow—in spite of the limitations of body and mind that we're projecting onto it.

We all know that the Self exists. Nobody has to tell us that we are; that we exist. The man in the story was aware that the rope existed. He simply misperceived it as something it was not. In the same way, we misperceive our Self as a combination of body, mind and their various aggregates.

The man's suffering came from experiencing his mind-created snake. So, too, do we suffer as a result of our assumption that we're a lacking and limited being, trapped in a body and subject to the mind and all its vagaries.

In both cases, we're seeing and experiencing something that isn't real.

The chapter on self-enquiry revealed a number of the ways in which we get tripped up by superimposition. Every time that we identify with the body and its qualities, such as its age or health, height or weight, we are superimposing "I", our sense of Self, onto an object, for the body is known to us as an object.

The moment you say, "I am young," "I am old," "I am tall", "I am short", and so on, you are superimposing the qualities of the body, an object, onto the Self; you, the subject.

We also do this readily with our thoughts, feelings and beliefs. By declaring, "I think," "I feel", "I believe", you are projecting these qualities onto the Self. Because of this misidentification, when the body or mind suffers, you believe that you, the Self, suffer.

Once again, the thing we're superimposing onto isn't affected by the superimposition. The rope remained a rope even though the man was convinced it was a ferocious snake and the crystal remained clear in spite of its proximity to the red cloth.

In the same way, the Self remains changeless and free even if you're projecting a body, mind and various painful thoughts and emotions onto it.

Self and Not-Self: The All-Important Discrimination

In the twilight world of maya, reality is not what it appears to be. What we experience with our mind and senses is conditioned by ignorance, and this ignorance is the root of our suffering.

Like the traveller frozen in terror at the sight of the rope-snake, we each fall victim to the universal superimposition of the Self onto the body-mind-sense complex; and all the fear, limitation and grief that comes along with this misidentification. As long as we are bound by this superimposition, we remain lost in illusion and subject to the sorrows of samsara.

The heart of Vedanta's teaching methodology, and the key to freeing the mind, is the ability to discriminate what is Real from what is only apparently real, or the Self from what we term the "not-Self".

These two categories, Self and not-Self, refer to the eternal subject, Consciousness, and the world of objects; to that which knows and that which is known; to that which sees and that which is seen.

In the Bhagavad Gita's thirteenth chapter, Krishna describes these categories as "the field" and "the Knower of the field."

The field refers to the material world; the universe of objects; both the outer world of physical objects, and the inner world of your thoughts, feelings, dreams and imagination. This all falls into the category of not-Self.

Here's why. Recall that matter is, by itself, inert. It requires another factor in order to enjoy life—and that is Consciousness.

It's important to reiterate that, contrary to popular assumption, Consciousness is not a property or product of matter. Consciousness,

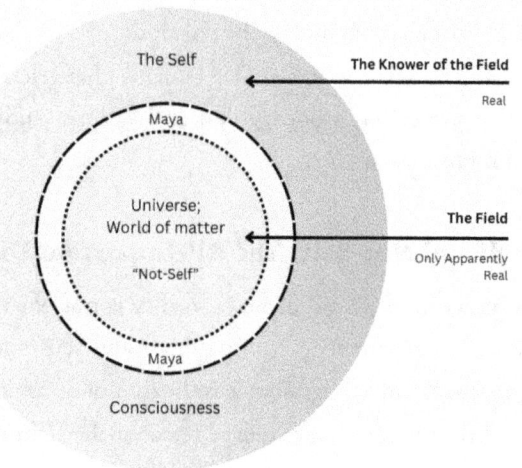

which is the very nature of the Self, is a transcendent principle. It relies on nothing else in order to exist. As the ground of Existence itself, Consciousness is self-existent, self-revealing and without limit of any kind.

It's the "combination" of Consciousness and matter, made possible by maya, that endows the material world with life and sentience.

To compare and contrast:

- The Self is conscious and sentient, while the not-Self, the world of matter, is inherently inert and insentient.
- The Self is one, whereas the world of objects is comprised of many.
- The Self is changeless, while the world of form is constantly changing.
- The Self has no attributes as such, while the world of form boasts an enormous variety of attributes.
- The Self is limitless, while everything in the material world is limited by space and time.

The essence of Self/not-Self discrimination is differentiating between the seer and the seen; between the Self and the objects appearing in it.

Anything that you perceive and experience as an object cannot be You, the Seer.

That includes the physical body. Because the physical body is an object known to you, it cannot be you, the subject. Realising the body is just another object appearing in your field of perception, you can negate it as not-Self. It's not you. It's just an object appearing in you!

The same is true of the subtle body; the mind, senses, intellect and ego. While not visible to the eye, you nevertheless experience the subtle body via your inner world of perception. Your thoughts, feelings, beliefs, desires, dreams and fantasies are all known to you as subtle objects of perception. Being objectifiable, they cannot be you, the subject. They are the seen and not the seer; the field and not the Knower of the field.

Through self-enquiry, all objects can ultimately be negated as not-Self.

This teaching is designed to shift your identification from the false to the true, or from the objects of gross and subtle matter to the Consciousness in which they are experienced—the Self; you!

Pivoting your sense of identity from the not-Self to the Self is the key to liberation.

The Bhagavad Gita states:

> That which is to be known is the Self. The Self has no beginning, is limitless and is neither existent as an object nor non-existent. Pervading everything, it dwells in all beings. [...] Both near and far, its nature is so subtle that most beings fail to perceive it. Though indivisible, it appears divided into separate beings and objects. It is the support of all beings and elements.

A Personal Epiphany

In my spiritual autobiography, "There Shines a Light", I describe a revelation that, for me, was incredibly liberating: the ability to differentiate myself, Awareness/Consciousness, from the objects arising in me.

These objects include both the gross and the subtle; the world of form, including my body and the environment around me, as well as the inner objects of my thoughts, emotions, memories, desires, fears and all mental formations.

I scrawled the following words in a notebook during a particularly rich and intense epiphany at Malaga airport of all places:

Constantly bring it back to *Knowledge of Awareness* and objects arising; the two categories of existence—*Reality* and appearance; *Formlessness* and form.

The objects are in Me, I am not in them, nor bound by them in any way.

I AM AWARENESS.

Awareness is everything—the only Reality. All else is just appearance in Awareness. Awareness gives life and sentience to the subtle and gross bodies. Awareness grants sentience just as electricity blesses a lightbulb with light. The lightbulb itself is inert, and so too are the body and mind without the presence of Awareness.

The crux of liberation is differentiating Awareness from that which appears in it.

I am Awareness and not the individual self; not the thoughts, the feelings, circumstances or experiences—all of which are objects arising and subsiding.

Gazing up at the sky and seeing the planes soaring overhead, I realised that Awareness was like the sky; vast and all-containing, formless and without beginning or end. All the objects appearing in this Awareness, including my thoughts, memories and feelings, were just like those planes happily gliding overhead.

The sky wasn't affected by anything at all, and I could see that neither was Awareness. It pervaded all but it wasn't affected by anything. Nothing could change it whatsoever, for it was without form and as all-encompassing as space. I realised that:

> I, as Awareness, remained the unchanging constant while all the forms around me changed and shifted in kaleidoscopic beauty. None of it affected me in any way; that much was clear to me. What a blessed relief; nothing in this world could change me, could hurt me, could touch me, the *real* Me, in any way.

Guided Exercise 5:
The Location of Objects

One of the Vedantic teachings that totally uprooted my understanding of reality was the location of objects teaching.

The mind and senses structure reality in such a way that we have the sense of being in the world; existing as one among billions of other people; each a distinct object occupying space and time.

Vedanta invites us to re-evaluate this assumption by reexamining the logic of our own direct experience.

Rather than simply telling you, I'm going to demonstrate this teaching by guiding you through several questions. Don't just read along; be sure to take part and answer each question honestly.

Take a look at whatever is on front of you. Right now, I have a computer screen in front of me, as well as a wall, a bookcase and a light. You might see a chair, a window, a table, mug, or any number of other things. Let's say you're looking out a window and see a tree in the garden.

Let's say I ask you, "Where is the tree [or whatever object you are looking at]?"

You'll most likely point ahead and say, "Why, it's out there, in the garden, several metres away". That would seem to be the logical answer.

What if I were to ask you, "Where are you experiencing the object?"

You'll probably still say, "Out there in the garden."

Here's the thing, though. How can you possibly experience a tree out there; outside of yourself?

If you think about it, you don't somehow project yourself out of your body in order to experience something at the other side of the room or in the garden, or at any other location.

We all tend to assume that we experience the world the same way as we look out a window. We assume that our eyes are a window to the world and we are looking out and seeing exactly what's outside.

In actuality, you're *not* seeing and experiencing the tree outside of yourself. You're experiencing the tree as a mental representation; as a thought in your mind. The senses are feeding data into the mind, which interprets and organises the data into an internal, mind-created representation of the object. The mind, in turn, is known by Awareness or Consciousness.

Awareness is that by which all things are experienced, including the world of objects. The sense that you're experiencing something in the world, *out there,* is a perceptual illusion. All objects appear not outside of you, but in the mind, which is illumined by Awareness, which is your carrier of reality; the medium by which you experience all things.

So, if I were to ask you again, "Where are you experiencing the tree?", you might now say, "In my Awareness."

Correct!

Here's the next question, "Where do you experience your Awareness?"

Take a moment to consider this by turning inward. See if you can intuit the answer by examining your own direct experience. Where exactly is this Awareness? Is it high or low, to the left or to the right?

"Why, it's just there," you might conclude. "It's everywhere!"

My final question: "What's the distance between you and Awareness?"

See if you can answer that yourself, right now.

Ultimately, I can almost guarantee that you'll answer, "There's no distance between me and Awareness!"

The implications are profound. That tree you thought you were experiencing outside in your garden? While it's obviously some distance from the body in three-dimensional terms, you're actually experiencing it within you, in your own mind, courtesy of Awareness. What's more, there's actually no distance between you, as Awareness, and the tree! The entire world appears in you.

This teaching hit home for me one day when I was driving into town for a hospital appointment. The roads were busy, with numerous delays, and I was starting to doubt that I'd make the appointment on time. All of a sudden, something switched in my mind and my entire view of reality turned inside out.

I'm not actually in the world, I realised. *This entire world is in me!*

We ordinarily assume that we exist as a material being living in an external, material world. But if you examine your own direct experience, you'll see that, in actual fact, the world is something that you experience inside of you—as Awareness. So, it's *not* out there; it's *in here!*

I immediately stopped worrying about my appointment (although I did actually make it in time). The sudden realisation that I wasn't some object in an external world that had to get from "here" to "there" was neutralised by the knowledge that, as Awareness, I never actually go anywhere at all. Awareness is ever-present and changeless. The objects appearing in it may chop and change, but Awareness itself never moves. It has no place to go, because it's already everything everywhere.

Guided Exercise 6:
Awareness and Objects

The world of maya is immersive, to say the least. Our senses are automatically hooked to their respective sense objects. That's why we so easily get consumed by both the outer world of form and the inner world of our own thoughts, emotions, memories and imaginings.

The illusion of being a body-mind-sense complex existing in a disconnected external universe is so intensely hardwired that it blinds us to our actual nature as Awareness.

This guided exercise is a helpful way to integrate the Self/not-Self teaching. It's the continuation of an exercise from Chapter Nine. The aim is to be able to differentiate the Seer, you, from the objects you are seeing.

1. Sit comfortably with your eyes open.
2. Become fully aware of the room in front of you. Allow your attention to rest upon the objects ahead of you, whatever they might be. Simply observe the sights in the form of shapes, colours and textures.
3. Now, while continuing to observe the objects before you, become aware of the fact that you're aware; that, in order to see and perceive these forms, Awareness must be present. Your attention is now split between what you are perceiving and the Awareness perceiving it.

4. Close your eyes.
5. Notice how the room full of objects has gone. It's no longer in your field of perception. But notice how Awareness is still present. The objects are gone, but Awareness remains. Regardless of whether there are objects or no objects, Awareness is present.
6. Move your attention now to the inner landscape of your mind; which you might experience as open, spacious "blankness" for lack of a better word.
7. Observing the screen of your mind, watch to see what your very next thought will be. Just hold an attitude of curiosity and be open to whatever thought might arise next.
8. Whereas you normally might experience an endless succession of thoughts, because you are now actively observing your mind, your mind may suddenly become very quiet.
9. Eventually, however, a thought will arise—either in the form of an image or visual form, or as a verbal thought, such as a word, statement or sound. It will likely be followed by another, and then another, appearing as a flow of thought
10. Don't have any expectations or judgements. It doesn't matter what images or sounds arise. The key is to simply watch and see what comes. Don't try to control the mind; just be its witness.
11. Now, allow your attention to split between what you are aware of and the fact that, as Awareness, you are aware of it. In order to perceive these thought forms, Awareness must be present.
12. Notice how regardless of the presence or absence of thoughts, Awareness always remains.
13. Turn your attention away from the thoughts now and take a moment to explore this Awareness.
14. Can you find a boundary, edge or limitation to Awareness? Or is it a vast, spacious and unconfined Awareness with no beginning or end?
15. Can you reach out and grasp this Awareness or is it beyond

reach? Does it exist in a certain location or is it expansive and all-pervading. What you'll find is that Awareness cannot be contained. It has no form and yet is the substratum in which all form, all thought, appears.
16. Ask yourself, is there is any distance between you and Awareness?
17. The inescapable conclusion is that there's no distance between you and Awareness. It not only exists within you; it is you. You are the Awareness! It's always present and pervades everything, with no beginning or end; the essence and totality of who and what you are.
18. Spend as long as you want abiding in Awareness as Awareness. Allow your mind to simply melt into this Awareness; to dissolve and merge into its source, removing all trace of duality.
19. When you are ready, gently open your eyes and bring your attention back to your body and the room around you.

This exercise helps demonstrate the two categories of existence: objects and the Awareness/Consciousness revealing them.

Whereas objects, whether gross or subtle, are always changing and may be present or absent, Awareness is always present and always the same. No matter what is happening outwardly in the world, or inwardly in your mind, you, as Awareness, remain unaffected and unchanged.

Awareness, the Self, is Real; it's always present and relies on nothing else for its existence. The world of objects, whatever form they take, is only apparently real. Just as the moon depends on the sun in order to shine, the world of form depends on the Self in order to exist, be known and experienced.

The ability to discriminate the Real from the only apparently real, or Awareness from the objects appearing in it, leads the mind from bondage to liberation. When practised with consistency and resolve, this discrimination breaks the false superimposition that has caused you to identify with form and reorients your identity from the object back to the Subject; the seen back to the Seer; the world of passing forms back to the ever-present and all-pervading Awareness that you are.

Summary

- The story of the blind men and the elephant demonstrates that reality is hard to understand because we only ever experience a small part of the overall picture. It's necessary to consider things from various angles. Vedanta does this by presenting a range of different teaching methodologies; ways to help us understand the nature of the Self and the world of form.
- The Reflected Consciousness teaching uses the analogy of the sun shining upon a bucket of water. The reflection we see in the water both is and isn't different from the original sun. We can think of the Self as the Original Consciousness. The mind and body serve as a reflecting medium for Consciousness. Like the bucket of water, the reflection differs depending on the nature of the reflecting medium. The source of the reflection, however, the Original Consciousness, never changes and is never affected by its reflection.
- The clay pot teaching highlights that whatever form a clay object might take, its basic essence and substance is clay, and that never changes. The objects can be many and varied, but all that's ever actually there is clay plus a certain name and form. The same is true of the Self and the world of form.
- We define Real (satya) as that which is independently existent. The only apparently real (mithya) is that which has a dependent existence, borrowing its existence from the Real just as the pot borrows its existence from the clay.

- The ability to differentiate the Real from the only apparently real is the key to freedom. Our suffering stems from misidentifying ourselves as the object (ie., the body-mind-sense complex) rather than the Subject (Consciousness/Awareness).
- An upadhi is an object which seemingly transfers its qualities to something else. For example, a red cloth behind a clear crystal transfers its quality of redness to the crystal. This is analogous to the way the three bodies and five sheaths seemingly make the Self appear to be limited to form and function.
- Ignorance causes us to superimpose our sense of Self onto the body-mind-sense complex. We take the body-mind apparatus to be "I", the Self, when, in fact, it is an object known to us. Anything objectifiable cannot be the Subject; the Self.
- The snake and the rope story is a metaphor for superimposition. Through ignorance, we mistake a coiled rope for a snake. So, the idea of "snake" is superimposed onto the rope. In the same way, the idea that we are a body-mind-sense complex is superimposed onto the Self and vice versa, causing a mutual superimposition. This superimposition causes suffering.
- The location of objects teaching demonstrates that we never experience objects *out there,* in the external world. Whether it's gross material forms or the subtle forms of our own thoughts and feelings, we only ever experience anything in our own Awareness.
- Vedanta teaches us to discriminate the Self from the not-Self; the witnessing Awareness/Consciousness from anything witnessed in the world of form, whether gross or subtle. Such discrimination leads to freedom.

15.
The Three Orders of Reality

> All worlds exist in the lower order of reality and I, the
> Eternal Self, exist in the higher order of reality.
> *Panchadasi*

Understanding the Self and its relationship to the world of form is without doubt one of the trickiest topics in Vedanta. After all, it calls for a radical reappraisal of reality and some truly multidimensional thinking.

How can it not? Nothing is ever what it appears to be in life. Basing our understanding of reality upon sense perception alone is a grievous mistake and the source of endless sorrow.

If you trust the senses alone, you'd conclude, as human beings did for the better part of our history, that each day the sun moves across the sky of a stationary Earth. It's a fair assumption to make because that's what we experience with our senses.

Knowledge, however, allows us to understand and contextualise our experience. Through knowledge, we know that, in actuality, it's not the sun that revolves around the Earth, but the Earth that revolves around the sun.

So, instead of unquestioningly accepting what the senses relay to us, Vedanta calls upon us to exercise some serious enquiry and critical analysis.

Ignorance got us into samsara and only knowledge can release us.

By taking appearance to be real, we believe ourselves to be nothing but a conglomeration of gross and subtle matter; a finite entity limited in space and time.

That's what happens when the upadhis of the gross and subtle bodies appear to condition the Self. Just as the proximity of red cloth to a clear crystal makes the crystal appear red, the presence of the three bodies makes the Self, Consciousness, appear to be a finite person.

This false superimposition, which occurs in the intellect, must be challenged and resolved, for it lies at the root of our existential suffering. The moment we assume ourselves to be nothing but a body and mind, we become subject to limitation, lack, sorrow, injury, disease and death.

This blatantly contradicts everything the scriptures tell us about what we truly are. In sharp contrast to our assumed, false self, they declare our real Self to be changeless, actionless, free of limitation, beyond birth and death, whole, complete and impervious to the boundless sorrows of samsara.

It may be a challenge reconciling this because it appears to contradict our everyday experience. How can we possibly be beyond action, desireless, changeless and untouched by anything in this world? The person that we experience ourselves to be in everyday life is, after all, driven by constant desire and action and is very much affected by worldly factors.

So, how can duality and Non-duality possibly coexist?

In order to resolve this apparent contradiction, it's helpful to understand what Vedanta calls the three orders of reality. These simultaneously existent orders or "levels" of reality are the Absolute, the empirical and the subjective. They do not exist separately and independently. Rather, like Russian dolls, they exist one within the other.

THE THREE ORDERS OF REALITY

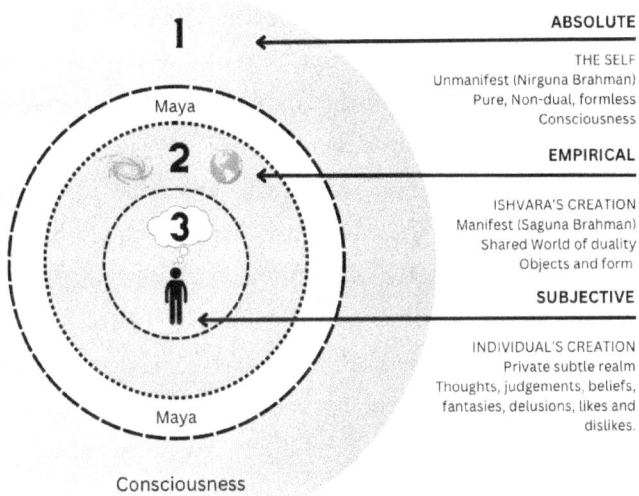

The Absolute Order of Reality
(Formless Consciousness)

The Absolute is the Self; Original Consciousness; all-pervading, self-existent, self-revealing and without form or differentiation. As you may recall, the technical term in Vedanta is Nirguna Brahman, meaning the Self without form and attribute.

In the words of the Katha Upanishad:

> The supreme Self is beyond name and form, beyond the senses, inexhaustible, without beginning, without end, beyond time, space and causality, eternal and immutable.

This birthless and deathless Self is self-existent because it relies on nothing else for its being. As pure Existence, it is the foundation, essence and totality of all that is.

Without beginning and end, with no boundaries or limitations of any kind, it is the One without a second; the essential Non-dual ground of Reality.

Nothing exists other than the Self. That's the meaning of Non-dual. The Advaita of Advaita Vedanta literally means "not-two". There is nothing beyond the Absolute. It is Reality itself; the sum total of everything in existence.

Got a headache yet? It's actually impossible to understand or grasp the Self with the mind because it's far subtler than the mind, intellect and senses. The Isha Upanishad explains:

> The Self is One. Ever still, the Self is swifter than thought, swifter than the senses. Though motionless, it can never be caught. Without the Self, life could not exist. It is within all and yet transcends all.

Although the mind and senses cannot capture it, we know that the Self exists because it is self-shining and self-revealing. It exists as our innermost sense of being; of existing. That's the one thing we can never negate: the fact that we exist; and the fact that Existence exists.

At the Absolute order of Reality, there's no maya; no form and division, no differentiation or duality of any kind. There's simply pure Non-dual Consciousness. This Consciousness is complete and absolute Wholeness.

A famous mantra from the Isha Upanishad (*Om Purnamadah Purnamidam*) declares the Self to be complete Wholeness; a Wholeness that can never be negated, lost or compromised. From Wholeness comes only Wholeness. If you try to remove any portion of that Wholeness, Wholeness still remains.

The realisation that this Wholeness must necessarily be our true nature yields liberation from all existential sorrow.

The highest truth of Vedanta is simply this: there's only one factor in existence and that is the Self, Brahman: pure Existence, Consciousness and Bliss.

The Empirical Order of Reality
(Ishvara's Creation)

Within this undifferentiated Absolute an entire world of objects and forms is superimposed. This is, of course, the world that we experience with our body, mind and senses.

This empirical, or objective, world is the result of maya; the creative principle inherent in the Self which can birth a universe of duality out of formless Non-duality. The Self plus maya equals the world of creation; the world shared by all living beings.

As we've seen, the Upanishads liken the empirical realm to a clay pot. The pot seems real enough; it has a name, form and function, but its reality actually belongs to the clay. It cannot exist without the clay, which is both the essence and substance of the pot.

In the same way, the essence and substance of the world of form is Brahman; the Self; Consciousness. It exists only because of the Self. Whereas the Self has an independent existence, relying on nothing else for its being, the world of maya, of form and function, has a dependent existence. It depends entirely upon the Self for its being.

In spite of the appearance of division and differentiation, the universe of form is not separate from the Self any more than the pot is separate from the clay. It is the Self, plus name and form. Whereas we term the formless Self Nirguna Brahman, the name for the Self with form is Saguna Brahman.

Another term for Saguna Brahman is Ishvara, or God. This entire universe and all the galaxies, stars, planets and creatures living upon them are the creation of Ishvara. The Self doesn't directly create them, because it has no will and is actionless. The creation happens when Consciousness combines with maya.

Everything in the phenomenal creation is Ishvara. As we learned in Chapter Eleven, Ishvara is both the intelligence that shapes the world of form and its very substance.

Although the mind and senses perceive duality and separation between all the manifold forms and objects, everything is actually one.

The macrocosmic gross body is the physical body of Ishvara. It's made up of all the physical objects in existence, including our bodies. The macrocosmic subtle body is Ishvara's subtle body. It comprises all the non-physical, subtle objects, including the sum total of all minds.

Both the gross and subtle worlds are born of the causal body; the unmanifest seed state which is the repository of all karma and the driving force behind creation.

So, while we each identify our particular body and mind as belonging to "us", in actuality, all things belong to Ishvara. All things are Ishvara.

Therefore, you needn't make pilgrimages to temples or holy shrines in order to find God. When you understand Reality as it is, everywhere you look you find God.

Ishvara is both the wondrous and pleasing things in life and also the less pleasing aspects of life. As the field of space-time inhabited by all living beings, Ishvara is birth, life, death and everything in between. Ishvara is up and down, inside and out, heat and cold, night and day.

Ishvara not only creates the phenomenal universe, but, as Controller of the laws of creation, manages everything in it. While the Self is actionless, all action happens through Ishvara, which is essentially a macrocosmic upadhi for the Self, lending the Self apparent form and function via the material realm.

We call this the empirical order of reality because it is readily observable and experienced by all beings. Ishvara's creation is a shared reality in which we are all subject to the same set of cosmic, physical and psychological laws.

All of us here, for example, live upon the same planet. It's because we have a shared, empirical experience that we can all agree on certain objective truths. The sky, for example, appears blue. Rain is wet. Sugar is sweet. All things in the empirical world follow their dharma, as determined by Ishvara.

It's because there's a level of constancy that we can take meaningful action and observe the pattern of cause and effect. Hence, duality allows us to work out the play of karma as it shapes and governs our lives (the topic of Chapter Sixteen).

The Subjective Order of Reality
(The Individual's Creation)

Finally, we have a third order of reality which is superimposed upon the previous. While inhabiting Ishvara's creation, the empirical or objective reality, the individual spins his or her own subjective reality.

This subjective reality is a world based upon our own personal thoughts, interpretations, dreams, imagination and delusions. It's a private, mind-created reality that we each project onto the objective world.

All things are inherently value neutral. An object has only the value that we ascribe to it.

Human beings, of course, go through life with an ingrained set of likes and dislikes; something that begins in early infancy.

If we deem something pleasurable or satisfying, this creates a "like" and the desire to keep on experiencing it. Thus, we actively pursue favourable objects. If we find something unpleasant or painful, this naturally sets up a "dislike". We become averse to the object and will actively avoid it in future.

So, whereas reality is, in itself, impartial and impersonal, the human mind interprets and categorises each and every object and experience it encounters. A thing becomes either "good" or "bad"; something to be pursued or something to be avoided.

The problem is we generally have a hard time separating our subjective interpretation of reality from the objective world itself. We cease seeing things as they are and instead see only our projections and superimpositions.

This accounts for the large part of human conflict throughout history. When we cannot view life objectively, we're unable to respond to situations, events and people with clarity and skilled judgement. We eventually lose sight of dharma and may inflict tremendous harm on ourselves and others.

Dharma, or right action, is essentially the law of Ishvara, enabling the smooth functioning of this complex yet harmonious and deeply interconnected ecosystem that is life.

Following dharma means responding to each situation in a correct, appropriate and timely manner. Dharma is our protector, because, by and large, following dharma keeps life on track and helps us avoid unpleasant and unfavourable results.

Adharma, on the other hand, which means contravening dharma, always brings suffering and calamity, individually and, ultimately, collectively.

The immense problems now facing humanity are largely a product of our own adharma. Instead of behaving with intelligence and sanity as we transact with the world, we've become consumed by our superimposed subjective realities.

This is particularly evident in the political sphere which, in many countries, is polarised in the extreme, with cult-like adherence to political and social ideologies and a willingness to dehumanise and inflict harm upon the so-perceived "other".

Rather than following dharma and responding appropriately to each situation as it presents itself, political leaders tend to pursue their own short-term gains with little regard for the future of the planet and the legacy we're handing to succeeding generations.

Losing Ourselves in the Subjective Realm

Humankind's unbridled worship of money is another example of becoming utterly lost in the subjective realm. There are many people out there willing to fight, kill and die in order to line their own pockets.

What they fail to realise is that money is just a concept. The monetary system was conceived as way of representing the value of goods, services and labour and replacing the barter system that had been used for the best part of human history. Money was invented to make life easier for us; not to utterly consume the human soul.

The currency we use is entirely symbolic. It has no intrinsic value. In fact, the only difference between a bank note and a Monopoly note is the belief that one is more valuable than the other. Its value has been arbitrarily ascribed to it—and if you don't believe me, then try using an American dollar in Azerbaijan.

In spite of having no inherent value, money has been elevated to godly status; something we are willing to make any sacrifice to acquire, including the future of the planet upon which we all depend (and which, as it happens, is actually Ishvara!).

Just as ignorance caused the weary traveller to inhabit the subjective reality of the so-perceived "snake", ignorance causes us to inhabit the subjective reality of being a lacking, limited and suffering individual, desperate to find happiness by pursuing objects in the empirical realm.

The effect of ignorance is pervasive. Ignorance clouds the intellect and conditions pretty much all human thought. Under its spell, we create a world of "good" and "bad" which often has more to do with personal predilection and our ingrained likes and dislikes than it does objective fact.

It's not just others that suffer when we become lost in the subjective realm. Many of us fall prey to the tyranny of our own thoughts of self-judgement and self-condemnation. We terrorise ourselves with the idea that we're "not good enough"; that we don't measure up to some mind-created ideal of perfection—or even adequacy. We fret that we're "not successful enough", "not wealthy enough", "too fat", "too thin" or an endless number of other things.

Tragically, many human beings live in their own mind-created hell; the bars of their prison comprised of nothing but their own thoughts, interpretations and judgements.

Superimposition and Fantasy

Living in this twilight world of maya, we can only ever see a fragment of the overall picture. Let's return once again to the snake and rope story. When the traveller stops by the well at dusk, there's enough light for him to see that there's something there; but not enough for him to see exactly what it is. His mind, however, takes what information it has and decides that it's a snake—and, bam, the snake becomes his reality.

What's actually there, at the empirical order of reality, is a piece of coiled rope. But the man is so certain of his conviction that his body and mind seize with dread and terror. He doesn't realise that he's slipped into an alternate, subjective world and lost touch with objective reality. Ignorance has blinded him to the truth and what he's experiencing is actually a lie.

This happens to human beings all the time. Deluded by maya, we're unable to process reality accurately. We see snakes where only ropes exist. We lose ourselves in a world of projection and superimposition; delusions that seem so real that we're often willing to stake our lives on them.

It's said that society has entered a "post-truth" age in which we can now pick and choose how we view the world. If empirical facts aren't to your fancy, you can simply look around for "alternative facts". Courtesy of the internet and social media, many people are becoming so immersed in conspiratorial thinking and manipulations of truth that we're losing the ability to reach any consensus about what's empirically real.

The Power of Knowledge

Knowledge is essential to our survival. We cannot successfully navigate life without accurate knowledge.

We have three basic means of attaining knowledge: perception, inference and testimony.

The first needs little explanation. We base much of our understanding of reality on what we directly perceive with the mind and senses. "Seeing is believing", or so we assume. As we've learned, however, direct perception can often be in error. The traveller in our story relied upon direct perception as he approached the village well—and he recoiled in terror as he perceived a deadly snake.

Inference is another important source of knowledge. It helps us contextualise our experience. For instance, if the traveller happened to live in a country without snakes, he would have been able to infer that what he was seeing might have looked like a snake, but couldn't possibly be a snake. Inference would reveal that what he was looking at must be a piece of rope.

The third means of knowledge is testimony, which means taking the word of a trusted source of authority. In the story, a villager appeared and assured the man that the snake wasn't real and was but a rope. The traveller had no reason to doubt the man, so he accepted this knowledge and the "snake" was instantly destroyed.

Problems can occur when people refuse to listen to the knowledge offered by others, even if they happen to be experts in a given subject. This is prevalent among people with limited skills of discrimination. Again, this is symptomatic of our culture's move to an increasingly pick-and-mix understanding of reality.

Even though astronomical data has proved beyond a shadow of doubt that the Earth is round and encircles the sun, you can still find people clinging to the idea that the Earth is flat. Blind to reason, they dismiss empirical facts because their belief supersedes all else. They're stubbornly inhabiting a subjective realm and have lost touch with the objective world of fact.

Reduce the Subjective to the Objective

A degree of subjectivity is inevitable as we navigate the transactional world. Over the course of a lifetime, we naturally form our own judgements, beliefs, likes and dislikes. The quality of our mind colours our interpretation of reality and we're all subject to certain blindspots.

It's essential, however, that we try to stay aligned with *what is* rather than what we *think about* what is.

Our commitment should always be to knowledge; to keeping our thinking aligned with Ishvara; with what is.

Wherever possible, we must reduce the subjective to the objective. This enables us to see with clarity and, as a result, we function far more harmoniously with life.

A human being cannot be free as long as they remain lost in the subjective order of reality; the realm of thoughts, projections and delusion. Fortunately, the petrified traveller was shown by a villager that the snake was only the product of his imagination. The light of knowledge destroyed his ignorance and the so-perceived problem vanished in an instant.

We need the lamplight of truth in order to break free of samsara; piercing our ignorance-induced projections and bringing us back to the objectivity of Ishvara. It's only when we're aligned with Ishvara, with what is, that we can then reorient our identity from the empirical to the Absolute; which is our true Self.

Real or Unreal?

To recap, the three orders of reality—the Absolute, the empirical and the subjective—exist simultaneously, one within the other.

The Absolute, Brahman, with its power of maya, gives rise to the empirical world of Ishvara. This is the world of the senses, a world of shared experience. We are all subject to the same set of physical laws by which Ishvara governs the creation.

Human beings don't just inhabit Ishvara's objective world, however. They also inhabit their own unique, subjective realm. If the empirical world is Ishvara's creation, the subjective world is the individual's creation. It arises from a person's particular interpretation of the empirical world and is shaped and coloured by their likes and dislikes, thoughts and judgements, dreams, imagination and fantasies.

Because the subjective realm exists only in the mind of the individual, no two subjective worlds are the same, whereas the empirical world of Ishvara is the same for everybody.

The subjective realm depends upon the empirical, because it requires the existence of a body-mind-sense complex—and that cannot exist without Ishvara.

The empirical realm, in turn, depends upon the Absolute because without the Absolute it would have no existence at all.

The Absolute, however, is the very ground of Existence and, as such, depends upon nothing else in order to exist. It exists entirely independently and is present with or without the other two orders of reality.

The empirical and subjective orders of reality are a product of maya and, as such, have a dependent existence. They are not, therefore, ultimately Real.

Only the Self, the Absolute, as the very foundation and ground of Existence, qualifies as Real.

A helpful metaphor is to think of a wave, the ocean and the water of which both are made. In this case, the wave represents the individual and the subjective order of reality. The ocean, which is the totality of all waves, represents Ishvara and the empirical order of reality. The water itself, which is the essence and substance of both the ocean and the wave, represents the Absolute.

When you're looking at the ocean and waves, all that's actually there is water. It doesn't matter how vast the ocean and how mighty the waves; neither could exist without the water.

Similarly, it doesn't matter what's happening in either the empirical world of Ishvara or the individual's subjective world. The Self, as the source and essence of all things, is transcendent: meaning it is—or rather, you are—always and ever free.

Summary

- The three orders of reality are the Absolute, the empirical and the subjective. Each exists simultaneously; the empirical within the Absolute and the subjective within the empirical.
- The Absolute order of reality is Brahman, or the Self—universal Consciousness; formless and all-pervading. The Absolute is the Unmanifest from which, by the power of maya, all form is manifest.
- The empirical order of reality is the manifest world of the senses; the shared world of name and form experienced by all sentient beings. This is Ishvara's creation.
- The subjective order of reality is the private world of our thoughts, dreams and imagination and is based on our personal interpretation of the empirical realm. Unique to each being, this order of reality is the individual's creation.
- Human beings have the tendency to lose themselves in the

subjective realm of their own thoughts, beliefs and interpretations which, coloured by ignorance, may be quite out of touch with the objective, empirical reality.
- The key to freedom is knowledge. We must attempt to resolve the subjective into the objective and view reality as it actually is, rather than as we think it is.
- What happens in one order of reality is specific to that order. The empirical realm exists quite independently of your thoughts, interpretations and delusions about it. Similarly, the Absolute exists independently of the happenings of the empirical world.

16.
Karma and Rebirth

> Karma is not fate, for man acts with free will, creating his own destiny. The Vedas tell us that if we sow goodness, we will reap goodness; if we sow evil, we will reap evil. Karma refers to the totality of our actions and their concomitant reactions, all of which determines our future.
>
> *Sivaya Subramunyiswami*

We've spent much of this section exploring the nature of the Self as pure Consciousness/Awareness. It's time now to take another look at the individual—the small "self"; the person living in the world of maya.

After all, in order to attain freedom, it's essential that we understand who or what is actually looking to attain freedom.

The Self doesn't seek freedom. It's already free. It doesn't want enlightenment, because it was never unenlightened.

It's a different story, of course, for the individual living in samsara.

This chapter will unfold one of the most important topics in Vedanta: namely, karma.

Everybody will be familiar with the word karma. It is not only used widely in spiritual circles but has also entered mainstream usage.

Astonishingly few people, however, actually know what it really means.

In the next few pages, we're going to demystify the topic, examining what karma actually is and how it relates to ignorance, rebirth and enlightenment.

The Creation of a Person

To recap what we've discussed in the preceding chapters, the world of creation is a product of pure Consciousness plus its inherent creative potential of maya. Inexplicable and beginningless, maya is that which allows the One to seemingly become many. It enables the Non-dual totality that is Brahman to appear as an entire cosmos of duality; the realm of objects and form we all experience with the senses.

The world of creation is a kind of virtual reality produced by macrocosmic ignorance; maya.

Within the creation exist countless embodied beings, from the mineral and plant kingdoms to animals and human beings, all the way up to what we call celestial beings (a topic beyond the purview of this book).

Ultimately, all beings and forms are Ishvara because Ishvara is the totality of the manifest universe; both the intelligence behind it and its very substance. To reiterate, Consciousness associated with the macrocosmic three bodies is Ishvara, or God—the creator and sustainer of the entire universe. At the same time, Consciousness associated the microcosmic three bodies is what we call the individual.

Think of a cloud in the sky. We look at a cloud and what we're seeing is the macrocosm; the entirety of "cloud". If you were to analyse the cloud closely, however, you'd see that it's made up of trillions upon trillions of droplets of water. Each of these droplets is capable of reflecting the light of the sun. There's one sun, of course, but there's no end to the number of reflections of that one light.

Ishvara is like the cloud. It's everything in the universe, including the very laws governing the universe. The individual beings that populate the universe are like the droplets of water. Where the "droplet" is capable of reflecting the light, in this case the light of Consciousness, we get a sentient being—what we call an individual or a person.

Every individual is comprised of the three bodies plus Consciousness, which is reflected by the subtle body, granting us life and sentience. We experience this reflected Consciousness as our inmost sense of being; of "I" or "am-ness".

Here's our fundamental delusion and the very root of samsara. Because our senses are hooked to the world of objects—and because we are subject to the ignorance of maya, which veils and obscures the true nature of reality—we take ourselves to be nothing but a body-mind-sense complex.

In our ignorance, we assume ourselves to be nothing but an individual; totally separate and disconnected from the rest of creation.

When we're under the spell of materialism, we believe that only what we can see is real. Impelled by ignorance, we superimpose our sense of Self onto the body-mind-sense complex and assume this body-mind-sense complex to be the Self.

Instead of knowing ourselves to be of the nature of pure Consciousness, we're barely self-aware at all. We buy into the illusion of separation and, in so doing, dream a personal world into existence. That's how the notion of being a person is born.

Our personhood is, as it happens, purely conceptual. If I were to ask you to show me the person you think you are, the person you assume yourself to be (and who others assume you to be), you wouldn't be able to do it.

Certainly, you can point to the gross body and stress the existence of a mind, intellect and ego, but where is the "person" in any of that?

It's nowhere to be found because it only exists as a concept.

From almost the moment you were born, you began attempting to build meaning out of sense perceptions, all the while desperately searching for somewhere to pin your sense of being, of "I" and "I-ness". Because the body is readily visible and the mind readily experienceable, that's where you have established your centre of identity.

Ignorant of the Consciousness/Awareness that is actually the very ground of your being, you've taken appearance alone to be real. You've taken your sense of "I am" and attached it to a lump of flesh and a variable and ever-changing assortment of personal stories based upon memory, interpretation and assumption.

You essentially cast a spell and dreamed the "person" you think you are into being.

When you identify yourself as something finite and limited, as the body and mind clearly both are, you assume that sense of finitude and limitation. This forms the basic, primal sense of lack and insufficiency at the core of the human psyche.

We feel limited and, because that's not our true nature, which is actually limitless and free, we cannot bear that sense of limitation.

If our nature was to be limited, we'd be perfectly happy with that because we accept and concede to what is natural to us. But that which is unnatural to us (which is to say, not of our nature) is unbearable, and so we seek to remove it any way that we can.

A fish is perfectly happy as long as it's under water because that's what's natural to it. The moment it's out of water, it frets and thrashes about because it cannot bear, or survive, what is unnatural to it.

We're no different. The source of our struggle is the limitation born of falsely identifying with the body-mind-sense complex. Because our true nature is limitlessness, limitation is unnatural to us— and so we are fiercely compelled to do whatever we can to eradicate it.

The primary way we seek to eradicate limitation is through action. We take action upon action upon action. It could be said that human life is characterised by action and its corresponding reactions. The Sanskrit word for this is *karma*.

Karma, Good and Bad

You might recall that karma literally means "action".

Everything you do is karma. From the moment you wake up in the morning and put on the kettle to make coffee to the moment you clean your teeth and climb into bed at night, your entire life is driven by action.

Krishna notes in Chapter Three of the Bhagavad Gita that, "No one rests even for a second without performing some kind of action."

Karma, of course, not only refers to the actions we undertake but also the results of those actions. It is, therefore, the pattern of cause and effect by which our past actions determine our present circumstances and our present actions determine our future life.

In simple terms, as we go through life, we each have a variety of experiences, good and bad. As the mind and psyche develop, the human being learns that some actions produce favourable results and other actions produce unfavourable results. As children, if we do something that earns praise and enthusiasm from our parents and caregivers, we're more likely to perform that action again. If, however, we do something that causes a negative reaction, we're inclined to avoid repeating that action in the future.

Karma falls into two categories; favourable and unfavourable, or what we call "good karma" and "bad karma".

Any action produces not only visible, known effects, but also unseen and unknowable effects. In other words, sometimes we do the right thing only to get a bad result. There's no getting around the complexities of life!

According to the scriptures, the best approach is to keep all our actions in line with dharma and universal values such as honesty, non-injury, kindness and consideration for others and the environment around us.

What matters most is our intention. The chapter on karma yoga explored how we can neutralise seemingly bad karma through our attitude of mind and by accepting all results with grace even if they aren't as we'd have hoped or intended.

Our actions are driven by our desires. We want something, whatever it might be, so we undertake action to get it. Alternatively, we might want to avoid something, so our actions will be an effort to avoid what we don't want.

An aversion is nothing but a negative desire. Perhaps you are motivated to clean your teeth in order to keep them healthy. Or perhaps you are motivated to clean them in order to avoid tooth decay and trips to the dentist. Either way, our desires and aversions, our likes and dislikes, are what drive our actions.

These desires and aversions are, in turn, determined by our thoughts. While we all inhabit the same empirical order of reality, we each have our own unique set of likes and dislikes, as determined by our past experiences.

We see life through the filter of our own thoughts, interpretations, judgements and beliefs. This accounts for the great diversity of human life and experience. Although we all live in the same world, each of us has a uniquely different experience of life based on our conditioning, thinking and the way we choose to interpret our experiences.

Free Will and Right Action

The reason human beings have such difficulty with karma is the fact that, unlike the animal kingdom, we have free will.

Animals have no problem with karma because their actions are naturally in harmony with their dharma; with their own nature. Fish swim, birds fly, snakes slither and monkeys chatter. They don't need to think about life; they simply live life, acting upon their inherent intelligence. You don't need to teach a fish to be a fish; it already knows how to be a fish, thank you very much. It's built into the design, courtesy of Ishvara. The fish has its own "fish dharma" and it will never violate that dharma.

Human beings, however, have both free will and are subject to ignorance; both the universal ignorance of maya and the individual ignorance particular to each person. This deadly combination can cause us to contravene the law of dharma, and whenever we act against dharma, we always cause suffering to ourselves and others. In other words, we create bad karma.

Following dharma, conversely, brings good karma. Giving to charity, for example, leads to good karma for both the recipient and the giver, who will feel good about themselves because they are following universal dharmic values such as kindness and generosity.

If you happen to steal money, you can be assured of bad karma. In the short term, you might benefit, because you have extra money to spend. There will be no escaping the negative karma of the act, however. If you get caught you will face punishment, including perhaps jail time.

Even if you don't get caught, you can guarantee you will experience negative psychological effects; if not guilt, then agitation and fear, as you're constantly watching your back and trying not to get caught.

The actions we undertake and the results we accrue have a pronounced effect on the mind and psyche. We become inclined to act similarly or differently in future. If donating to charity makes you and others feel good, you will most likely keep doing so in future. Generally, a positive result inclines you to repeat an action and a negative result disinclines you to repeat the action.

Let's say you've never tasted chocolate cake your entire life. One day, somebody gives you a slice, you take a bite and realise that you *love it!* This pleasurable reaction will create a desire to eat more chocolate cake. Each time you act upon that desire, and eat more cake, you strengthen the desire until it becomes a tendency or a conditioning.

Understanding Vasanas

We call this tendency a *vasana*. A vasana is a deep-rooted imprint or groove in the psyche. It's the impression left by past experience which compels us to repeat or avoid that experience. Each time we act upon a vasana, we reinforce it.

The vasanas are stored in the causal body, which is the unconscious or seed state from which our thoughts and actions sprout. They are basically the subtle manifestation of karma.

We all have vasanas and they determine just about every aspect of our lives. Your tendency to clean your teeth when you get up from or before you go to bed is a vasana you've programmed into the mind. It's not something you ever have to deliberate on. The vasana is so strong it compels you to act without so much as a thought.

Our vasanas reflect our likes and dislikes. You don't have to think about the foods you like to eat and the foods you like to avoid. You've already got food vasanas, in the form of ingrained likes and dislikes, and these determine all your culinary choices. When you view the dessert menu and you happen to see the words "chocolate cake", your chocolate cake vasana springs into action and, before you know it, you're tucking in to a hearty slice of chocolate cake.

You can, of course, develop vasanas for pretty much anything imaginable. These vasanas are the unconscious tendencies which mould and shape the mind and determine the trajectory of our lives.

When overindulged, vasanas can become problematic. Your preference for chocolate cake, for example, could turn into an overwhelming desire, or even an addiction.

Any kind of addiction, whether it's to food, alcohol, drugs, pornography, smartphones or extreme sports is basically a vasana that has gotten out of hand.

The more such vasanas are strengthened by repeatedly giving into the desire, the harder it becomes to break free of them. We begin losing control of our own psyche.

Such loss of control can be disastrous, not least because of the mental and emotional turbulence it causes. When we lose control of the mind and psyche, we are liable to transgress dharma and, as has been stressed again and again, even the slightest violations of dharma lead to negative consequences. To put it simply, we're basically creating bad karma for ourselves and quite possibly others too.

In and of themselves, vasanas are neither good nor bad. They simply are. It's how they manifest and whether or not they are aligned with dharma that determines whether they are beneficial or harmful to us.

We experience two types of vasana: non-binding and binding.

Non-binding vasanas manifest as simple preferences. When given the choice between regular sponge cake and chocolate cake, you choose the chocolate because that's your preference. You won't be too upset if there's no chocolate cake left, because—*c'est la vie!*

A binding vasana, however, true to its name, binds the psyche. When the object of your desire is unavailable, you experience stress and mental or emotional agitation. If the chocolate cake isn't available, you might rage at the chef or go home in a terrible mood and make everyone around you as miserable as you feel.

The psychology of Vedanta aims to render the vasanas non-binding by neutralising our desires and aversions, thus robbing them of the ability to incapacitate the mind. This is important for a number of reasons. After all, a disturbed and restless mind, driven by the push and pull of desire and aversion is simply not capable of internalising Self-Knowledge, which is the key to liberation.

Seen and Unseen Results

We all develop an instinctual understanding of karma from the time we are children. We're taught that actions have consequences and, depending on the nature of the action, those consequences can be desirable or undesirable.

Basically, if you do good things (which is to say, follow dharma) you tend to get good results and if you do bad things (by violating dharma), the results are invariably bad.

Here's a simple example. If, as a kid, you work hard at school, you're likely to get good grades. This will please your teacher and parents alike. When others are happy with us, we're generally happy with ourselves—because, in actual fact, much of what drives human behaviour is the desire to be seen positively in the eyes of others.

Once again, karma has both a visible, immediate result and a longer term, invisible result.

The immediate result is clear in this example. It can be harder, if not impossible, to determine the longer term results. After all, life is complex, with many factors at play. It could be that in ten years or so, your academic success earns you a place at a prestigious university. Perhaps by applying yourself at school, you fall in love with a particular topic that will determine your future career.

The seed is planted the moment we take an action, but we never know when that seed will grow and bear fruit. Sometimes the results are immediate; other times the karma may not fructify for many years, or even lifetimes. The results are determined by Ishvara alone and, as the dispenser of all karma, Ishvara takes all factors in the field into consideration.

That underscores why karma yoga is so important. Karma yoga trains us to accept the results of our actions with equanimity and grace, recognising that there are always factors outside our control and which do not easily bend to our likes and dislikes.

By recognising Ishvara as the dispenser of karma, we can accept all results as legitimate and proper, even if they aren't as we might have intended. This attitude insulates us against tremendous stress, uncertainty and agitation.

Karma and Rebirth

The law of karma spans not just a single lifetime, but multiple lifetimes.

While the gross body is mortal and lives only a single life, the subtle and causal bodies are relatively eternal.

At the time of death, only the physical body dies. The subtle body is impervious to death and, driven by its unresolved karma, will associate with another gross body and begin another life. So, what happens at death is little but a change of scenery for the subtle body.

This cycle of reincarnation is driven by our unresolved karma. As long as we have karma to work out, the cycle continues. That's why, even if a person appears to evade the consequences of their bad deeds, there's no escaping karma. The seeds sown in this lifetime will eventually fructify, even if it's several lifetimes hence.

The law of karma helps explain the disparities we experience and observe in human life. Our karma determines our life experience, from the constitution of our body and mind, to the environment and circumstances in which we find ourselves. Some are born into wealth and luxury, while others are born into poverty and deprivation. Some are born healthy while others are born with disabilities or health defects.

It's important to never view karma as some kind of punishment or cosmic retribution for past actions. That is a distortion and misunderstanding of the teaching. You should never judge others in less fortunate circumstances than yourself, because you are not privy to the intricacies of the working of karma.

It's often our seemingly bad karma that is instrumental in helping us to learn and grow in life; to become better and more compassionate people and to commit to spiritual growth. People who apparently enjoy an overabundance of good karma may have less incentive and impetus to work on themselves and to progress psychologically and spiritually.

By understanding karma, we can accept what life has given us and do our best to ensure that our present actions positively shape our future.

We have no say over the past. However, it's entirely up to us how we choose to view our present circumstances; and how we can act today to plot a better trajectory for tomorrow.

When we understand karma, we realise the importance of always keeping our actions aligned with dharma. That means doing the right thing in the right way at the right time by observing universal dharmic values (as outlined in Chapter Six).

Very often, when looked at from a strictly materialist perspective, life seems incredibly unfair. It's a sad fact that many of society's most successful businesspeople and politicians rise to the top by harming and exploiting others with sociopathic disregard. Often such people appear to get away with their adharmic actions and never face due retribution.

There's no escaping karma, however. Even if such individuals appear to squirm their way out of facing the consequences of their adharma, you can rest assured it will carry through to future lifetimes in which they will have to balance the karmic book.

Similarly, some people live honest, dharmic lives, yet rarely seem to reap the rewards they deserve. Needless to say, the positive karma they accrue through good living will also carry through to future lives.

The Three Types of Karma

There are three basic types of karma. You might think of them as accumulated karma, present life karma and future karma.

The first type, accumulated karma (called *sanchita karma* in Sanskrit), is basically the store of all karma from our previous lives. This is the karma that has yet to fructify or manifest. It remains in seed or potential form in the causal body.

From this stored karma, a specific portion is allocated to a particular lifetime. This is our present life karma (*prarabdha karma*); the karma that will express during our current lifetime. This karma determines the circumstances of our birth and lifetime, from our particular type of body, our parents, environment, health and the experiences responsible for shaping our lives.

While working through the karma allocated to this lifetime we do, alas, accumulate new karma and this is called future karma. This future karma (*agami karma*) will either manifest during our current lifetime or will be carried over and be added to the store of our accumulated karma.

When the karma for a particular lifetime is exhausted, the gross body expires and the subtle body will, driven by its accumulated karma, move on to associate with another gross body. As Krishna states in the Bhagavad Gita, "Just as worn-out old clothes are cast aside, the indwelling Consciousness discards worn-out bodies, replacing them with new ones."

So, the cycle continues. The entire creation is basically a field for the outworking of karma. The seeds are planted and, over many lifetimes, these seeds germinate, grow and flourish. Each action begets more actions and each of these comes with results both good and bad.

Again, in the Bhagavad Gita, Krishna says that maya causes all beings to spin around as if mounted on a wheel. This is sometimes called the wheel of samsara.

Binding us to the wheel of samsara is the need to continually perform action in order to remove the aching sense of lack and incompleteness caused by self-ignorance.

This manifests as the vasanas; the subtle tendencies and compulsions which shape our mind, heart and destiny. These vasanas, which are stored in the causal body and express through the subtle body (as desires, attachments and aversions) are basically what drive our karma.

Mercifully, human beings are also gifted with free will. We have the ability to consciously shape our future karma by our choice of actions in the present (although, as always, it's ultimately Ishvara that determines the result of those actions). We also have the potential to break free of the wheel of samsara altogether—to attain liberation; thereby neutralising all karma forever.

Freedom From Karma

Vedanta is a tool for attaining liberation. The scriptures are resolute that liberation is only attained through Self-Knowledge.

This stands to reason. Our problem is self-ignorance; taking ourselves to be what we are not. The only logical solution is, therefore, to correct this ignorance by understanding what we truly are.

Karma belongs only to the individual in maya. It does not belong to the Self; Consciousness. As long as you take yourself to be an individual, a person subject to birth and death, you remain chained to the wheel of samsara.

The happiness and wholeness you're so desperately seeking in life is nowhere to be found other than within you.

It's imperative you understand that nothing in the material world is capable of delivering lasting happiness.

How can it? Everything in the world is, after all, subject to duality; every upside has a downside and nothing remains the same for long. Does it really make sense seeking permanent happiness in an impermanent world? Or is that just a recipe for perpetual disappointment and sorrow?

The Katha Upanishad states:

> The Self-existent Lord oriented the senses to turn outward. Thus, we look to the world outside and fail to see the Self within us. Seeking liberation, the sage withdraws his senses from the world of changing form, looks within and beholds the Eternal Self.

Whether we know it or not, it's always the Self that we're seeking, for the Self is of the nature of Bliss or Wholeness.

Limitless and complete, beyond injury and death, beyond sadness and grief, beyond the pull of duality, the Self that you are is completely untouched by anything in this world of form.

It has no karma!

Karma pertains only to the body and mind. That which enlivens the body and mind, the Self, is actionless because there is nothing other than it.

As we've said, when you identify with the body-mind-sense complex, you adopt their limitations, defects and failings.

When you identify as the Self, however, you come to realise that the Wholeness and Bliss you sought in the world was only ever within you as the very essence of your being.

That's freedom right there.

Because the Self is never separate from us, we always have access to this Wholeness, regardless of what's happening in the world of objects.

Speaking as the Self, Krishna states in the Bhagavad Gita's fourth chapter:

The one who knows Me as his own Divine Self overcomes bodily identification and attachment and is not reborn into this world.

Ignorance chains us to karma. Our misidentification with the body and mind is so great that it blinds us to our true nature, contracting the vastness of our being into an assumed pseudo-self. The only remedy is the knowledge, "I am Consciousness; I am Awareness."

Self-Knowledge eradicates the individual's store of accumulated karma. When you no longer identify as a finite person, there's nobody there to lay claim to that karma. You realise that karma pertains only to the body-mind-sense complex; and that belongs to Ishvara, not you.

You are the Self—and, as the Self, you are not bound by karma, either good or bad. Your karmic account, so to speak, is closed because there is, essentially, no longer an addressee on file.

Self-Realisation doesn't affect the present life karma associated with your particular body-mind, however. If it did—if enlightenment erased your present life karma—the gross body would instantly die.

For those liberated while living, the body-mind-sense complex continues to live out the rest of its allotted karma. As with all beings, when the karma exhausts, the lifetime ends.

That doesn't present a problem to the liberated soul, however.

When you know that you are the Self, you are no longer compelled to seek wholeness and happiness from worldly objects.

That immediately takes the pressure off life, eradicating the stress of samsara and insulating you against even the toughest of karma. Life becomes a thing of ease and grace when you surrender to Ishvara's will whilst effortlessly living in accord with your nature and with dharma.

Upon liberation, you no longer accumulate future karma. That's because Self-Realisation removes the sense of egotism, doership and ownership which characterises the unenlightened mind.

You simply allow life to unfold around and through you, with the knowledge that Ishvara alone is the doer; both the agent of action and the dispenser of the results of that action.

The fruit of liberation is the ability to enjoy life, free of the crippling burden of having to seek happiness and fulfilment outside of yourself. This will be explored in greater detail in the final chapter.

When liberated, once the karma of your current lifetime plays itself out, no further rebirth into the world of form is necessary. Your karmic balance has been wiped and no new karma has been accrued. In short, you are no longer strapped to the wheel of samsara and rebirth.

The key all along is Self-Knowledge. If, as the saying goes, knowledge is power, then Self-Knowledge is nothing less than liberation.

Summary

- Ignorance causes us to feel a gaping sense of lack and insufficiency at the core of our being. We seek to get around this by taking action in the world of form. We take action after action, all with the desire to be free of self-limitation. Action and its results are called karma.
- Karma falls into two categories: favourable or unfavourable; good or bad. It also produces two types of effect: immediate, clearly visible effects and unseen effects which often take time to manifest and are harder or impossible to predict.
- Our actions, our karmas, are driven by our desires and aversions, which are, in turn, determined by our thoughts.
- While animals and plants automatically follow their dharma, human beings have free will. The combination of free will and

the ignorance into which we're all born often causes us to violate dharma and create bad karma for ourselves and others.

- Our vasanas are conditioned tendencies; grooves in consciousness caused by our past actions, predisposing us to either repeat or avoid an action in the future. Stored in the causal body and manifesting in the subtle body as our desires, compulsions, cravings and aversions, the vasanas are essentially our karmic imprint.
- Vasanas can be good or bad; non-binding or binding. Non-binding vasanas express as preferences, whereas binding vasanas are compulsions; often with the ability to completely overpower the mind.
- The law of karma subjects the subtle body to continued rebirth and association with new gross bodies. This happens in order for the store of our accumulated karma to fructify and work itself out.
- Karma and rebirth explains the disparities we experience in human life. Our karma determines the constitution of our bodies and minds and the circumstances of our lives. Some people are born with significant meritorious karma whereas some are born into more challenging and painful lives.
- Karma is not some force of cosmic retribution and is not a punishment from God. Like the grit in an oyster, seemingly bad karma is actually an opportunity to help the individual soul to grow and progress psychologically and spiritually.
- The three types of karma are accumulated karma, present life karma and the karma we generate in this lifetime which will be carried over to our store of accumulated karma and will manifest in future lifetimes.
- The only way to free yourself from the wheel of karma and rebirth is to realise your nature as the Self, which, being of a different order of reality and always whole and complete, is

completely transcendent of karma.

- When you know with the entirety of your being that you are the Self, your karmic account is closed and no further karma accumulated. The karma for this current lifetime will continue to play itself out, but after that no further rebirth is necessary, for you have realised your identify as the Self and attained liberation from samsara.

17.
The Ultimate Truth in Three Words

> The only means of release from all limitations is the Knowledge of the unity of the individual consciousness with Brahman. This Knowledge is born of the study of the Great Statements such as "I Am That".
> *Adi Shankara*

As you may recall from Chapter Ten, the essence of Vedantic teaching, and the key to liberation, is encapsulated by three short words: "I Am That."

This most famous of Upanishadic proclamations is deceptively simple, yet loaded with meaning. As Shankara says, this statement dispenses the highest of all Knowledge; the Self-Knowledge by which one attains release from all bondage.

Inspired by talks by the brilliant Swami Paramarthananda, this chapter unfolds the full meaning of these three words and takes a deeper look at the nature of the individual and the Self and, most crucially, their fundamental unity.

Original Consciousness

Any living being, all the way from Ishvara down to the tiniest of animals or plants, consists of three components:

1. **The Three Bodies** (A Reflecting Medium)
2. **Reflected Consciousness**
3. **Original Consciousness**

Let's work in reverse and start off with the third and most important of these factors: the Original Consciousness. This is basically an English term for Brahman or the Self. It's a subject we've now spent considerable time exploring.

This changeless, limitless Consciousness pervades the entire universe, both manifest and unmanifest, and is the primary subject matter of the Upanishads.

Containing all things, yet contained by nothing, Consciousness is the ground and support of all that is. It's described in Sanskrit as the *adhistana*, which literally means the "base, support or substratum" of all things.

Put simply, the Self is Existence; Reality itself. There is nothing it is not.

All that exists in maya exists only because it borrows existence from the Self, much as the moon borrows the light of the sun. The moon, of course, has no luminosity of its own. In order to shine, it must serve as a reflecting medium for the light of the sun.

In a similar way, all beings, in order to enjoy life and sentience, must serve as a reflecting medium for the light of Consciousness. They rely upon Consciousness for their very being. Let's be very clear: nothing in creation exists independently of the Self.

Ishvara

When maya is operant, this limitless, unmanifest Self, the Original Consciousness, appears to take on name and form. An entire universe of objects is birthed into being! The visible arises from and exists intertwined with the Invisible.

Consciousness associated with the three macrocosmic bodies (the gross, subtle and causal body) is called Ishvara.

As it happens, the word "That" in our Upanishadic statement refers to Ishvara.

There's nothing in the phenomenal world that isn't Ishvara. Indeed, the entire universe is Ishvara's body and the entirety of the subtle realms are what we might term Ishvara's mind.

All-knowledge and all-power, Ishvara is both the Intelligence that fashions the universe and the very substance of which it is created.

As that which ordains and controls the laws of the universe, including the laws of dharma and karma, Ishvara is the Divine Intelligence that grows seedlings from seeds, leaves on trees and your body from the tiniest of embryos to what it is today.

Of course, Ishvara, which is the Self with form, cannot exist by and of itself. It arises from and depends upon the ultimate ground of Existence; the Absolute; the Self without form.

The entire maya world exists only because of the Self; Consciousness.

Maya depends upon Consciousness, but Consciousness does not depend upon maya, which may or may not be manifest at any given time.

Consciousness is key. Without Consciousness, nothing exists.

In the world of maya, the three bodies are granted life and sentience by their capacity to reflect Consciousness. If the forms of the material world lacked the ability to reflect Consciousness, we'd have no living beings and no phenomenal reality whatsoever.

The Individual

Just as Ishvara is the three bodies plus Consciousness at a macrocosmic level, the three bodies plus Consciousness at a microcosmic level comprise the individual self.

The "I" referenced in "I Am That" refers to the individual being; the person associated with the three bodies—ie., you and I.

As we saw back in Chapter Nine, all individuals possess a gross, subtle and causal body. These instruments actually belong to and are a part of Ishvara; Ishvara being the totality of the phenomenal world. The closest analogy is to think of a cell in a body. Although each cell has an individual existence, they do not exist independently of the body of which they are part.

The same is true of the individual and Ishvara. As individuals, we're each cells in the body of Ishvara; a kind of infinite cosmic organism.

Everything the individual has and is materially belongs to Ishvara. Indeed, Ishvara created, maintains and will eventually reclaim the body. It governs not only the body, but also the mind. The very thoughts that you think are determined by Ishvara, in the form of your karma. As the dispenser of the results of karma, Ishvara is very much the one holding the reins.

We owe our lives to Ishvara and we depend upon Ishvara for everything. All things phenomenal belong to and are governed by Ishvara as the Universal Body and Cosmic Mind.

The ego's notion of ownership and doership is but an illusion. Just as we don't actually own anything here, despite the ego's capacity to initiate actions, we're not ultimately the doer, either.

In order to be the doer, an autonomous agent of action, the ego would need to be in control of the environment and all the laws of creation—a job that belongs solely to Ishvara.

In summary, the overt meaning of "I Am That" is I, as a person, am non-separate from Ishvara.

All the things I believe I have, own, and do, actually belong to Ishvara; the source, substance and support of my being in this world of maya.

The upshot is God created everything; therefore, everything is God.

The differences between the individual and Ishvara come down to the differing upadhis or reflecting mediums (ie., the three bodies). Courtesy of the upadhi, the individual upadhi is limited in space and time, whereas Ishvara, as both the intelligent and efficient cause of the universe, is space and time. The individual has limited knowledge and power, whereas Ishvara has limitless knowledge and power.

Yet, as we'll see, the differences between them are purely notional when considered from a greater vantage point.

The Waves and the Ocean

When you look at the ocean, you'd almost be forgiven for thinking that the waves possess an existence of their own.

Each wave, after all, occupies a certain point in space and time. They have their own form, shape and speed, and a beginning, middle and end. The waves rise up from the ocean and eventually crash down upon the shore before dispersing completely.

Of course, the waves don't exist independently of the ocean. They couldn't exist without the ocean and are the very form of the ocean.

That's not to say that the wave is the ocean. It can claim to be of the ocean, but not the ocean itself, which is the entirety of all waves.

The ocean and the wave are one and yet not the same.

The ocean is vast and encompassing, while the wave is comparatively small and limited. The ocean is relatively eternal, while the wave exists for but a brief moment in time.

All difference between the two, however, is negated by the knowledge that both are nothing but water. Their form differs, but the essence is one.

The ocean and wave analogy is used to help us understand the relationship between the individual and Ishvara. Vedanta likens individual beings to the waves on the ocean; the ocean being Ishvara itself.

Like the wave, each individual is part of Ishvara, yet obviously isn't Ishvara in its totality.

If you, as an individual being, were Ishvara, you'd have access to all Ishvara's knowledge and the powers of omniscience and omnipotence. Clearly that cannot be said of any mortal being.

When looked at from the standpoint of their upadhis, the three bodies, they seem immensely different. One is limited and the other is not.

But, like the wave and the ocean, both are the same in essence. Just as the wave and ocean are both nothing other than water, the individual and Ishvara are nothing other than Consciousness.

The Original Consciousness is one and the same in both.

This Consciousness expresses differently due to the differences in the reflecting medium. That explains how the individual and Ishvara are at once different and yet the same. It's the same Consciousness with a different reflection.

The reflection teaching helps us understand the unity in apparent diversity and how duality can ultimately be resolved into Nonduality.

In short, everything in the universe lives only because the Self enlivens it with its eternal being.

Consciousness pervades the three bodies and, by its mere presence, brings life, sentience and aliveness to them. It's able to do this because the three bodies serve as a reflecting medium for Consciousness.

The Mirror

Imagine that you're in a darkened room. There's a gap in the curtains and a mirror facing the window. When angled a certain way, the mirror is capable of reflecting the sunlight from outside, therefore illuminating the room.

The mirror is a reflecting medium. It has no light of its own, but, positioned the right way, it becomes a reflector of light.

The light in the mirror is both different and non-different from the original light of the sun. In a sense, it's the same light. There aren't, after all, two suns.

This reflected light differs in some crucial aspects, however.

First of all, it relies entirely upon the reflecting medium and will only exist as long as the mirror is capable of reflecting it.

The quality of the reflection also depends upon the quality of the reflecting medium. If the mirror happens to be clean and clear, the reflection will be pristine and pure. If, however, the mirror surface is covered in grease and grime, the reflection will be dulled, or there may not be much of a reflection at all.

There's another key way in which reflected light differs from the original light. While there's only one sun, one original light, its reflections can be countless in number. One sun can simultaneously be reflected by a trillion different mirrors across the world.

A Clear Mind is Essential

The same is true of the Original Consciousness and the reflected consciousness that functions through the body-mind-sense complex.

There's one Original Consciousness, yet trillions of different mirrors capable of reflecting that Consciousness. That's how, out of unity, we experience a world of plurality.

While all beings are reflecting the same Consciousness, the reflection differs substantially according to the composition of each reflecting medium. Specifically, the reflection of Consciousness is filtered or conditioned by the quality of a person's subtle body—ie., mind.

Just like the mirror, some subtle bodies are relatively pure, clear and, thus, highly reflective, whereas others are damaged and encrusted with many layers of mud and grime.

These differences are the result of a person's karma. Some have enough meritorious karma to reflect the light of the Self in radiant splendour, while others muster only a distorted and impure reflection.

That's why Vedanta places such emphasis on the cultivation of a pure and qualified mind. In order to know the Self, the mirror of your mind must be sufficiently primed and prepared.

You may need to spend considerable time and effort removing the dirt that has accumulated over years and lifetimes of struggling in samsara. For it's only with a reasonably clean and reflective mind that you can successfully understand and internalise the Self-Knowledge which leads to liberation.

The Price of Ignorance

By now, it should be clear that the core human problem is that we are born in almost total ignorance. An impeccable illusionist, maya obscures the true nature of Reality from us.

We're not aware of the Original Consciousness which is actually the truth and source of our being.

Instead, we take appearance to be real. We perceive a body and assume that, because we can see and touch it, it must be what we are; together with a less tangible, but no less problematic, mind.

We come to believe, as we're trained to in this materialist age, that the body is our primary identity, that it evolved from crude matter and that this somehow gave rise to consciousness. We assume that the mind and consciousness are properties of the body; so that when the body dies, we die.

It's little wonder we suffer. This concept of mortality causes a crippling sense of fear and lack. We cannot be happy as long as we feel such lack, so we take action after action in the transactional world in an attempt to find happiness, wholeness and freedom from our existential despair.

We chase phenomenal objects, whether in the form of money, possessions, relationships, achievements or sensual pleasure; in the desperate hope these things will erase our inner sense of lack.

Even if we do succeed at getting what we want, it'll inevitably fail to remove that basic sense of insecurity. After all, we know that whatever we gain will eventually be lost and, ultimately, the body itself, our most prized of possessions, will forsake us and die.

It's these desires and fears, attachments and aversions and the subsequent action they compel that drives our karma. Identified solely with the body-mind-sense complex, we perform karma and accrue the results, both good and bad.

This karma, in the form of the vasanas and mental conditioning, keeps us tied to the wheel of death and rebirth. The reflected consciousness, shining within our subtle body as our innermost sense of individuality, of am-ness, clothes itself in body after body as it seeks to satiate its desires and resolve its karmic debt.

The Real Problem

The source of our problem is that while we're aware of the first two components of our being—the reflecting medium (the three bodies) and the reflected consciousness (the sense that we exist)—we're unaware of the truth of our being; the Original Consciousness; the only thing that's ultimately Real.

Returning to the mirror analogy, this is akin to believing that the sunlight comes from the mirror itself. The mirror has no light of its own. It can only reflect the original sunlight. Because we're in a darkened room, it maybe doesn't occur to us that there must be a source of light outside the room, hidden from view, yet slipping through the curtain onto the mirror.

Ignorance obscures the Original Consciousness from us. Although it's self-revealing and always present, it's subtler than the mind and senses and cannot be perceived as an object.

We can only know it by removing self-ignorance and ceasing to identify with the finite aspects of our being.

Vedanta argues that in order for anything to exist, there must be independent ground of of Existence—and that is the Self.

Try though you might, you cannot have an effect (and the entire universe is an effect) without a cause.

That cause is the Self—Consciousness; Reality itself.

It's not until we come to recognise the existence of the Original Consciousness, of which our cherished individual consciousness is but a reflection, that we come to know what we truly are, and this Knowledge alone leads to freedom.

The problem of mortality is solved by realising that, while the reflecting medium is temporary and time-bound, the Original Consciousness, that which we are, shines forever.

The gross body obviously has an expiry date, although the subtle body is relatively eternal and will skip from body to body as it seeks to work out its karma.

At the time of either liberation or the dissolution of the universe, the subtle body will merge back into the unmanifest causal body.

Indeed, at the end of the universal cycle, Ishvara itself resolves back into its unmanifest seed state. Until, that is, karma again stirs the gunas into motion, causing the universe to once again manifest.

With or without the world of maya, the Original Consciousness, the Self, endlessly shines, for it exists entirely independently of the world.

Whereas the reflected consciousness relies upon a functioning reflecting medium, the Original Consciousness depends on nothing for its existence.

Entirely self-existent, limitless and eternal, Consciousness is without beginning or end.

The Self knows no death because it was never born.

It is Reality, and it abides eternally.

It is the same in all; the inmost Existence and *beingness* of both the individual and Ishvara; the worldly and the Divine.

The Full Meaning of "I Am That"

"I Am That" has both an overt and an implicit, implied meaning.

We've already explored the overt meaning. To summarise, "I" refers to the individual. "That" refers to Ishvara; the creator and controller of the material realm. "Am", of course, negates the difference between them.

While there are obviously immense differences between the individual and Ishvara from the standpoint of the three bodies, they are essentially one. Everything that the individual has and is belongs to Ishvara, from our body to our thoughts and karma. It's all given to us by Ishvara and ultimately belongs to Ishvara.

The deeper, implied meaning of "I Am That" can only be understood in the light of Self-Knowledge.

The implied meaning of "I" is not the individual, but the pure Consciousness that is our true nature. As we've seen time and again, when we cease to identify with the material aspect of our being, we are free to claim our true nature as the Self; Consciousness.

Similarly, "That" doesn't just refer to Ishvara. It also refers to pure Consciousness; the Original Consciousness that pervades the entire cosmos and is the sum total of all things in existence.

The three bodies, which reflect Consciousness, are incidental attributes. They are a product of maya, are finite and may or may not be present. Consciousness, however, always remains. With no beginning or end, it always abides as the indestructible core of our being. This Consciousness is our true identity. It's what always remains.

Tattva Bodha declares:

> There is no contradiction regarding the essential oneness of the individual and God from the standpoint of pure Consciousness.

From the perspective of the water, there is no contradiction between the wave and the ocean. They are both simply water. Similarly, the individual and God are two expressions of the same Consciousness that is the very heart, essence and totality of Existence.

Choose Your Identity

The purpose of this teaching is to, in the words of a prayer from the

Isha Upanishad, "Lead us from the unreal to the real, lead us from darkness to light and lead us from death to immortality."

Immortality is not something that can be gained by any particular action or attainment.

The only way to "gain" immortality is through the Knowledge that you are already immortal.

Were the ocean wave sentient, it would have a choice. It could either continue identifying as a wave and, thus, be separate, time-bound and subject to its own imminent dissolution. Or, in the light of Self-Knowledge, it could choose to identify as *water*, and be comparatively immortal!

The name and form is temporary, but the essence abides. The moment the wave realises that its form is only incidental and that, in actual fact, it is simply water, it never need fear its own mortality again. It can simply and freely enjoy rising up and merging back into the ocean.

As an individual, you have the same choice as to where you place your identity.

Will you continue labouring under the delusion of maya and identify solely as the body-mind-sense complex?

If so, a tremendous price must be paid. For, as long as you identify with the instrument, you accept its limitations as your own. You remain subject to the pains and sorrows of duality, not least sickness, loss, ageing and eventual death; a life forever blighted by the insecurity that is the hallmark of samsara.

Why identify with the finite, ultimately unreal, part of your being when you can instead identify with the Infinite; the ultimate Truth of what you are?

It's a choice nobody else can make for you.

You can continue labouring under the ignorance of maya, or you can heed the words of the scripture and the testimony of the seers and enlightened beings across the ages.

The entire spiritual journey is one of shifting our point of self-identification from the finite to the Infinite; from the false to the Real; from the limited reflected consciousness to the limitless Original Consciousness that is the essence of all beings.

Direct and Indirect Knowledge

Here's the caveat. It's not enough simply to know the Self.

You must take this Knowledge and wholeheartedly, resolutely claim it as your own. You have to own it, thereby transforming Self-Knowledge into ironclad certainty.

Indirect knowledge must be converted to direct knowledge in order to beget freedom. Indirect knowledge is knowing of the Self. Direct knowledge is knowing that you *are* the Self.

There's a world of difference between the two, because only direct knowledge will end your search and yield the bountiful fruits of liberation.

The all-important final section of this book will now set out how you can take this Self-Knowledge, all that you've learned so far, and convert it to absolute conviction. In other words, you're about to put all of this into practice, turning Self-Knowledge into lasting freedom.

Summary

- The entire teaching of Vedanta can be summarised by three short words: I Am That.
- All beings in the world of form consist of three components: the three bodies, which are a reflecting medium, reflected consciousness and Original Consciousness.
- Original Consciousness is the Self; the Absolute; pure Existence/Consciousness. It is the ground of all being.
- Consciousness associated with the macrocosmic three bodies is Ishvara. Ishvara is the entirety of the creation, both gross and

subtle.
- Consciousness associated with the microcosmic three bodies is the individual. All that the individual is and has, specifically the three bodies and all our karma, actually belongs to Ishvara.
- The first meaning of "I Am That" is I, as an individual, am non-separate from Ishvara, or God.
- The individual and Ishvara seem to be different when looked at from the perspective of the three bodies; Ishvara being vast and limitless and the individual being small and limited. However, just as the wave and the ocean are united in that both are water alone, the individual and Ishvara are united in that both are Consciousness alone.
- The second, implied meaning of "I Am That" is that I, the individual, am Consciousness and Ishvara, the totality, is also Consciousness. This can only be understood by one with Self-Knowledge.
- It's up to us to choose where we place our sense of identification. Why identify with the temporary and finite aspect of your being, which brings sorrow, when you can identify with the limitless and Infinite truth of your being, which brings liberation?
- Indirect knowledge means you know *of* the Self. Direct knowledge means you know you *are* the Self. Indirect knowledge must be converted to direct knowledge in order to yield liberation.

Part Three

From Knowledge to Freedom

18.

The Enlightenment Protocol

> As gold heated in a furnace loses its impurities and achieves its own true nature, so the application of Self-Knowledge rids the mind of the impurities of delusion, enabling true liberation.
>
> *Adi Shankara*

We're about to get practical! As we highlighted in the previous chapter, Self-Knowledge alone is rarely enough. In order to convert this Knowledge to liberation, it must be rigorously applied to the mind with consistency and skill.

This chapter provides a framework for doing just that.

By the end of the chapter, you'll have a suggested daily Vedanta practice and a six week syllabus, complete with recommended reading, listening and resources, as well as a toolbox of exercises, meditations and techniques for helping apply this Knowledge.

The aim, to use a computer analogy, is to uninstall your old operating system, based on ignorance and lack, and install a new one.

This new operating system is the culmination of all that you've learned so far. It's based on true Self-Knowledge and the reorientation of your identity from the lack and limitation of the false ego-self to the Wholeness and Freedom of what you truly are: pure Consciousness.

The Necessity of a Teacher

A lot of people try to self-study Vedanta. That's fine to begin with, because most people discover the teaching themselves in the course of their own spiritual reading, learning and exploration.

There comes a time, however, when it's necessary to find a teacher.

The reason is simple. Your suffering is the result of ignorance. Ignorance exists in the intellect and conditions all your thoughts, beliefs, interpretations and your very worldview.

If you approach Vedanta and attempt to teach yourself, the teaching will be filtered by the intellect's preexisting ignorance. Put simply, you'll be inclined to interpret it according to what you think you already know.

That's just what human beings do. The untrained mind is a confirmation bias machine! People generally, consciously or unconsciously, only seek information that correlates with what they think they already know. This means that, scarily often, the mind doesn't *really* want to know the truth as much it wants to be right and to confirm its existing viewpoint.

Ignorance all too readily masquerades as knowledge and the mind often cannot tell the difference. Without a teacher, the moment you come across a part of the teaching that you don't understand or don't like, you're liable to reject it (or, worse still, reject Vedanta in its entirety) because it doesn't "resonate", which is to say, align with what you already think is true.

A good teacher will cut through ignorance with the sharpened blade of discrimination and be there to help and guide you when you get lost in doubt or confusion. They'll be able to resolve your doubts, clarify your understanding and explain what you might otherwise have disregarded out of hand because ignorance clouded your perspective.

As Krishna advises in the Bhagavad Gita:

> Always seek a teacher who has attained Self-Realisation. With reverence and devotion, ask the proper questions and this wise soul will share the vision of Truth and teach you Knowledge of the Self.

It can be difficult to find a good, genuine teacher of traditional Vedanta outside of India. Many don't have access to legitimate teachers in person. Fortunately, the internet has made it possible to connect with, learn from and communicate with teachers all across the world from the comfort of your own home.

A teacher should be Self-Realised, although there's no objective test to determine if a person is Self-Realised. Be judicious and get a sense for how a teacher conducts him or herself. A Self-Realised person will behave with kindness, unpretentiousness and a lack of egotism and ambition. Importantly, they must well versed in the scriptures and should be from a recognised lineage in the Shankaracharya teaching tradition.

I recommend teachers from the lineage of Swami Dayananda Saraswati of Arsha Vidya. Dayananda's approach was impeccably pure and arguably the most in line with what Adi Shankara actually taught. While some schools, such as the Ramakrishna Mission, tend to view Vedanta as a philosophy, Dayananda reasserted Vedanta's status not as a philosophy or object of study, but a means of knowledge. You'll find a list of recommended teachers in the Appendix 3, so feel free to investigate their teachings.

In general, I suggest avoiding non-traditional teachers who advertise themselves as "Advaita" or "Non-dual" teachers. Usually they're not part of a recognised lineage and don't teach from the scriptures. Many simply cherry-pick ideas here and there and repackage it as their own teaching.

Vedanta is a complete, comprehensive body of knowledge and must be delivered as such; all the way from A to Z. Although nontraditional teachers may have charisma and magnetism, simply dispensing the odd inspiring quote from the Upanishads will do little to erase ignorance in the long term.

A true Vedanta teacher must be adept at wielding the teaching and capable of filling in the entire canvas. While the core of the teaching is the nature of the Self as Consciousness, they should be teaching all the topics covered in this book, from dharma and karma yoga to the nature of Ishvara and maya. As a student, you deserve no less than the full curriculum. Don't sell yourself short.

The Pyramid of Self-Realisation

The pyramid above is a map of the entire spiritual path. It show the steps that must be taken in order to prepare the mind for Self-Knowledge.

As you can see, Vedanta sits at the top of the pyramid. Tempting though it might be, you cannot jump to the top without first making your way up through the preceding steps. Like any building, this pyramid is only as strong as its foundation.

We've repeatedly stressed that Vedanta only works if the mind has been adequately prepared to receive Self-Knowledge. Much like a job or educational course, certain qualifications must be in place in order for Vedanta to bear fruit.

These qualifications were explored in the fifth chapter. To recap, it's important to develop the mental qualities of:

1. **Discrimination:** the ability to discern the true from the false and the fleeting from the eternal.

2. **Dispassion** with regard to the world of objects and the inner world of our thoughts and feelings.

3. **Discipline:** including discipline of the mind and senses, the ability to withdraw from sense objects, endurance in the face of adversity, faith in the teacher and teaching and the ability to concentrate the mind.

4. **Desire** for liberation above all else.

You'll be pleased to hear that perfection is neither expected nor possible. The aim isn't to try to become some holy saint. You do, however, need to learn the basics of mind management and cultivating the above qualities as best you can. It's not easy, for sure, but it's a necessary challenge and a decidedly noble pursuit.

Even if that's all you do, and you don't go on to pursue Self-Knowledge, you'll be astonished at how sweeter and less stressful life becomes and how much more happiness and contentment you experience. Why? Because you'll finally have learned to govern your mind, psyche and emotions rather than be a slave to them.

When it comes to enlightenment, success or failure ultimately comes down to the presence or absence of these qualifications.

A seeker may spend years, or even decades, diligently studying Vedanta. If the qualifications are lacking, however, the teaching will never be much more than words and concepts. Such a student won't enjoy the fruits of Self-Knowledge—because their mind simply isn't able to assimilate it.

An untamed mind, ravaged by an endless ocean of desires, attachments and fears, and subject to recurrent emotional storms, simply won't have the focus, commitment and clarity to stick with Self-Knowledge.

Therefore, as a seeker, it's imperative that you bring your mind under control and work hard to develop the qualities listed above. A reasonably peaceful, steady, discerning and dispassionate mind is a tremendously powerful asset in all ways.

As you can see from the diagram, the steps leading up to Vedanta are dharma, karma yoga and upasana yoga.

These don't lead to enlightenment in themselves, but are intended to purify the mind, getting it sufficiently qualified for Vedanta's three stage process. Although we've already explored these in the course of this book, a summary of each now follows.

Dharma and Values

Dharma sits at the base of the pyramid because it's the foundation upon which all else is built.

Without dharma, we have nothing. In order to succeed and be happy in life, it's essential that we follow dharma with unrelenting resolve.

The cost of violating dharma is always too high. We face not only outer consequences for even the smallest transgressions but also inner consequences in the form of guilt, anxiety and fear.

To recap, there are three types of dharma:

1. Universal dharma.
2. Situational dharma.
3. Personal dharma.

Universal dharma means adhering to universal values such as honesty, non-injury, kindness, compassion and straightforwardness. Chapter Six presented a list of dharmic values outlined by the Bhagavad Gita. It may be helpful to refer to this list with regularity, and see which of these qualities you have in sufficient measure and which need work.

Situational dharma means responding appropriately to each situation as it presents itself. It means doing our best as we navigate the various roles and duties we assume in life, whether as a parent, a child, an employer or employee, a teacher or a student.

Our personal dharma relates to our inherent nature. It means that we act in alignment with who we are and play the role we've been allotted in life to the best of our ability.

Following our personal dharma means not trying to be somebody that we're not. Each individual has certain proclivities, talents and passions and it's important to honour our nature, in accordance with dharma, and play our unique part in the grand tapestry of creation.

Following dharma makes life much easier because we don't have to figure things out on our own. We just have to do what's right in any given situation based upon universal values of good conduct (which, if you're ever in any doubt, are outlined in scriptures such as the Bhagavad Gita).

When desire and dharma clash, dharma must always emerge triumphant. Make that your sacred duty and commitment!

Taking A Values Inventory

Until your values are fully aligned with dharma, your life won't work particularly well. You'll find yourself stressed and beset by conflict and confusion.

Most of our values are instilled into us at a very young age. We don't choose these values. They're chosen for us. Some will inevitably be false or harmful values. Why else would otherwise intelligent people base their self-worth on their bank balance, the way they look or what other people think of them?

Even though, at one level, you may know that such things don't matter, if you still have a value for them, even a partial value, it'll clash with other, more important values. This always results in inner conflict and confusion with regard to your actions.

Conflict arises when spiritual seekers have an only partially assimilated value for liberation but a fully assimilated value for seeking happiness through worldly gain.

Which of the two values will win out; the partially assimilated value or the fully assimilated value? No contest; whichever value is strongest will win.

Your values determine your priorities and your priorities determine your actions. Clarity is essential. Muddled values cannot lead to anything but a muddled, unsuccessful, conflict-ridden life.

So, it's vital that your values are aligned with dharma and in harmony with who you are.

That's why it's important to take a values inventory.

Tempting though it may be, please don't skip this step.

I recommend getting out your journal and taking some time to figure out what's most important to you in life and what you truly value in the depths of your heart.

Ask yourself, "What do I most value?" "What's most important to me in life?"

Try to identity and weed out any false values that come up in this process. These include unhealthy values that may have been conditioned into you from a young age; such as materialism, greed, the need to be right or to be viewed a certain way. Is that really, truly important to you? Or have you now come to realise that what you really want in life is to be free?

As we've learned, lasting freedom comes only from Self-Knowledge—so that, upon reflection, should be your highest value. It's only then that you'll develop the necessary fourth qualification: the desire for liberation.

This desire shouldn't be a weak or middling desire. That'll only lead to weak and middling results. It must become a blazing, all-consuming passion. It's the strength of your desire for freedom that fuels your resolve, keeps you committed and provides the necessary energy, focus and determination to keep going until you've reached your goal.

So, through the process of journalling, try to expose those lesser values; the ones that aren't even "your" values at all, but were programmed into you by other people and society at large.

Find out what you truly value above all else, the light of your own Self, and commit to fully realising and actualising that.

Regularly take a look at the fourfold mental qualifications and, with complete honesty and candour, ask yourself which of these qualities you most need to strengthen.

Incidentally, don't ever beat yourself up. Given the culture we live in, most of us have grown up with what are, in many cases, the polar opposite of dharmic values. We're generally encouraged to be ego-driven, passionate, materialistic and desire-based. Our culture has little value for genuine spirituality, which is often derided and ridiculed.

Be objective and dispassionate. If you lack a certain quality, it can be cultivated. The tools for doing that now follow.

Karma Yoga

The Bhagavad Gita spends a great deal of time discussing karma yoga as a means of purifying the mind.

Traditionally, only ascetics who renounced worldly life altogether were deemed suitable candidates for Vedanta, the path of liberation through Self-Knowledge.

However, Krishna makes it clear that those with an active life of worldly karma, such as jobs and families, are still capable of attaining enlightenment—as long as they refine and purify the mind by converting all karma, all action, to karma yoga.

To recap, the three steps of karma yoga are:

1. Cultivate gratitude for all that you have and all that you've been given.
2. Perform all your actions as an offering to Ishvara.
3. Relinquish attachment to the results and accept what comes with grace and equanimity.

Karma yoga sanctifies all action. Actions are no longer taken simply to satisfy your personal desires and aversions. Instead, you perform your actions in worship of God as you go about daily life.

Swami Paramarthananda says that karma yoga converts your entire life to a field of service. Your every action, whether grand or mundane, becomes a way of paying the "rent" to Ishvara and expressing gratitude for the many blessings you've been given.

Because these actions are given to Ishvara, the results of those actions belong to Ishvara too. You recognise that Ishvara alone determines and dispenses the results of all actions.

The only appropriate response is, therefore, to accept those results, whatever they may be, as coming from God. This attitude of mind removes significant stress, resistance and reactivity, enabling you to respond to situations with objectivity and evenness of mind.

Over time, the practice of karma yoga, converting daily action into service and accepting the results with good grace, neutralises the mind's binding desires and aversions. You naturally become more objective, discriminating and dispassionate; all essential qualities for liberation.

For seekers with worldly karma—which is, let's face it, almost everyone—karma yoga is non-negotiable. Without it, your mind will be subject to both internal obstacles (in the form of your desires, fears and attachments) and external factors (in the form of circumstances, other people and the various hardships and stresses of life).

Karma yoga is necessary to help manage the mind and to gradually convert all personal desires into the desire for liberation.

As a reminder, the five principles of karma yoga offered in the scriptures are:

1. Worship of God in any form.
2. Unconditional respect, support and regard for your parents and elders.
3. Worship of the scriptures.
4. Service to humanity.
5. Service to nature, the environment and all living beings.

Live by these five principles and you cannot go wrong.

Upasana Yoga

Upasana yoga means meditation upon Ishvara. It's another term for what we call *bhakti*, or devotion.

When your life is driven by dharma and your actions converted to worship via karma yoga, you'll find your mind naturally becomes more discriminating and refined.

It becomes ever clearer that what you really want cannot be found in the world of objects. What you're ultimately seeking is the very source and essence of the objects themselves: God; your own Divine Self.

Upasana yoga is the next step up from karma yoga, although one is not a substitute for the other. Karma yoga focuses on action and upasana yoga harnesses the immeasurable power of love and devotion. It further establishes the calm, contemplative disposition required for a seeker of liberation.

As you'll recall, how a person thinks of and worships God depends upon their level of understanding.

Because it's extremely difficult to conceptualise God as formless and all-pervading, for many, it is helpful to visualise God as a particular form.

Hence, worship of Ishvara usually begins with worship of a personal deity. This can be done through a daily devotional ceremony, through prayer, meditation and the reciting of mantras and names of God.

Keeping the mind fixed upon God, in whatever form, has an incredibly healing, nourishing and purifying affect on the human psyche. It neutralises the ego and helps prevent spiritual narcissism; a common problem among seekers who fail to understand and embrace the devotional component of Self-Realisation.

As your understanding grows, your knowledge of Ishvara expands from a specific form to the cosmos itself, encompassing everything in creation: every star, planet and galaxy; every being, every form, every flower and blade of grass. The entire world becomes your temple of worship when you learn to see God all around you.

The final and highest understanding of Ishvara is as Brahman, the formless Self; the very source of all being. For that, we have the three stages of Vedanta, as we're about to outline.

Krishna makes it clear in the Bhagavad Gita that the highest devotion is not just to realise God, but to realise your oneness with God.

Upasana yoga in combination with karma yoga is excellent for helping dealing with emotional difficulties. You recognise that, at the individual level, you are utterly dependent on Ishvara for all your needs, much as a baby depends on its mother. You allow Ishvara to shoulder the burden, drawing upon the strength of God, which is, of course, Infinite.

Morning and Evening Ritual

Many people lead busy lives. Depending on your karma, you may have a job, a family and various other commitments and demands.

It may, therefore, be a challenge integrating Vedanta into your already full life. That's why it's important to make a real effort to incorporate some practice into your daily routine.

Regardless of how busy your day, this must be considered as important and non-negotiable as showering or brushing your teeth. After all, physical cleanliness is important, but equally so is spiritual and mental/emotional cleanliness.

What follows are suggested morning and evening rituals that can be easily integrated into daily life. They needn't take long, but you can, of course, take as much time as you like. Structuring these routines into your day will ensure that you start your day well and end it well.

Morning Ritual

1. Gratitude and Values. The first thing to do upon waking is remind yourself that, firstly, you are alive! You've been given the gift of another precious twenty four hours and it's up to you to use them wisely. Always remember that life and time are precious and limited. Death is a certainty for all living beings, but the

time of that death is uncertain. Knowing this, ask yourself, "What is most important to me? What am I living for?" Allow yourself to be clear on your true values, goals and priorities, and plan your day accordingly.
2. Perform your daily devotional ceremony [see Chapter Twelve]. The suggested ceremony in Chapter Twelve is deliberately short and need only take two to three minutes. You can, of course, create your own ceremony and spend as much time doing it as you wish.
3. Attune. Become aware that God exists within you, as the core of your being, and all beings. Affirm that you are neither the body, mind, nor the intellect or ego; but the Awareness or Consciousness in which these instruments appear and have their being.
4. Love. Place your hand upon your heart and, taking a couple of deep breaths while focusing on the heart, allow a feeling of love to arise within. Consciously direct that love to your own body and mind, and then imagine bathing your loved ones in that love, before extending it across the planet to all beings, all creatures and the planet itself.
5. Close. To close, chant Om three times, either aloud or mentally.

Evening Ritual

1. Gratitude. Give thanks for the day. Even if it has come with its challenges and difficulties, thank Ishvara for all that did go right and for all the blessings you have, such as a roof over your head, food, heat and people that love you.
2. Forgiveness. A powerful way of disentangling from the day and clearing up any unresolved karma is to place your hand upon your heart and focus your energy and attention there for a few breaths. With focus and sincerity, mentally affirm that you are

sending out forgiveness to anyone who may have hurt or caused you pain and sorrow. Recognise that to err is human and to forgive Divine. Ask for forgiveness from anyone you may have inadvertently hurt or wronged. Send out love once again to your loved ones and to the world at large. Be sure to bathe your own body-mind in the warm glow of that love.

3. Personal Deity. [Optional] You can light a candle and spend some time connecting with your personal deity; your symbol of the immense light, power and love that exists at the very heart of your being. Recognise that you are not separate from this Divinity. It shines within you as the very essence of your being.

4. Contemplate. Take a moment to read through Shankara's *Nirvana Shatkam* [see Appendix 2], allowing yourself to reflect on each verse and let the Knowledge permeate your mind and heart.

5. Reflect. [Optional] If you have done any Vedantic study during the day, and hopefully you have, take a moment to reflect on the teaching and any key insights that arose. This can be done by referring to your Vedanta journal.

6. Close. To close, chant Om three times, being aware that you are offering a salutation to your own innermost Self.

These two rituals form a nice bookend to your day. You can adjust and tailor them to your preference.

The key is taking some time to turn your attention inward, to claim your highest nature, sanctify your day and heal your mind by tapping into the limitless love within you.

Next, we're going to kickstart your Vedanta practice by suggesting a syllabus of sorts, complete with recommended texts and resources for beginner, intermediate and advanced student alike.

Vedanta Stage 1: Listening

The first stage of Vedanta is called *shravana*, which means listening.

Put simply, you sit down and listen carefully as the teacher unfolds various scriptural texts, explaining each verse, and gradually revealing Vedanta's vision of Reality.

At this point, you may already have a teacher, in which case they'll be able to direct your course of study. If you don't, however, you needn't worry, because there's much truth to the old adage that, "When the student is ready the teacher appears."

Once again, to get you started on your path, you'll find a list of recommended teachers and audio/visual resources at the back of this book in Appendix 3.

A common tendency which should be avoided is to haphazardly watch online videos, simply clicking on whatever comes recommended. A YouTube algorithm should not be your teacher.

It's important to start at the beginning and work your way through the Vedanta syllabus. The teaching is set out in a carefully sequenced manner, allowing your understanding to gradually take shape, grow and strengthen. Tempting though it may be, you cannot jump to the end with Vedanta and expect to it make sense.

A traditional Vedanta teacher will start with the appropriate introductory texts and spend considerable time explaining each verse.

The pace is slow. Some teachers may only get through a single verse in an hour. There's absolutely no hurry, however.

When it comes to Vedanta, the tortoise always beats the hare. The hare may dart ahead, dazzling with an initial burst of energy and enthusiasm, but the tortoise knows to pace itself for the duration. It'll still be ambling forward long after the hare has burned itself out.

Suggested Texts

For Beginner Students

- *Tattva Bodha* (Knowledge of Truth) [text]. This text, composed by Adi Shankara, is the perfect starting point as it introduces most of the main terms and concepts in Vedantic teaching in a short, concise manner. See Appendix 1 for this author's translation of the text. If you would like to read some other translations of Tattva Bodha, highly recommended are the versions with commentary by the late, great Swami Dayananda Saraswati of Arsha Vidya, James Swartz (available online at shiningworld.com) and Swami Tejomayananda.
- *Enlightenment Made Simple* by Rory B Mackay [book]. The book you're now reading! As comprehensive yet accessible an introduction and overview of the main concepts of Vedanta as you will find. Don't just chuck it aside once you've finished. This is a book that will reward repeat readings.
- *Essence of Enlightenment* and/or *How to Attain Enlightenment* by James Swartz [books]. These books were my entry into Vedanta; written masterfully by an experienced Western student of the venerable Swami Chinmayanada. They offer a perfect overview of the teaching that is easy to understand and accessible.
- *Vedanta - The Big Picture* based on talks by Swami Paramarthananda of Chennai (edited by Rory B Mackay) [book]. This is a slim, easy to read volume that again covers the main concepts in a concise manner and introduces a lot of the Sanskrit terminology which is helpful to learn.
- *Introduction to Vedanta - Understanding the Fundamental Problem* by Swami Dayananda Saraswati [book]. A good primer by one of the most important and influential Vedanta teachers of the past century.

- *Advaita Made Easy* by Dennis Waite [book]. A nice, short introduction to some of the core tenets of Vedanta.
- *Bhagavad Gita - The Divine Song* by Rory B Mackay [book]. A clear, accessible and stripped down translation of one of the three source texts of Vedanta. The in-depth commentary gradually unfolds virtually all the key concepts of Vedanta. It starts at the beginning and works its way to the more advanced subject matter. Certainly, for beginners, the first six chapters plus commentary are highly recommended.

For Intermediate Students

- *Atma Bodha* by Shankara [text] is a seminal work, exploring the nature of the Self with a range of metaphors and analogies. *The Fire of Self-Knowledge: Commentaries on Atma Bodha* by James Swartz [book] provides excellent commentaries on the verses and comes complete with illustrations.
- *Vivekachudamani* and *Aparokshanubhuti* [texts] are two more classic texts written by Shankara. Both are best read along with the commentary of a teacher.
- *Bhagavad Gita - The Divine Song* by Rory B Mackay [book]. The first six chapters are ideal for beginners and the remaining twelve chapters and commentary will fill in everything else for intermediate and advanced students.
- *The Teaching of the Bhagavad Gita* by Swami Dayananda Saraswati [book]. An excellent and enlightening distillation of the Gita's main themes.
- *The Upanishads* by Ecknath Easwaran [book] is an easy to digest introduction to the main Upanishads complete with introductory commentary to each of Upanishad.
- Swami Nikhilananda's translations of the Upanishads are also excellent. Especially recommended are the *Katha, Kena,*

Svetashvara and the *Mandukya Upanishads*. Many of Nikhilananda's books can be found on Amazon and eBay.
- Also recommended: *The Yoga of the Three Energies* [book] and *The Yoga of Love* [book] by James Swartz and *The Basics of Self-Inquiry* [book] by Isabella Viglietti-Swartz.

For Advanced Students

- *Panchadasi* by Vidyaranya Swami [text] is an essential work for advanced students with a firm grounding in the teaching. The study of this text should be guided by a competent teacher and commentaries can be found among the recommended audio/video resources in Appendix 3.
- *Inquiry into Existence - The Lamp of Self-Knowledge* [book] by James Swartz is a superb, in-depth commentary on the above-mentioned Panchadasi inspired by the lectures of Swami Paramarthananda.
- *Mandukya Upanishad with Gaudapada's Karika* [text]. One for advanced students, Gaudapada's commentary presents what we call non-origination theory, perhaps the highest and subtlest level of understanding reality in Vedantic canon.
- *Mandukya Upanishad with Gaudapada's Karika* by James Swartz [book] features commentary on Gaudapada's commentary and helps make this profound teaching easier to understand and digest.
- *Bhagavad Gita Home Study Course* by Swami Dayananda Saraswati [multi-book series]. This astounding nine-volume collection is based on in-depth talks given by Swami Dayananda on the intricacies of the Gita. Covering just about every aspect of the teaching imaginable, it's a lengthy treatise and Sanskrit heavy but also highly recommended for advanced seekers.
- *Avadhuta Gita* and *Ashtavakra Gita* [texts] are two scriptures

which poetically explore the nature of Non-dual reality from the perspective of the liberated soul. Neither are teaching texts (which is to say, not ideal for beginners), but they make great tools for meditation and contemplation.

- *Avadhuta Gita - Song of the Liberated Soul* by Rory Mackay [book] comes with commentary on selected verses.
- *Ashtavakra Gita* by Swami Chinmayananda [book] comes with full commentary. Another more simple and stripped down translation is *The Heart of Awareness: A Translation of the Ashtavakra Gita* by Thomas Byrom [book].

How to Be a Good Student

As a student, your job is to approach the teaching with openness, humility and the desire to learn.

It's important to adopt what Zen practitioners call "beginner's mind". Consider it a challenge to leave your existing knowledge, ideas and opinions the door. You can always pick them up again later if you wish.

For the duration of the teaching, it's essential that your mind be available, open and willing to learn. A glass cannot be filled if it is already full of water, and the mind is no different.

You can only ever learn as much as you're willing to learn. Hubris can be one of the greatest enemies of the seeker of liberation. The basic, sobering fact is if you already knew the Truth, you'd be enlightened and would have no need for Vedanta. It can be difficult for the ego to admit that we don't know; but that humble recognition is what opens the door to genuine knowledge.

To be a good student means to keep your mind qualified, open, earnest and eager to learn. It means respecting the teacher and trying not to unduly monopolise their time and attention. It means to be mature and conduct yourself with the appropriate thoughtfulness, integrity and diligence. Above all, you remain committed to your goal: freedom through the application of Self-Knowledge.

Keep a Vedanta Journal

You may want to invest in a notepad or journal as you begin your journey.

Keeping a spiritual journal can be an valuable practice in and of itself. You'll find it helps organise the mind and keep you focused and on track.

How you use the journal is up to you. I recommend being creative, playful and taking plentiful notes as you learn.

It's essential that you take the teaching and internalise it. Hearing or reading something once is almost never enough. You need to deeply contemplate the Knowledge, and keeping a journal will aid in this.

You can include any "lightbulb" moments and keep summaries of key concepts and teaching metaphors. It can be particularly helpful to summarise the teaching in your own words, helping the many layers of knowledge sink into the mind.

You can also include your favourite quotes, and any verses or statements you find particularly insightful and illuminating.

Your Daily Practice

The daily morning and evening rituals suggested a few pages back are a way of purifying, calming and concentrating the mind.

Such rituals help integrate Vedanta into your life. They aren't Vedanta itself, however. Vedanta is the threefold process of listening, reasoning and contemplation.

If you happen to be a householder, with various work and family obligations, your challenge will be setting aside the necessary time each day to sit down and focus your mind on the teaching.

Whether it's over a cup of tea first thing in the morning, or at night when the kids are in bed and the day is winding down, you need time each day when you can devote yourself to Vedanta.

That might involve listening to audio/visual content, reading the scriptures, a book or writing in your Vedanta journal.

As well as exposing your mind to the teaching through texts, commentaries and lectures, it's also important to spend some time in meditation.

The benefits of meditation are many and varied. It helps sharpen and refine the mind, is highly beneficial to the body and overall health and well-being and is a perfect antidote to the stress of daily living.

Vedantic meditation has another, even more important benefit. It allows you to take Self-Knowledge and integrate it into the mind; aligning your mind, heart and innermost sense of identity with the pure Awareness or Consciousness that you are. This Knowledge must be consistently applied to the mind in order to yield benefit, and that's precisely what Vedantic meditation does. The next chapter provides a crash course in Vedantic meditation.

First, here's a suggested daily routine for incorporating Vedanta into your day.

Morning

- Upon rising, perform your morning ritual (outlined above).
- If possible, read, listen to or watch a little Vedanta over your breakfast or morning coffee. Alternately, read through your Vedanta journal. This starts your day by aligning your mind with spiritual Truth.

During the day or evening

- Make the time to do some Vedanta practice. Aim for at least an

hour, but, if push comes to shove, any time is better than none. Work your way through whatever text or book you are on, or watch and listen to the teaching being unfolded by a qualified teacher. Immerse yourself in this and keep notes in your journal.
- Practice Vedantic meditation (see the next chapter).

Evening

- Before bedtime, perform your evening ritual (outlined above).
- Take a moment to contemplate the teaching and return to the Knowledge, "I am not the body, mind, intellect or ego. I am the Self; pure Awareness; pure Consciousness". This is the highest of all truths; the Knowledge that alone leads to liberation.

A Six Week Syllabus

Here's a suggested six week course of study for a beginner student.

The text is Tattva Bodha. You'll find a clear and concise translation of this text in Appendix 1.

Traditionally, a Vedanta teacher will chant each verse in Sanskrit and then spend time revealing its meaning before moving onto the next verse. While you may grasp the essentials just by reading it yourself, it's necessary that you understand the full nuance and meaning of the text—and for that, you need a teacher.

So, to accompany your study of Tattva Bodha, please go to the audio/visual resources section in Appendix 3.

Select the teacher of your choice and go to their website or YouTube channel and find their commentary on Tattva Bodha (I believe just about all of them have such commentaries available; many are available for free but some may need to be purchased). You will follow this as you work your way through the text.

Week 1 - Dharma

- Each day, do your morning and evening ritual.
- Begin your study of Tattva Bodha using the text and selected audio/visual commentary. Listen to, or watch, as much as you like or have time for each day. Be consistent but don't go too overboard; pace yourself like the tortoise.
- The first topic in Tattva Bodha is the mental qualifications required for liberation. Make sure you thoroughly understand each of them.
- Because dharma is the base of the pyramid of Self-Realisation, this week, re-read Chapter Six of this book: "Values and Dharma". Take notes and write a summary of this topic in your own words.
- Sometime this week, conduct a values inventory. With as much objectivity and candour as you can muster, take a look at how well your life and actions are aligned with universal, situational and personal dharna. Highlight any areas in your life that require work and be willing to make the necessary changes.

Week 2 - Karma Yoga 1

- Each day, do your morning and evening ritual.
- Continue working your way through Tattva Bodha.
- This week, we shall focus on karma yoga; essential for helping purify the mind and cultivate the necessary qualifications. Re-read Chapter Seven, "Karma Yoga". Take notes and write a summary of this topic in your own words.
- Commit to living your life as a karma yogi. Begin practising stages one and two immediately. This means cultivating gratitude for all that you have and offering all your actions, however mundane, to Ishvara as a form of gratitude and worship. As a karma yogi, you no longer do things simply to get a certain

result. You instead convert your life into a sacred offering. This helps qualify the mind and neutralise binding attachments and aversions. Notice the effects of this shift in mindset.

Week 3 - Karma Yoga 2

- Each day, do your morning and evening ritual.
- Continue working your way through Tattva Bodha.
- Continue to perform all action as karma yoga. This week, begin to implement the third step of karma yoga. This means letting go of attachment to the results of your actions and accepting what happens, whether seemingly good or bad, as being the will of Ishvara. Spend some time in contemplation of the deeper Intelligence at work in life, knowing that misfortune invariably contains the seeds of fortune, and vice versa. Recognise that accepting what happens doesn't mean passive fatalism. As a karma yogi, you don't simply give up if things don't immediately go your way. What you strive to do, however, is to let go of emotional reactivity and continue to act in alignment with dharma, offering all your actions to Ishvara and taking the results in a spirit of equanimity.

Week 4 - Upasana Yoga 1

- Each day, do your morning and evening ritual.
- Continue working through Tattva Bodha. If you've come to the end of Tattva Bodha, consider going over the text and your notes or invest in one of the books recommended for beginners above.
- Continue practising karma yoga throughout the day.
- Re-read Chapter Twelve, "Devotion." Take notes and write a summary of this topic in your own words.
- In addition to practising dharma and karma yoga, incorporate upasana yoga, or meditation upon Ishvara, which is the third

means of preparing the mind for liberation. Begin practising the meditation on a personal deity from Chapter Twelve. Do this every day this week.

Week 5 - Upasana Yoga 2

- Each day do your morning and evening ritual.
- Continue working through Tattva Bodha. If you've come to the end of Tattva Bodha, consider going over the text and your notes or invest in one of the books recommended for beginners above.
- Continue practising karma yoga throughout the day.
- Incorporate the second upasana yoga meditation from Chapter Twelve; meditating on Ishvara as the cosmic form.
- As you go about the day, endeavour to see life with new eyes. See the beauty of Ishvara shining in all forms, from the clouds and skies, to trees and flowers and, of course, shining as the innermost essence of all people and animals. Allow yourself to feel reverence for all of creation.

Week 6 - Guna Management

- Each day do your morning and evening ritual.
- Continue working through Tattva Bodha. If you've come to the end of your study, consider going over the text and your notes or invest in one of the books recommended for beginners above.
- Continue practising karma yoga throughout the day.
- Select any of the Vedantic meditations from Chapter Nineteen and make this a daily practice.
- Re-read Chapter Thirteen, "The Three Energies". Take notes and write a summary of this topic in your own words.
- Consider how these gunas, the three qualities, are at play in your life. Take stock of your home and work environment, your diet and leisure time and find ways you can minimise the agitating

effect of rajas and the dulling effect of tamas. The goal is to cultivate a strong, stable and sattvic mind; a mind fit for Self-Knowledge. Be willing to make any necessary changes to facilitate this.
- For further reading, read the fourteenth chapter of the Bhagavad Gita and the corresponding commentary from my book *Bhagavad Gita - The Divine Song*. For more depth on this topic, consider the book *The Yoga of the Three Energies* by James Swartz.

This six week syllabus provides a solid foundation for any new student. Each week highlights the importance of preparing the mind for Self-Knowledge; covering the essentials of dharma, karma yoga and upasana yoga. It's structured in such a way that you won't just be learning Self-Knowledge; you'll be living it.

What next?

Once you've finished Tattva Bodha, I recommend the Bhagavad Gita as a good second text. You may find my book *Bhagavad Gita - The Divine Song* helpful as it contains a comprehensive commentary in the form of an essay at the end of each chapter. To accompany your study of the Gita, simply select the teacher of your choice from the audio/visual Resources in Appendix 3.

Vedanta Stage 2: Reasoning

The Sanskrit term for the second stage of Vedanta is *manana*, which means "thinking", "reflection" and "understanding".

If the first stage is about acquiring Self-Knowledge, the second stage is making sure that you understand this Knowledge.

It's not enough simply accepting the teaching on blind faith. You must understand and comprehend what's being taught. Faith alone will not liberate the mind. It'll simply create another belief system for the mind to acquire and defend.

Knowledge must become conviction in order to free the mind. You have to know beyond a shadow of doubt, and with the entirety of your being, that what Vedanta teaches is true, or else it simply won't work.

So, never feign understanding when you're actually plagued by doubts, confusion and misunderstanding. That's why you need a teacher; somebody who can resolve your doubts and answer any questions to your satisfaction.

So, whereas the teacher directs stage one, the basic unfoldment of the scriptures, it's up to the student to take care of stage two; and to, with the help of the teacher, satisfactorily resolve any doubts that might arise.

It's important to note that most questions will automatically be answered by the teaching in the fullness of time. Patience is always rewarded. So, don't be too quick to jump in with your questions. Keep listening and you'll see how the teaching is designed to answer questions as they naturally arise. If, however, you find yourself stuck and unable to grasp something, don't hesitate to approach the teacher for assistance.

You'll find Chapter Twenty answers a number of frequently asked questions, hopefully eliminating some of the more common doubts and misunderstandings.

Vedanta Stage 3: Contemplation

We've now covered stages one and two of Vedanta. The first stage provides the Knowledge. The second stage ensures that the student fully understands the Knowledge. The essential third stage is to consistently reflect and meditate upon that Knowledge until it is fully assimilated by the mind and heart.

The Knowledge "I am the Self" must be taken and fully internalised until not a trace of doubt lingers. Only then will it erase the suffering of samsara. This final stage happens to be the subject of our next chapter.

Summary

- Vedanta is a complete body of knowledge. It must be taught by a teacher and not self-taught. Without a teacher, you are liable to fall victim to confirmation bias and disregard any parts of the teaching you don't understand or don't like.
- The pyramid of Self-Realisation has its foundation in dharma. Once committed to practising dharma in all regards, the next step is karma yoga. The third step is upasana yoga. This prepares the mind and leads to the gateway to Self-Realisation: the three-stage process of Vedanta.
- The first stage of Vedanta is listening. Avoid self-study and haphazardly watching videos online. Explore the teachers and audio/visual resources found in Appendix 3. Some key texts and books are recommended in this chapter for beginner, intermediate and advanced students.
- The student of Vedanta must approach the teaching with a beginner's mind, humility and the eagerness to learn.
- Be sure to set aside time each day to expose your mind to the teaching, whether through reading the scriptures or books, listening to audio/visual content or practising meditation.
- The second stage of Vedanta is reasoning. This means making sure you understand what is being taught and resolving any doubts, questions or misunderstanding.
- The final stage is deep contemplation of what has been taught. This is necessary in order to alchemise Self-Knowledge into lasting freedom.

19.
Vedantic Meditation

> The Self, my dear, must be realised—must be heard of, reflected on and meditated upon. By listening, reflecting and meditating upon the Self, all things are known. [...] Through this meditation, the aspirant wins an Infinite world.
>
> *Brihadaranyaka Upanishad*

The practice of meditation has its roots in the most ancient of the Vedas.

The true aim of meditation, according to the scriptures, has nothing to do with its physical or mental health benefits, of which there are unquestionably many. These are but a welcome byproduct for the seeker of liberation. The spiritual seeker uses meditation not as a way of relaxing or sharpening the mind, but as way of applying Self-Knowledge to the mind.

It's worth highlighting that meditation itself doesn't directly lead to liberation. The key to liberation is Self-Knowledge; the removal of self-ignorance and the realisation that what you are is already utterly whole, complete and free.

This Self-Knowledge is acquired through the first stage of Vedanta, by listening to the teacher and coming to understand the message of the scriptures. The second stage should resolve any areas of confusion, doubt or misunderstanding. The final stage is to fully consolidate and integrate that Knowledge into the depths of your mind and intellect.

That's where Vedantic meditation comes in.

Vedantic meditation, or *nididhyasana* in Sanskrit, is the deliberate and sustained contemplation of your identity as the Self; pure Awareness/Consciousness.

While, for some rare and highly qualified seekers, simply hearing the Knowledge is enough to yield liberation, most people must spend some time converting this Knowledge into ironclad certainty. Without taking Self-Knowledge and consistently applying it to the mind, it will likely remain an intellectual fancy; an abstract notion that does little to remove one's suffering.

Vedantic meditation enables you to fully integrate and actualise the Knowledge that what you are is not the body, mind or any of their aggregates, but the Awareness, the Consciousness, in which they appear. It's not until your sense of identification pivots from the body-mind-sense complex to Awareness that you truly enjoy the fruits of liberation.

Once you've added sugar to coffee, you need to give it a stir in order to taste the sweetness. Similarly, once Self-Knowledge has been added to the mind, it needs a good stir in order to permeate the psyche, neutralising the many layers of ignorance and enabling you to finally taste the true sweetness of your own essential being. This Knowledge is stirred, so to speak, through the practice of Vedantic meditation.

Practising Meditation

Most forms of meditation are object-focused. Some techniques use observation of the breath or the sensations in the body, the recitation of a mantra or some kind of visualisation.

The upasana meditations from Chapter Twelve focused on the Self in the form of an object; first as a personal deity, and then as the cosmos itself.

Upasana meditation is excellent for beginner and intermediate students. It aims to concentrate, refine and expand the mind, preparing it for the most potent of all meditation: Vedantic meditation, or the contemplation of your identity as the Self.

Whereas upasana yoga is object-focused, Vedantic meditation is subject-focused. It involves turning your attention away from all objectifiable phenomena and fixing it upon the subject—you; Awareness.

This is the necessary final step of Vedanta's threefold process.

Other forms of meditation may be helpful for various reasons. Whether it takes the form of mindfulness, relaxation or concentration, meditation has multiple benefits that can help you prepare the mind and develop the necessary qualifications for Self-Knowledge.

You can, therefore, continue doing whatever meditation method works best you. After all, it's essential that you're able to sit comfortably, relax and concentrate both body and mind. This shouldn't be seen as the aim of meditation in itself, however. It's simply a way of helping you to settle down, calm the mind and senses and withdraw your attention from the outer world.

Once you've managed to do that, you are ready for Vedantic meditation, as revealed by Krishna in the Bhagavad Gita's sixth chapter:

> With a tranquil mind and an open heart, the meditator contemplates the Self, having That as the ultimate goal, while withdrawing the mind from all else.

Shankara, in his commentary on the Katha Upanishad, describes this meditation as "concentration of the mind upon the Self after withdrawing it from all outer objects."

This means continually contemplating your nature as Awareness.

Gaudapada called it "uniting the tranquil mind with the Self", thus allowing the mind to "become" the Self—or, rather, recognise that its nature is the Self; pure, simple, always present, ever-shining Awareness/Consciousness.

Vedantic meditation means taking a stand in your true nature as the Self. It means owning what you are until this Knowledge is fully assimilated by every level of the mind and psyche.

The guided meditations that follow are different ways of implementing this practice. You can experiment to see which you find most helpful.

Guided Exercise 7:
Vedantic Meditation 1

The following exercise forms a basis for Vedantic meditation. It combines a preparatory relaxation with upasana visualisation and the all-important incorporation of Self-Knowledge.

1. Find a comfortable, quiet and undisturbed place to meditate. Always sit comfortably with your back upright but not rigid; your countenance poised yet relaxed.
2. Consciously withdraw your attention from the world of the senses and direct it within. Set aside all worldly concerns, letting go of the past and future and bringing your full attention to the present moment.
3. Become aware of your breath. Simply be aware of the inflow and the outflow of your breath. Allow it to settle of its own accord, much like the rhythm of the tide; effortlessly flowing in and out. If you feel the need to calm the body and mind, breathe in as normal, hold for a second and lengthen your exhale. Notice how

this effortlessly relaxes you both physically and mentally.

4. While keeping your attention on the rhythm of your breathing, mentally chant the syllable Om as you breathe in and again as you breathe out. Allow its sacred vibration to elevate the mind and open the heart. The syllable Om is an expression of the Self; of that which is Real and True.
5. Turn your mind and heart to the Self; the all-pervading Awareness or Consciousness that is your innermost essence and being.
6. You may want to first visualise this in the form of your personal deity, or simply as a resplendent form of light, shining like the sun, radiating beams of light all around. Feel its light filling your mind and gently flooding your entire body. Allow it to permeate your being; as your mind and senses merge into it.
7. You're now aware that this Divine light is unfathomably vast and expansive, encompassing and pervading the entirety of the universe and all of creation.
8. Sense this boundless light pervading the entire cosmos, illuminating and shining in the heart of all beings as the innermost light, the innermost Consciousness and Existence of all things. This Divine light shines eternally as both the form and essence of all that is. It is Ishvara, God; the Self with form; that which created and is the entire universe.
9. Recognise that the Self is ultimately the invisible; the formless and all-pervading Existence in which the world of form appears and upon which it depends. This Awareness or Consciousness is Existence itself...infinite, eternal and unaffected by anything in the world of form.
10. This Awareness pervades all things and shines as the innermost light, life and being of all things. All beings live only because the Self shines within them. All beings are enlivened by this one, eternal Awareness.

11. The Self, Awareness, is only one. Complete, Whole, Non-dual and Infinitely Full. Contemplate your oneness and unity with this Eternal Self; the nature of which is Existence, Consciousness and Bliss. Recognise that you are the Self. Realise that you are without blemish or defect, beyond birth and death, changeless and limitless, unbound and eternally free.
12. "I Am That". Affirm inwardly, "I Am That".
13. Affirm, "I am Consciousness. I am Awareness...the only Reality."
14. Keep your mind fixed upon this Knowledge. Allow it to soak into your mind and heart; to fully permeate the entirety of your being. "I Am Consciousness. I am Awareness. All else is unreal."
15. When you are ready to end the meditation, gently bring your attention back to the body and the room around you. Don't, however, unconsciously throw away this Self-Knowledge. Instead, keep it with you and reflect on it frequently as you peacefully, consciously resume your day.

I suggest doing this meditation daily for at least three months. The intent isn't to generate a "high" experience, although you should find it particularly enjoyable. Once again, the true purpose of meditation is to apply Self-Knowledge to the mind, allowing it to seep into every level of your being, reorienting your sense of identity from the finite body-mind to the infinite Awareness by which all is experienced.

Guided Exercise 8:
Vedantic Meditation 2 (Short Version)

This is a shortened version of the above meditation and can be practised in only a few minutes.

1. Sitting comfortably, set aside all worldly concerns and allow your

attention to move within.

2. Take a few moments to observe your breath, allowing it to relax and settle of its own accord. As you breathe in, breathe in stillness and peace, and as you breathe out, consciously let go all cares and concerns, allowing them to flow out of you as you release the breath. Do this until you find your body and mind peaceful, calm and open.
3. With your attention fully within, open your heart and mind to the Self; the all-pervading Awareness/Consciousness residing within as your innermost essence and being.
4. Know this Self, this light of Consciousness that you are, as unfathomably vast and expansive, encompassing and pervading the entirety of creation.
5. Sense this boundless Consciousness pervading the entire cosmos, illuminating and shining in the heart of all beings as the innermost light, the innermost being of all things. This pure Consciousness or Awareness is Existence itself...infinite, eternal and unaffected by anything that happens in the finite world of form. All beings live only because the Self shines within them. All beings are enlivened by this one, eternal Awareness.
6. The Self, Awareness, is only one. Complete, whole, Non-dual and Infinitely Full. Contemplate your oneness and unity with this Eternal Self, the nature of which is pure Existence, Consciousness and Bliss. Realise that you are the Self. Realise you are without blemish or defect, beyond birth and death, changeless and limitless, unbound and eternally free.
7. "I Am That". Affirm inwardly, "I Am That". "I Am Consciousness. I Am Awareness. All else is unreal."
8. Take some time now to allow this Knowledge to permeate your mind, heart and entire being.
9. When you are ready to end the meditation, return your attention to your body, become aware of the room, and slowly resume your

day, allowing this Self-Knowledge to stay with you.

Guided Exercise 9:
Contemplating Truth

Vedantic meditation is not about silencing the mind. While the mind should be calm and focused, the goal is not to achieve a completely thoughtless state. The true aim is to use the mind to deeply contemplate Self-Knowledge.

Meditation Statements

This meditation uses a statement of truth as a meditation object. A selection are listed below. You can use whichever statement you like, working your way through each of them, or you can find one of your own, as long as it affirms your true nature as the Self.

Once again, the words Awareness and Consciousness are used interchangeably and point to the same thing. Some people prefer one over the other. Use whichever of the two works best for you, or both.

Limit yourself to only one statement per meditation. The aim is to keep the mind fixed upon it, allowing you to completely and thoroughly contemplate its meaning.

- I Am That [Awareness/Consciousness]
- I Am the Self
- I Am Pure Awareness
- I Am Pure Consciousness
- Consciousness Alone Exists
- I Am Pure Consciousness; all else is unreal.
- I Am Existence; I Am Reality.
- Everything Arises in Me; in My Awareness
- I Am Not the Body, Mind or Ego; I Am the Awareness in Which

They Appear
- As the Self, I Was Never Born, As the Self, I Will Never Die
- My Self, Awareness, Shines As the Heart of All Beings
- This Entire Universe Appears In Me
- I Am Eternal, Ever-Free, Limitless Consciousness
- I Am Free, Unbound Awareness; I Am That
- All I See Appears in Awareness; Awareness Alone Is Real
- I Am Eternal, All-Pervading Consciousness

Contemplation Meditation Practice

1. Find a comfortable place to meditate and try to avoid interruptions and distractions. Sit comfortably and do what you need to settle the body and mind.
2. Consciously withdraw your attention from the world of the senses and direct it within. Set aside all worldly concerns, letting go of the past and future and bringing your full attention to the present moment.
3. In your mind, visualise a vast blue sky; clear, open and expansive, without a cloud in sight. This spacious open sky has no beginning or end and no limitations. Like space, it pervades and encompasses all things. Allow your mind to merge into that sky; to become the sky; to become wide, open and without any boundary or limitation. If any thoughts distract you, see them as little clouds and let them simply drift across the sky of your mind.
4. Take a moment to attune yourself to the Awareness/Consciousness that's within you, that is you, pervading your entire being, blessing you with life, light and sentience.
5. Select a meditation statement from the choices above, or something similar. Repeat the statement in your mind several

times, slowly and purposefully. Keep your attention upon this statement, allowing your mind to fully contemplate and comprehend its meaning and implications. If your attention wanders, simply and gently redirect it to your meditation statement. Allow your mind to become fully absorbed by this statement. Allow it to gradually permeate your being as you reflect deeply upon its meaning.

6. Continue doing this for as long as you wish; steadily and purposefully contemplating the words and their meaning.
7. When you are ready to end the meditation, simply bring your attention back to your body and physical surroundings. Make a special effort to retain this Self-Knowledge as you go about your day.

Guided Exercise 10:
Applied Self-Enquiry

This is an advanced meditative self-enquiry adapted from the book *Adhyatma Yoga* by Swami Satchidanandendra Saraswati. Try to fully grasp each step before moving onto the next.

1. Find a comfortable place to meditate and try to avoid interruptions and distractions.
2. Close your eyes and consciously withdraw your attention from the world of the senses and direct it within. Set aside all worldly concerns, letting go of the past and future and bringing your full attention to the present moment.
3. Notice that when your eyes are closed, the outside world vanishes. Your experience of the outside world happens via the five senses: sight, sound, touch, taste and smell.
4. Without the sense organs, there would be no world for you.

Aside from the information provided by these sense organs, there is no proof whatsoever of an external, independently existent world. You experience the world within you. You cannot experience it outside of you; which is to say, independently of your senses. Let go, then, of clinging to the outer world and contemplate this: the sense organs are the "Self" by which the external world is known. This Self is within; it pervades all things; it exists independently of all things; and is subtler than all things.

5. Now, try to find the source of your sense organs. What is it that enables the senses to be known? The information delivered by the sense organs is known by the mind. Without the mind, no sensory information would be possible. The mind is, therefore, the "Self" of the senses. This Self is within; it pervades all things; it exists independently of all things; and is subtler than all things.

6. Beyond the mind, with its various thoughts, feelings and agitations, is the intellect. The intellect is that which takes the experience of the mind, analyses and interprets it, and determines courses of action. Without the intellect, the mind would be unable to function. Intellect, therefore, is the "Self" of the mind. This Self is within; it pervades all things; it exists independently of all things; and is subtler than all things.

7. Beyond the intellect is the ego; the centre of your "I-sense"; the sense of being an individual, autonomous being. The ego personalises the intellect. Thoughts are no longer just thoughts; they are "my" thoughts; "my" ideas; "my" beliefs. Pleasure and pain are experienced by the senses and mind—and the ego, through its sense of identification, owns the pleasure and pain. It becomes the "enjoyer" and "experiencer" of the functioning of the senses, mind and intellect. Where there is no ego, as in deep sleep, there is no trace of any kind of world. Ego is, therefore, the "Self" of the intellect. This Self is within; it pervades all things;

it exists independently of all things; and is subtler than all things.

8. Beyond the ego is that which witnesses the ego. How else would the ego be known? Ego exists as the innermost "I-sense", but that "I-sense" is known to you by the witnessing Awareness. Your identification with ego will cease when you realise that, as Awareness, you are witness to the ego, and to the intellect, the mind and the sense organs. Awareness is, therefore, the "Self" of the ego. This Self is within; it pervades all things; it exists independently of all things; and is subtler than all things. This Self is that by which all is known.

9. Knowing the truth that all is perceivable only by Awareness, which itself cannot be perceived, take a stand in Awareness; your own Self. Ramana Maharshi declared, "To know the Self is to be the Self and to be the Self is to cease identification with the not-Self."

10. The Self, Awareness, is that in which all things appear, from the ego, mind and thoughts to the outer world perceived by the senses. All these components exist in the Self, in Awareness, and can only be experienced by virtue of Awareness. Their existence depends upon Awareness. Awareness pervades all things, just as water pervades the waves and the entire ocean.

11. Just as the desert mirage has no existence or substance apart from the sand, all phenomenal experiences have no existence apart from the Self. We can, therefore, conclude that the Self is the Absolute and unchanging Reality and the world is but a false appearance.

12. Abide in Awareness as Awareness. Recognise you don't have to do anything in order to become the Self. The Self is always present, always immediate, always self-luminous and available. The only effort needed to "attain" the Self is to remove your false identification with the objects appearing in the Self, from the body and sense organs to the mind, intellect and ego. In order for

the Truth to be known, all you must do is to negate the false.
13. Remain in this contemplation as long as you wish, before resuming your day. Try to reflect upon this Knowledge as frequently as possible, allowing it to deeply sink into the mind, heart and psyche.

Guided Exercise 11:
Awareness Meditation

This meditation is an expansion of the Awareness meditation in Chapter Ten. The aim is to redirect the mind to its source, Awareness, and keep it merged there as long as possible.

1. Find a comfortable place to meditate and try to avoid interruptions and distractions. Sit comfortably with your back upright, relaxed and not rigid.
2. Consciously withdraw your attention from the world of the senses and direct it within. Set aside all worldly concerns, letting go of the past and future and bringing your full attention to the present moment.
3. Become aware of your breath and allow it to settle of its own accord. Simply be aware of the inflow and the outflow of your breath like the rhythm of the tide. If you feel the need to calm the body and mind, simply lengthen your exhale slightly by a few seconds and notice how this effortlessly relaxes both body and mind.
4. Turning your attention within, become aware of the fact you are aware. Know that Awareness or Consciousness is always present, regardless of what you are or aren't aware of. The objects come and go, but Awareness remains. This is the Awareness that illuminates your waking world. This is the Awareness that illuminates your dreamworld. And it's also the Awareness

present in the objectless realm of deep sleep. Even when there's no object to be aware of, Awareness is always present.

5. See if you can locate Awareness. Does it have a specific location? Does it have a beginning or an end? Or is it, in fact, present everywhere, pervading all things?
6. Does this Awareness have a shape, form or colour? Or is it without attributes, form or qualities of any kind? Does it have an age? Is it a young Awareness or an old Awareness? Or is it just Awareness? Does it have a gender? Is it a male Awareness, a female Awareness, or neither?
7. Does Awareness lack anything? Is there anything that can be added to it or taken away from it? Or is it whole and complete in itself?
8. Is there any distance between you and Awareness? Or are you, in fact, one and the same?
9. For the remainder of the meditation, simply, gently, effortlessly keep your mind and attention focused upon Awareness; which is you! Become absorbed in it. Abide in Awareness as Awareness. Know Awareness. Rest as Awareness; simple, immediate, direct, self-evident Awareness; the light by which all things are known.
10. If your mind begins wandering, simply redirect it back to Awareness of Awareness. Expansive, spacious, encompassing and free; Awareness is you; the very ground of your Existence. Know yourself as That which knows. Observe yourself as That which observes. Take a stand in Awareness. Abide in Awareness as Awareness.
11. Meditate in this way as long as you like. When you are ready, simply bring your attention to back to the room and to your body, while continuing to retain the Knowledge and direct recognition that you are the Awareness in which the entire world appears.

Make Your Life Your Meditation

The above meditations are formal, seated meditations that can be practised at an allotted time each day. Ideally, however, your entire life should become your meditation.

Recall that your goal is liberation through Self-Realisation. Self-Realisation means to realise and fully abide as your Self; Awareness. The first two stages of Vedanta impart and clarify Self-Knowledge. The third and final stage is to consistently contemplate and reflect upon this Knowledge until it's accepted as self-evident fact.

The Katha Upanishad makes the following promise:

> The wise, who, by means of concentration on the Self, realise the timeless, effulgent Self—which is beyond the senses, unmanifest and which illumines the intellect and enlivens the body—do indeed leave sorrow far behind.

The key statement here is "concentration on the Self". All this time, you've laboured under the delusion of being nothing but a crude mix of mind and matter. Self-Knowledge reveals the body and mind to be but temporary, finite instruments through which the Self transacts with the world.

Shifting your sense of identification from these limited objects to the limitless subject, Awareness, naturally takes time. That's why it's essential that you continue contemplating the Knowledge, "I am Awareness; I am Consciousness" until it completely overwrites the intellect's old patterns of ignorance and misidentification.

You must be committed for the duration. It may only take minutes to hear Self-Knowledge. It then may take hours, days or months to fully understand it and eradicate any doubts and confusion. The final stage, the full assimilation of that Knowledge may take years—and that's okay.

Liberation is the ultimate attainment. It is that by which one attains all that is to be attained in life; complete satisfaction, contentment and Wholeness. It is, therefore, unquestionably worth any investment of time, energy and effort that might be necessary.

If you need any more motivation, consider these words of Shankara:

> He who has recognised Brahman as himself, as the very Witness manifest in one's own mind—what happens to him? The scriptures say that the knower of Brahman attains or enjoys everything without exception, all that is desired is now attained.

Final Tips For Practising Self-Knowledge

Here are some principles and techniques to deepen your integration and assimilation of Self-Knowledge.

- Self Remembering. As you go about your day, train your mind to have a dual focus. That means being aware not only of the outer world of objects and the inner world of your mind and senses, but also aware that you are the Awareness in which these objects appear. The objects themselves come and go, moment to moment, but the Awareness that you are is always present and never changes.
- In the midst of daily living, keep the thought "I am Awareness" or "I am Consciousness" looping in your mind. Let it be your mantra. Contemplate its meaning as often as possible.
- Enquiry into the Changeless. Notice how Awareness is never touched by anything and never modifies to experience. In fact, the Awareness looking down at your adult body right now is the very same Awareness that perceived your body as an infant. All the objects perceived by Awareness are subject to change, but

you, Awareness, are changeless.
- Learn to discriminate that which changes from that which never changes. All objects are temporary and time-bound—but you, Awareness, are always present.
- Recognise that, contrary to popular assumption, Awareness doesn't somehow appear in your body and mind. Rather, your body and mind appear in Awareness. Notice how this is true in your own immediate, direct experience. Everything that you experience you experience in Awareness. You have to! There's no other way of experiencing anything. This means that *you don't appear in the world. The world appears in you.*
- Recognise that absolutely anything can be subtracted from you except Awareness. People, objects and experiences come and go every moment of the day, but through it all Awareness remains—because that is what you are.
- Train your mind to practice self-enquiry until it becomes an automatic reflex. Whenever your catch yourself identifying with your body, mind, thoughts, feelings or beliefs, recognise that these are objects appearing in you; the subject. They aren't you. They are known to you. This discrimination of the subject, you, from the objects appearing in you, is one of the pivotal Vedantic techniques for liberating the mind.
- Whatever your current experience, make it a habit to ask yourself: *"How do I know this?" "By what is this revealed?" "What is it that knows/sees/feels/hears?"* The answer will always be Awareness—and you are that Awareness.

Be consistent in the contemplation of your identity as Awareness and you will soon begin noticing results. Bit by bit, you loosen the bonds of your misidentification with the body and mind. You begin to experience the freedom of a far vaster and truer identity; the spacious Awareness in which all things come and go; the Self—the source of all love, bliss, contentment and joy.

Don't just take my word for it, though. Find out for yourself! Like most things of value in life, it will take work; steady, consistent, diligent work. So, start right now and make your life your meditation.

Summary

- Vedantic meditation differs from other forms of meditation in its purpose. Whereas most meditation techniques aim to relax the body and mind and perhaps develop concentration, Vedantic meditation is used to attain Self-Realisation or liberation.
- This meditation or contemplation is the third and final stage of Vedanta. Once Self-Knowledge has been acquired and all doubts resolved, this Knowledge must be applied to the mind via sustained meditation.
- Vedantic meditation allows for the full integration and assimilation of the knowledge "I am Awareness/Consciousness".
- The secret of Vedantic meditation is to continually contemplate the Self and your identity as the Self, while withdrawing the mind from all else.
- This removes the last vestiges of self-ignorance and reorients your identity from the mind-body-sense complex to pure Awareness/Consciousness.

20.

Troubleshooting, FAQs and Pitfalls on the Path

Arise, awaken! Find an illumined teacher and open your
mind to the light of Truth. As sharp as a razor's edge, the
spiritual path is hard and difficult to traverse.
Katha Upanishad

The road less travelled comes with challenges, to be sure. You'd think it should be easy given that what you're seeking you already are—the Self; something you already have and can never lose!

Indeed, the secret of enlightenment is knowing that you don't have to add anything to yourself in order to be free, for you already have and are everything you could ever possibly want and desire. The source of all freedom, joy, contentment and love is already there, within you. It is you!

Liberation is owning this knowledge. It's the realisation that your very nature is freedom.

In the end, all you need do is remove the ignorance that's prevented you from apprehending what you truly are; not a limited mortal form, nor a mind full of thoughts, desires and sorrow, but the ever-present, self-shining Awareness in which these rise and subside like bubbles in the ocean.

When you remove the false, what remains is Truth. You finally see things—the world, Reality and your own Self—as they truly are and no longer through a distorted mirror of ignorance.

Ignorance, however, can be a relentless foe.

That's why it's important to work with a qualified teacher. They know the territory, are aware of the dangers, and can guide you safely to your destination. A good teacher will help you work through any doubts or questions and, once it all "clicks", it's then up to you to meditate upon that Knowledge until it truly sinks in.

This penultimate chapter takes the form of a troubleshooting guide, a collection of frequently asked questions and a warning of one of the biggest dangers along the path: enlightenment sickness.

Enlightenment Troubleshooting Guide

Q: Help! It isn't working! I've tried hard but I'm absolutely no closer to liberation!

A: Check the following solutions.

1. Are You Qualified?

Everyone knows the cliché of calling a technical helpline and immediately being asked: "Are you sure it's properly connected and switched on?"

The Vedanta equivalent of this is: are you qualified? Have you sufficiently prepared the mind for Self-Knowledge?

The teacher's job is to teach. The student must come prepared, however. Your job is to sufficiently tame the mind by following dharma, clarifying your values and practising karma yoga.

This, in time, leads to a peaceful, sattvic and steady mind. You find that life becomes easier, simpler and emotional disturbances less consuming and frequent.

It's not that the external world changes. It's your ability to handle it that changes. A qualified, refined mind is a mind capable of receiving, understanding and internalising the Knowledge, "I am Awareness".

The fifth chapter of this book is one of the most important. Refer to it often. See how well you're managing to develop the qualities of discrimination or discernment, dispassion, discipline of the mind and senses and the desire for liberation.

It's admittedly no easy feat, particularly when one must deal with the stresses and strains of worldly living. It is, however, essential that the mind be appropriately prepared for Self-Knowledge. It's only then that Self-Knowledge translates into tangible and lasting freedom.

When it comes to enlightenment, it really is the presence or absence of the mental qualifications that determines success or failure.

This isn't a one-time fix, either. Like everyone, your qualifications will naturally fluctuate over time. That's why it's necessary to exercise continual vigilance, to remain committed to dharma and to keep practising karma yoga and upasana yoga. These transformative tools prime the mind for the integration and assimilation of Self-Knowledge, which alone leads to freedom.

2. Are You Patient?

As the saying goes, Rome wasn't built in a day. Sometimes students have unrealistic expectations. They're looking for a quick fix and instant gratification. Needless to say, there's no shortcut to any place worth going. It takes time to reorient your sense of identity from a deeply ingrained sense of lack and limitation to the freedom and expansiveness of simply being Awareness.

The irony is, yes, you already are the Self! At times, this realisation may hit you with such force that it stuns the mind, enabling you to taste the bliss of a spiritual epiphany. This happens when your mind and heart fall into alignment with the Truth of who you are.

The problem is you can almost bet that the gravity of ignorance will soon misalign the intellect once more, yanking you back into misidentification with the ego-self and the seemingly endless problems that come with this false identity.

Be patient and consistent. Take everything one step at a time. There's no hurry to get where you're going (because ultimately you're already there; you just don't know it yet!).

Unless you happen to be blessed with an extraordinarily pure and disciplined mind, it will take time to go through the process of acquiring, understanding and assimilating Self-Knowledge.

The first stage of Vedanta, listening, can take months or years. The second stage, reasoning, may take even longer. It's important not to sidestep any doubts or confusion. You have to fully grasp what is being taught in order for it to work. The final stage, the contemplation and integration of this Knowledge may take an indefinite amount of time (which isn't to say that you won't begin seeing the results of Self-Knowledge, because you surely will).

To give students a very rough approximation of how much time may be needed, Swami Paramarthananda talks of the five-ten-fifteen rule. According to the Swami, the listening stage might take up to five years. The reasoning stage may require up to ten years. Finally, the contemplation stage may need as many as fifteen years. That said, it is recommended that you continue practising the final stage indefinitely, just to keep the mind in check and prevent ignorance from again taking the reins. We'll explore this phenomenon when we discuss enlightenment sickness.

3. Have You Adopted a Beginner's Mind?

It's impossible to fill a jug that's already filled to the brim. Some spiritual seekers spend a lifetime going from this path to that path, and this teacher to the next teacher. Over time, the mind assumes that it's accumulated a great deal of knowledge and wisdom.

This can lead to a certain spiritual pride which makes learning difficult. For how can a student learn when they already think they pretty much know it all?

This can be a profound problem for many seekers. Under the spell of confirmation bias, that most slippery of cognitive biases, they seek only teachers and teachings they "resonate with"; or, in other words, which confirm what they already believe is true. They engage in pick-and-mix spirituality; selecting the ideas they like and discarding those they dislike or don't understand.

How can such a person learn when they already think they have the answers?

Vedanta is a complete teaching—and it only works if you follow the instructions and do it Vedanta's way.

It takes a while to paint the whole picture and to understand every aspect of the teaching. Some neophyte students, subject to impatience, may prematurely assume that just because they don't "get it", Vedanta hasn't "got it!"

It's imperative that, as a student, you approach the teaching with the humility of a beginner's mind. At least temporarily, while listening to the teaching, you must set aside what you think you already know in order to open your mind to what is being taught.

That said, Vedanta doesn't work on blind faith. We don't tell you to shut down the mind. Rather, we insist that you use it. You must engage your intellect in order to fully understand what's being taught.

It does require an initial faith; but it's a faith pending the results of your own investigation.

The student needs to show up with an open, curious mind and be willing to listen to what's being said.

Remember that ignorance conditions the mind—and if you were already free, you wouldn't still be seeking liberation.

It's a sobering fact for the ego to admit, but it's not until you recognise that you *don't know* that you're finally open to knowledge.

So, be humble, be open and be willing to set aside your existing beliefs and ideas in order to expand your mind.

4. Are You Seeking Experience or Knowledge?

One of the pitfalls the spiritual seeker can easily fall into is the idea that enlightenment is an *experience:* a greater, elevated experience; the experience to end all experiences!

The human being is, by nature, experience hungry and this extends to the spiritual sphere, where some students go to extraordinary lengths—kundalini yoga, tantra, shamanism, all kinds of meditation, *shaktipat gurus* (yogis capable of transferring bursts of energy), and so on—in order to get a spiritual high.

Enlightenment should never be viewed as some kind of experience you can generate for yourself. Certainly, liberation will have a massive affect on the way you experience yourself and life, as we'll see in the final chapter. But it's not some kind of supercharged, cosmic state of ecstasy that you're seeking. All states and experiences, no matter how wondrous and exalted, are mithya, meaning only apparently real. They belong to the world of form; and the Self, that which you seek, is beyond form.

Nothing in the world of mithya lasts. The deepest *samadhi* (state of absorption in meditation), no matter how blissful, inevitably has a beginning and end. You can be enjoying the most sublime meditation and then a fly lands on your nose and—bam, the experience is over.

Spiritual epiphanies and experiential highs are wonderful, but do not, in themselves, constitute liberation. If anything, they can actually hinder it. Why? Firstly, all experiences are finite and fleeting;

what has a beginning will necessarily have an end. Secondly, it's very easy to become attached to such experiences; and attachment only ever leads to bondage.

If you feel you need anything in order to be free, then you're not free. Freedom means you don't depend on anything outside of you for your happiness and wholeness.

When you're free, you don't need to experience any particular state in order to be whole and complete. Instead, you realise that you are whole and complete regardless of your current experience.

Therefore, remember that enlightenment isn't about experiencing spiritual highs or heightened states of consciousness. Liberation is solely the result of Self-Knowledge; of knowing who and what you truly are and taking a stand in your nature as Awareness; the one thing that depends on nothing else for its existence.

5. Do You Have Enough Desire For Liberation?

One of the most crucial qualifications for enlightenment is the desire to be free. The stronger your desire to be free, the more focused and motivated you'll be to do what needs to be done and follow through with your spiritual goal.

As we saw in the chapter on values, when a value isn't strong enough or is countermanded by other, competing values, the value is only partially assimilated.

It's not uncommon for spiritual seekers to have a desire for enlightenment but also the desire to attain worldly success and material goals, whatever they might be. This creates inner conflict. The value that wins out will be the one that's strongest.

Who determines which value is strongest? You do!

Assuming, that is, you assert your will and consciously choose what's most important to you rather than allowing your unconscious conditioning to determine your priorities for you.

Your goal to be free must be so strong that it supersedes all other goals. If it's not, you'll find yourself frittering away your time and energy pursuing various conditioned likes and dislikes.

Therefore, be clear on your highest value, your greatest goal, and commit to that with passion and persistence. Take to the heart these words from the Buddhist Master Dogen:

> Life and death are of supreme importance. Time swiftly passes by and opportunity is lost. Each of us should strive to awaken! Take heed, and do not squander your life.

Frequently Asked Questions

Q: Why don't other traditions talk about qualifications?

A: Most teachings and teachers want to appeal to as wide a range of people as possible. Telling potential students that the teaching won't work unless they first have an appropriately qualified mind would most certainly throw a spanner in the works.

Many modern teachers will promise that anyone can attain enlightenment, even though, if you look into their success rate, the number of people attaining liberation through their teaching is not encouraging, to say the least.

Therefore, try not to see the qualifications as a bad thing. They actually explain why out of the millions of people seeking enlightenment, so few ever do. The fault lies not in the cruel hand of fate. It lies in the readiness or lack of readiness of the mind to accept, understand and integrate Self-Knowledge.

That can be remedied if you so choose. The application of dharma, karma yoga, upasana meditation and guna management will prepare the mind for liberation—and, as a happy byproduct, they're also magnificent stress busters!

Chapter 20: Troubleshooting, FAQs and Pitfalls on the Path

Q: Just how qualified must my mind be in order for Vedanta to work?

A: Perfection is neither required nor necessary. All things in the world of duality are imperfect by nature (or, you might say, perfect in their imperfection).

That includes the individual being, which will always be subject to some issue or another. At a personal level, many of us have an incredible amount of psychic debris, dysfunctional conditioning and unresolved hurts and wounds from childhood and beyond.

Those with particularly severe issues and mental health problems should seek the intervention of a competent psychologist or mental healthcare professional. Vedanta is a tool for Self-Knowledge and isn't designed to deal with mental health afflictions beyond ignorance of our nature.

In general, for most people, the tools of karma yoga, upasana meditation and guna management should be sufficient for managing the mind, along with cultivating the dharmic values outlined in Chapter Six.

Q: Isn't Vedanta a kind of spiritual bypassing?

A: A valid question. In the Bhagavad Gita, Krishna says:

> The shifting qualities of sattva, rajas and tamas shape the things of this world, but I remain unconditioned by them. These qualities of creation exist in Me, but I am not in them.

Some might call this spiritual bypassing. It's actually just knowledge of Reality. Vedanta is essentially a spiritual recontexualising, which means seeing things from the perspective of the Self rather than the individual body-mind-sense complex.

Vedanta is not about ignoring or failing to deal with our personal issues, duties and responsibilities. Indeed, removing our misidentification with the ego enables us to deal with life with far greater ease and efficiency, for we know that regardless of what might be going on in or around the body-mind, we, ourselves, are unaffected.

One of the prerequisites for liberation is living a life of dharma. Dharma means performing our duties in the world and dealing with whatever situations and problems arise in an appropriate and timely manner.

That's one of the key messages of the Bhagavad Gita. Arjuna, the Gita's protagonist, attempts to get out of his duties and bypass his problems by seeking renunciation (something that isn't aligned with his nature and duty). Krishna will not let him. He states that, above all else, Arjuna must do his duty. That applies to all of us.

There's no getting around the fact that we all have certain duties and responsibilities to take care of in the world. When done in the spirit of karma yoga, we don't bypass our problems. We face them head on, responding appropriately to each situation as it presents itself. We allow dharma to guide our actions and leave it to Ishvara to take care of the results of those actions.

Q: How do I overcome attachment to worldly objects?

A: The issue of attachment can be a problem for many people.

First of all, it's important to note that there are two types of desire: non-binding and binding desires.

Non-binding desires are the manifestation of our likes and dislikes and exist as simple preferences. We naturally prefer one thing over another, although it shouldn't cause too much suffering if you can't get it. Such preferences are natural and unlikely to cause significant problems.

Binding desires, however, take the form of compulsions, addictions and cravings. This results in attachments of varying degrees of strength. If something happens to get between you and the object of your desire, you may experience a significant degree of mental and emotional turmoil. If the attachment is strong enough, the resultant suffering may be enough to completely incapacitate the mind. It's these binding desires and their subsequent attachments that should be minimised.

The spiritual practises offered by Vedanta naturally help eradicate binding attachments: specifically, living by dharmic values, karma yoga, upasana yoga, guna management and meditation. These naturally foster discrimination and dispassion; two key qualities of a pure mind.

It also helps to practise objectivity. Practising objectivity means viewing the object of your attachment with complete impartiality. It means stripping away whatever subjective values and qualities you've superimposed onto the object. By reducing an object to its own status, you see things as they are rather than as you think they are or want them to be.

If that still doesn't lessen the bonds of attachment, you might spend some time contemplating the downsides of that particular object. We only want a thing because we've been sold on whatever upside and benefits it might confer; but what are the downsides and disadvantages of that particular object? Consistently focusing on the less appealing qualities of an object will easily reduce your attachment to it.

Q: Can I pursue Vedanta if I belong to another religion?

A: Absolutely. Vedanta is not at odds with religion. It's a means of knowledge for understanding the nature of Reality. You can still worship whatever God or deities you have grown up to love and revere. Vedanta does not delegitimise other religions, although it does recontexualise them.

It is, however, important to be able to let go of dogma and to open your mind to what Vedanta teaches. It can be all too easy to judge and evaluate the teaching through the lens of your preexisting beliefs and ideas. Instead, it's important to set aside what you think you already know in order to hear what Vedanta is saying. Strive to be open, curious and eager to expand your understanding.

Q: How do I explain Vedanta to friends, family and other people?

A: Whereas Buddhism was successfully exported across the world and is known by all, the average person is unlikely to have heard of Vedanta. Even many spiritual types may give you a quizzical look when you mention it.

That's in spite of the fact that Vedanta's core principles can be found at the root of various other traditions and approaches, including Buddhism (which borrows most of its key concepts from the Vedas), Theosophy, various New Age teachings and the modern Advaita or Non-Duality scene.

You might describe Vedanta as the philosophical basis of Hinduism, which is at least something people can grasp. You could also tell a curious person that Vedanta is neither a religion nor a philosophy but a different way of understanding the nature of Reality and who we are, based on the teaching of the ancient Vedas.

Q: Is it necessary to believe in God?

A: This is a common issue, particularly for Westerners disillusioned or even wounded by conventional religion and who find themselves uncomfortable with the notion of God. A common mistake is that instead of simply throwing away illogical, unhealthy and outdated notions about God, people throw away God itself.

Vedanta provides a highly logical and multifaceted understanding of what God is. You needn't get hooked up on God as a particular name or form, but you do need to open yourself to the basic teachings.

There's no getting around the fact that for the universe to exist there must be both a creative principle and a substance from which it is made. Any effect automatically presupposes a cause. That cause is Ishvara; the Self plus the power of maya.

Of course, you don't need to use the word "God" if you don't want to. Use whatever word or term you're comfortable with. Vedanta generally uses the term Ishvara. It's just a name for the unnameable. Heck, you could use the name Ken or Sandra if you wanted!

There's no getting away from Ishvara. Ishvara is the very environment around you, and the micro-environment of your own body and mind. It's the substance and essence of everything in the material world; and the force by which the stars shine, the planets spin, rivers flow and your body circulates blood and digests food. Ishvara, God, is everywhere all around and within you. Everything existent is God. So, it's not a matter of belief but a matter of what is.

While the ignorant abuse and distort the idea of God, waging childish battles over "my God" and "your God", Vedanta is resolutely clear that God is everywhere and in everything. In fact, there is nothing but God.

Q: Can Vedanta help me deal with my everyday, worldly problems?

A: Vedanta is a means of Self-Knowledge; nothing less, nothing more. It has nothing whatsoever to do with personal development or material attainment. That said, the preparatory practices, such as karma yoga, dharma and managing the gunas, are superb at neutralising the stresses of daily life and making life flow with greater ease, simplicity and objectivity. This is a pleasant side effect of preparing the mind for Self-Knowledge.

Q: How does Vedanta address the issue of evil?

A: Vedanta describes evil as adharma; the polar opposite of dharma, the moral law underpinning the creation. Adharma arises from self-ignorance and humankind's abuse of free will.

Ignorance blinds us to the fact that when we harm another we're actually harming ourselves, for there is only one Self inhabiting various different forms. This "original sin", the inability to see ourselves as we truly are, creates a fundamental sense of lack and fear and this lies at the root of pretty much all a person's desires, attachments and aversions.

Dharmic people know that, irrespective of their desires, they must always follow dharma and abide by righteous, lawful conduct. The Vedas describe dharma as our protector because it protects us, others and the environment from unnecessary harm and suffering.

Those who ruthlessly pursue their personal desires at the expense of dharma might be described as evil. Driven by self-ignorance, overpowered by selfishness and lacking care and empathy for others, they are willing to inflict suffering on others and the world around them. Such adharmic people should be avoided and stopped where possible for the safety of others and the integrity of society.

Evil, then, is not a product of Ishvara. It arises from ignorant mankind's misalignment with Ishvara, which is synonymous with dharma.

Q: If everything is Consciousness, why don't I experience your mind and thoughts?

A: At the Absolute order of Reality, there's only one universal Consciousness. At this relative order of reality, the empirical world of maya, Consciousness functions through many different body-mind-sense complexes; each of which serves as a reflecting medium.

You don't experience my mind and thoughts because, while we both reflect the same Consciousness, our respective reflecting mediums, the three bodies, are different. Your thoughts and feelings are specific to your reflecting medium; mine are specific to mine.

Enlightenment Sickness: The Number One Pitfall on the Path

Traditionally, Vedanta was only taught to advanced seekers who had spent significant time purifying, refining and polishing their mind and intellect.

This wasn't out of elitism or snobbery. The reason was simple. Only those with relatively pure minds are likely to grasp and assimilate the teaching. Such students are also far less likely to succumb to potential pitfalls on the path. Enlightenment sickness, or spiritual narcissism, is perhaps the number one pitfall and something that every spiritual seeker should be aware of.

When properly integrated, Self-Knowledge should humble the ego into submission with the realisation that it is, in fact, only apparently real (mithya). Despite masquerading as the epicentre of your being, the ego-self is actually a hollow phantom; an epiphenomenon with no inherent existence of its own. It is, along with the other components of the subtle body, just an appearance in Consciousness; not Consciousness itself.

Unfortunately, ignorance rarely dies an easy death. The ego will most certainly cling on for dear life even as the light of Self-Knowledge threatens to usurp its reign.

If the ego hasn't been sufficiently neutralised by spiritual practice—and one's identification with it negated by self-enquiry—problems almost certainly lie ahead.

The ego, always seeking to elevate itself and to consolidate a stronger and more solid sense of identity, will happily seize upon the

Knowledge, "I am the Self; limitless and unbound" and use it to create a new identity for itself; a kind of spiritual super-ego.

This is like a self-assured wave claiming to be the ocean. Yes, the wave is part of the ocean and both the wave and the ocean share the same essential nature: water. The wave cannot claim to be the ocean, however. It ought to be humble, for it is just part of the ocean and completely dependent on the ocean for its existence.

In the same way, the ego cannot claim to be the Self. The Self is the Self; Consciousness is Consciousness. The Knowledge "I am the Self" is meant for those who have first negated the ego identity. Rather than giving the ego something to *add* to itself and to claim as its own, the Knowledge "I am the Self" ought to shift one's identification *from* the ego *to* the Self.

Those who understand that they are the Self, and who identify as the Self, are liberated. On the other hand, those who still believe they are the ego, and yet claim to be Self, are dangerously deluded. They've inadvertently inflated the ego to godlike proportions.

This is called enlightenment sickness. I tend to call it spiritual narcissism because the individual in question isn't actually enlightened; they just think they are.

It's a subtle yet dangerous distortion of Self-Knowledge and is the reason this teaching is only intended for highly mature and qualified seekers.

Unfortunately, spiritual narcissism is all too common in the spiritual arena. All it takes is a single epiphany; somebody gets taste of the limitlessness of their true nature, and then their ego butts in, deciding it's hit the jackpot. The ego declares, "I'm enlightened," "I'm the Self", "I'm God" and then feels the need to broadcast to the world how enlightened—and, therefore, how special and exalted—they are.

Of course, they've missed the point entirely. Being the Self is neither an accomplishment nor some unique achievement. How could it be when we're all the same Self?

Those under the spell of spiritual narcissism may think that they're free, but that "freedom" is based on an erroneous sense of feeling superior to others. Such people are still very much driven by samsara and the need to attain recognition, validation, power, money and influence in order to feel happy and content.

Unfortunately, their inflated sense of power often makes them prone to acts of adharma because they feel normal rules of conduct no longer apply to them. They often misuse the teaching "I am not the doer" to justify exploiting and abusing others, whether for money, power, sex or all of the above.

Spiritual narcissists often have a degree of charisma which they use to build followings; usually innocent and genuine spiritual seekers with a tendency to see only what they want to see in their exalted "guru".

Spiritual narcissism or enlightenment sickness is the ugly side of spirituality. It can be easy to spot if you have sufficient discrimination and dispassion. Cult leaders have been doing this throughout the ages; casting a spell over naïve disciples often with the flimsiest or most nonsensical teachings. Sometimes, however, they're not as easy to spot, because they are less overt in their exploitation.

The bad news is that enlightenment sickness isn't easy to spot in oneself. In order to see it, you need a high degree of dispassion, self-honesty and objectivity.

The good news is that if you have a qualified teacher, are versed in the scriptures and have sufficiently purified your mind to meet the qualification criteria, this malady is far less likely to occur.

The crux of Vedanta is understanding and claiming the Knowledge, "I am the Self", with the full understanding that the Self is

Consciousness or Awareness and is not subject to lack or limitation of any kind.

Prior to claiming this Knowledge, it's essential that you first negate the body, mind, intellect and ego as mithya, unreal, or "not-Self". These are simply components of the gross and subtle body; instruments through which you, as Consciousness, transact with the world. It's essential that you divest any sense of identification from these instruments and place that identification where it belongs: Consciousness alone.

Left unchecked, the ego will try to own Consciousness, but Consciousness belongs entirely to itself. Consciousness does not rely upon the ego. It exists with or without the ego. The ego, however, relies upon Consciousness for its existence.

Consciousness is satya (real) and the ego, like anything perceivable as an object, is mithya (unreal).

The nuance here is subtle. That's why it's important to have a competent teacher and to follow the teaching to the letter.

In our fiercely individualistic society, an attitude of "anything goes" often spills even into the spiritual field. This is catnip for the ego and an often irresistible invitation for it to, either wilfully or ignorantly, misinterpret and distort spiritual teaching for its own ends. That's something that must be avoided at all costs.

If at any point you catch yourself leaning into spiritual narcissism, first of all congratulate yourself for having the objectivity and self-awareness to notice it!

Then, go back to the beginning, double down on the preparatory spiritual practises such as karma yoga, find a teacher if you haven't already, and start afresh with a beginner's mind.

It doesn't matter that you slipped. Everyone does at some point. Simply dust yourself off, be humble and start over again.

Every day is a new life, every moment a fresh start, every second an opportunity to realise the Infinite Wholeness you are.

Summary

- If you're having trouble progressing on the path, first of all, always check in to make sure you have the necessary qualifications. It also pays to cultivate patience, a beginner's mind, be sure you're clear that you are seeking knowledge rather than some experiential state and make sure that you have sufficient desire for liberation.
- The qualifications are what determines success or failure. Perfection is not necessary, however. The key is to learn basic mind management through the practice of karma yoga, dharma, upasana yoga and meditation.
- Vedanta is not spiritual bypassing. It is spiritual recontextualising based on a radical new understanding of Reality.
- Attachment to worldly objects can be overcome by dharmic living, karma yoga, meditation, the practice of objectivity and, if necessary, contemplation of the downsides of a particular object.
- Some seekers struggle with the concept of God and tend to reject it altogether. Vedanta provides a logical and clear understanding of the nature of the Self, Reality, God and the universe. You needn't get hung up on the word "God", however. Use the term Ishvara, or any other word you like.
- Vedanta is not designed to eradicate mental health problems or to facilitate personal development or material gain. It's strictly a means of Self-Knowledge. The preparatory practises do, however, come with all kinds of benefits; a pleasing byproduct of preparing the mind for Self-Knowledge.
- One of the biggest pitfalls on the path is enlightenment sickness or spiritual narcissism. This happens when the ego co-opts the knowledge "I am the Self" and uses it to create a new, inflated ego identity for itself.

- At worst, enlightenment sickness can cause people to use their newfound spiritual identity to seek fame and dominance over others; as in the case of corrupt spiritual teachers and cult leaders. If the student hasn't sufficiently purified their mind prior to seeking Self-Knowledge, the teaching can be misused by the ego in a number of ways, including as a justification for adharma.
- Enlightenment sickness is very common and is only ever a thought away. If you catch yourself falling into this subtle form of ego inflation, congratulate yourself for noticing it, go back to the beginning and double down on the preparatory spiritual practices. Be diligent and self-aware and realise that every moment is a new beginning and a fresh opportunity to shift your identity from the ego to the Self.

21.
A Life of Freedom

> It is true that the body is perishable, but within it dwells the imperishable Self. This body is subject to pleasure and pain; no one who identifies with the body can escape this pleasure and pain. But those who know they are not the body pass beyond pleasure and pain to live in abiding joy.
> *Chandogya Upanishad*

By now, it should be clear that enlightenment means liberation; specifically, liberation from the fundamental sense of lack, incompleteness and insecurity which is a product of ignorance and common to virtually all human beings.

Whether we're aware of it or not, and most people aren't, everything that we do in life is motivated by the desire to be free of this innermost sense of bondage.

Worldly people generally seek freedom by devoting their lives to the pursuit of objects—whether it be money, possessions, attainments, success in work and love, or endlessly indulging the senses in the hope of finally satisfying their hunger.

Unfortunately, samsara is a state of perpetual frustration. While sometimes we manage to attain the things we want, oftentimes we don't and, either way, the fundamental problem remains; that gnawing wound of dissatisfaction with ourselves and our lives.

There are rare souls, however, who, driven by an unquenchable spiritual thirst, dare to go against the grain. Having already decided that, whether we win or lose, there's nothing in the world capable of delivering lasting happiness, they take an altogether different approach.

They turn within and seek a solution inside themselves.

This was spoken of thousands of years ago in the Katha Upanishad:

> The self-existent Lord created the senses to turn outward. That's why we look to the world outside and fail to see the Self within. The wise, guided by the scriptures, withdraw their senses from the world and, seeking immortality, direct their attention within and behold the deathless, ever-present Self.

The scriptures make it clear that our problem is not a material one. Assuming that we have a roof over our head and enough to eat, we don't suffer because we lack all that we want materially. We suffer because we don't know who we are.

Under the spell of self-ignorance, we take ourselves to be a limited, lacking entity subject to birth, death and all manner of limitations in between. We lose ourselves in the relentless ocean of samsara; rising up and down like restless waves, living and dying in ignorance again and again.

The only way out of this cycle of suffering is to challenge the misassumption at its root; the superimposition of limitless Consciousness onto the limited body and mind.

That's what Vedanta is for. It's hopefully clear by now that Vedanta isn't a philosophy; an idle intellectual curiosity; something to be studied, discussed and debated. Rather, it's a means of Self-Knowledge; a tool for removing ignorance and revealing the brilliance of our own pure, unbound, changeless and eternal Awareness.

The Brihadaranyaka Upanishad promises this:

> Those who realise the Self attain the peace that brings complete self-control and perfect patience. They see the Self in everyone and everyone in the Self. Evil cannot harm them, for they overcome all evil. Karma cannot bind them, for they transcend all karma. Free from evil, unbound by karma, taintless and free from doubt, these knowers of the Self inhabit the world of the Eternal.

The Upanishads are resolute in their promise. Self-Realisation alone leads to lasting liberation from sorrow. The Chandogya Upanishad affirms:

> One who realises and contemplates the Self sees the Self everywhere and rejoices in the Self alone. Such a soul lives in freedom and is at home wherever they go.

Furthermore:

> The Self is one, though it appears to be many. Those who realise and contemplate the Self go beyond death and decay; beyond separateness and sorrow. They see the Self in everyone and obtain all things. [...] Integrated Knowledge of the Self transforms bondage to freedom and sorrow to joy.

Over the course of this book, we've explored both the problem and solution to humankind's existential suffering. The key teachings of Vedanta have been introduced. Also, crucially, we've addressed the importance of both preparing the mind and taking the time to integrate and assimilate this Self-Knowledge.

This closing chapter explores the fruits of Self-Knowledge, the seven stages of the spiritual path and what living a life of freedom really means.

The Seven Stages of the Spiritual Path

One of Vedanta's seminal texts, Panchadasi, written in the fourteenth century by Sri Vidyaranya, outlines the spiritual path in seven stages.

The 7 Stages of the Spiritual Path

SAMSARA
1. Ignorance
2. Veiling / Concealment
3. Projection

KNOWLEDGE
4. Indirect Knowledge
5. Direct Knowledge

LIBERATION
6. Freedom From Limitation
7. Total Fulfilment

Let's run through each stage and see how we go from ignorance and suffering to the total fulfilment of knowing ourselves as limitless and free Consciousness.

Stages 1 to 3: Samsara

Samsara means sorrow or suffering. It's a state rooted in a deep and pervasive sense of lack and insufficiency. The samsari, never satisfied with him or herself, is constantly compelled to take action, to seek and acquire various objects, in order to overcome that sense of insufficiency.

The Sanskrit term comes from the root *samsri*, which means "to revolve; go round; to pass through a succession of different states".

At a basic level, it's the drive that compels us to keep seeking happiness outside of ourselves. We desire various things that we believe will bring happiness, so we constantly engage in action, and must then deal with the results of that action.

Samsara also refers to the cycle of rebirth, by which the subtle body continually associates with new gross bodies as it seeks to work out its karma and find that elusive happiness and liberation.

Panchadasi describes samsara as having three basic components or stages: ignorance, veiling or concealment, and projection. All three, however, are experienced simultaneously.

Stage 1: Ignorance

In a spiritual context, ignorances relates specifically to self-ignorance.

At the macrocosmic level, ignorance is maya itself; that by which the Self, formless, undifferentiated Consciousness, appears to become an entire universe of form and objects.

At the microcosmic level of the individual, ignorance causes faulty thinking, misidentification with the body and mind, and seemingly endless entanglement with karma.

Maya itself cannot be destroyed by the individual, for it is a power inherent in the Self. Self-ignorance, however, can be eradicated. Therefore, liberation is possible even within the maya world.

Ignorance is near universal. All beings (with exceedingly rare exceptions) are born ignorant. We are not born with Self-Knowledge. We experience a body and mind, thoughts and emotions, so we conclude that we are this body, mind, thoughts and emotions. In our ignorance, we create a false or pseudo-self, sometimes called the ego-self.

Although the Self is actually self-evident and always available as the very Awareness by which all is experienced, we fail to realise this Self. That's the true source of our problems, and, as we're about to see, the second stage of samsara.

Stage 2: Veiling/Concealment

Maya has two basic powers: the power of veiling or concealment and the power of projection.

Veiling means that it prevents us from seeing reality as it actually is.

While we're aware of the fact that we're aware, alive and conscious, we don't realise that these are qualities of the Self; ever-present Awareness or Consciousness.

Deluded by materialism, we mistakenly conclude that Consciousness must be a part, product or property of the body and mind. If the Self exists, we assume, it must belong to, or *be*, the body and mind.

Or perhaps we deny that the Self exists at all! Atheists fall into this category. They believe that appearance alone is real and, because the Self cannot be experienced by the senses, they deny that it exists at all.

Stage 3: Projection

So, maya veils and distorts our experience of reality, which then makes us victim to projection. Projection is a result of faulty thinking. Because we cannot see what is actually there, the mind attempts to fill in the missing blanks.

The classic example is the snake and the rope. As you'll recall, because the traveller can't see properly in the murky twilight, he mistakes the rope for a snake. He knows there's something there, but it's concealed from him, just as maya conceals our true identity from us. His mind attempts to extrapolate what's there and he ends up "seeing" a snake. The snake, of course, only exists in his mind. It's an act of superimposition caused by ignorance; by his inability to see reality as it actually is.

All human beings are subject to this superimposition. We know that we exist but, thanks to maya, we don't know what we truly are. The Self is subtler than the mind and senses and, therefore, cannot be perceived by them.

What we do see and experience is the body-mind-sense complex, so we assume that this body-mind-sense complex must be who and what we are. We superimpose the Self, Consciousness, onto what are, in actuality, merely instruments through which Consciousness expresses.

Through an act of gross self-misidentification, we reduce ourselves to nothing but a body and mind. We become a person.

Because the body and mind are, by nature, mortal and limited, our sense of self is blighted by lack and insecurity. Seeing only a world of form and objects, we believe we must pursue objects in order to be happy. We become lost in samsara and the constant need to find more, different and better and, worse, to somehow elevate ourselves in the eyes of ourselves and others. This traps us in a loop of karma, driven by desire and aversion and a desperate sense of incompleteness and sorrow.

Eventually, something will happen to sow a seed of spiritual awakening. Perhaps we hear a spiritual teacher speak of the Self or we chance upon a scriptural quote or passage. At this point, we may begin to acknowledge that there is a Self beyond the body and mind.

However, as long as we're subject to maya's twin powers of concealment and projection, we'll only interpret the teaching according to our current level of understanding—which is conditioned by ignorance.

Therefore, we're likely to buy into all kinds of fantasies and delusions about what the Self is and how it is to be "attained". Rather than finding a teacher and allowing the scriptures to guide our understanding, we project our concepts and ideas onto the Self and consider ourselves knowledgable. It doesn't help that, as we saw in Chapter Three, so many enlightenment myths, often highly tantalising, circulate the spiritual marketplace like counterfeit currency. That's where discrimination comes into play; an essential quality all seekers must develop.

Stages 4 to 5: Two Types of Knowledge

Once gripped by a desire to realise the Self and attain enlightenment, the individual will hopefully, in time, find a valid and time-tested means of Self-Knowledge. Vedanta is arguably the most direct and comprehensive of these. When the student is ready, they find Vedanta, or, as it often seems, Vedanta finds them. They approach a teacher and commit themselves to the attainment of Self-Knowledge, which alone frees the mind.

These next two stages highlight the two types of Self-Knowledge.

Stage 4: Indirect Knowledge

Self-Knowledge invariably starts off as indirect knowledge. We begin learning about the Self. We learn that we are, of course, far more than a body and mind and that these are but instruments enlivened and illumined by Awareness/Consciousness.

We learn what Swami Paramarthananda calls the five capsules of Vedanta, namely that:

1. The Self is of the nature of eternal, all-pervading Consciousness.
2. This Consciousness is the only source of lasting peace, happiness and security.
3. By its mere presence, Consciousness gives life to the body and through the body experiences the material universe.
4. Consciousness is not affected by anything that takes place in the body or the material world.
5. Life is a burden when we don't know our true nature as Consciousness. By knowing what we truly are, life becomes a blessing.

Assuming the seeker is qualified, the more they hear, the more interested and committed they become. They develop faith in the knowledge that the Self exists and is all-pervading Consciousness; the same in one and all.

A lot of seekers get stuck at this stage and may prematurely abandon their quest for freedom. They have Self-Knowledge, which is good, but their knowledge remains indirect. Unfortunately, indirect knowledge alone does not translate to liberation.

Stage 5: Direct Knowledge

One of the pitfalls of the path is the widespread belief that the Self is something we need to experience through yoga, meditation or various other means and methodologies.

Implicit in this assumption is the mistaken belief that you aren't currently experiencing the Self; that the Self is something you have to become, acquire or attain through action and experience.

This belief can easily be negated. If the Self is Consciousness, and you are the Self, then you must already be experiencing the Self.

How can you ever *not* experience the Self? If you sometimes did and sometimes didn't, then it wouldn't be your Self. You, the Self, are not variable; you can never *not* be You!

You can never *not* be experiencing Consciousness because Consciousness underlies and is the very carrier of your every experience. It is ever present as your innermost being; as your very Existence. So, the idea that you aren't already experiencing the Self is simply ignorance.

Here's the crucial distinction. Indirect knowledge is knowing *of* the Self. Direct knowledge is knowing that you *are* the Self.

So, how do you convert indirect knowledge to direct knowledge?

That's what the third stage of Vedanta is for: the consistent contemplation and meditation upon your nature as the Self. You must repeatedly expose your mind to this Knowledge until it finally and resolutely sinks in.

To use an analogy, you can mix all the ingredients for a cake and put it into a cake tin. Unless, however, you fire up the oven and cook it for the necessary time, it'll never become a cake. It'll simply remain a gooey mixture of flour, eggs, butter and sugar. The heat of the oven is necessary to transform it into the desired product.

Similarly, the heat of Vedantic meditation, the deep contemplation of your nature as Consciousness, is required to liberate the mind and heart from the sorrows of samsara. This is done by not only knowing about the Self, but fully and irrevocably claiming your identity as the Self.

You confidently accept and own the great Upanishadic proclamation, "I Am That"!

Stages 6-7: Liberation

Here's the key to liberation in three short sentences:

The scriptures declare the Self is free. You are the Self. Therefore, you are free.

When this Knowledge sinks in, it begins overwriting your old template of ignorance and eradicating your identification with the body-mind-sense complex.

This leads to stages six and seven, which have been the goal of spiritual seekers across the millennia: liberation or enlightenment!

The first of these two aspects of liberation is freedom from limitation and the second is complete satisfaction and fulfilment; the sense that everything that is to be attained in life has been attained.

Stage 6: Freedom From Limitation

Assimilated Self-Knowledge removes false identification with the body-mind and negates the idea that "I am a person"; mortal, finite and subject to perpetual lack and limitation. It's this fundamental misassumption that breeds samsara's hallmark sense of limitation. Because the root of the problem isn't one of experience, but of ignorance, only knowledge can remedy it.

Self-Knowledge is knowing that the Self, Consciousness, is the source of all fullness, peace, fulfilment and happiness. When your sense of identification shifts from your personhood to the self-evident, self-shining Consciousness illuminating all experience, this limitation disappears along with it.

As your sense of "I" shifts from the reflected consciousness to the Original Consciousness, the person you long identified with is revealed as nothing but a perceptual error.

With enlightenment, the ego-self isn't destroyed at such. It is simply seen as the illusion that it is. It was never really there to begin with; you just thought it was. Similarly, the three bodies won't suddenly vanish. They'll continue functioning until your karma for this lifetime has run its course.

In spite of what some people claim, the universe is not eradicated at the time of liberation. It's just seen for what it truly is; the play of Ishvara. Karma continues its dance, until such time as it doesn't.

What is destroyed with liberation is the sense of limitation and insecurity that comes from identifying as a finite entity subject to gain and loss, happiness, sorrow and an eventual demise.

In time, your sense of doership, of being an agent of action, is also removed by the realisation that Ishvara created the three bodies along with the entire field of creation. All action, all doership and ownership ultimately belongs not to the individual, and not to you as Consciousness, but to Ishvara.

This falling away of the sense of doership doesn't mean that actions won't still take place. As long as you possess a body and mind, worldly transactions are necessary and unavoidable. What changes is this: you know all action and the results of that action are taken care of by Ishvara.

Knowing this, you experience the "actionless action" or the "doing-less doing" spoken of in the Bhagavad Gita and other scriptures. The realisation that all action is initiated, and its results dispensed, not by you, but by Ishvara, removes the individual's crippling burden of doership.

This means that you're free to simply enjoy life.

You no longer feel compelled to seek happiness in the world of objects, for you know that true and lasting happiness is only to be found in your Self.

What a great liberation this is!

You already have and are everything you could ever possibly seek!

What's more, the Self is always available to you and nobody can ever take it from you.

You are free to enjoy the Wholeness that is your very nature as Consciousness.

You no longer act to gain happiness. You act from happiness.

Knowing the Wholeness that you are, instead of trying to extract as much as you can from the world, you freely give to the world.

When you know that, as the Self, you have and are everything, you never feel the need to exploit or seek anything from others.

The desperate scramble to acquire and attain worldly things, as dictated by your likes and dislikes, is no longer the motivating force in your life. Instead, you're free to simply give, to love and to enjoy life; free of the burden of seeking, striving and acquiring.

Again, it's not that action won't happen through you. Life in the transactional world is karma; action after action after action. You'll still do all that you need to. You'll simply no longer be reliant upon anything external in order to feel whole and complete in yourself.

With time, you become increasingly secure in the Knowledge that, as Awareness, nothing in the world can touch you. Fear evaporates and, so too, does desire. Desires may still arise in the mind, but you no longer find yourself compulsively compelled to pursue them. You can simply watch them drift by like clouds in the sky, knowing that you have nothing to gain or lose by their fulfilment.

In the Bhagavad Gita, Arjuna asks Krishna to describe those who have attained enlightenment. Such souls, Krishna says, are free from attachment and discontent and are no longer compelled to chase sense objects in order to attain happiness. They remain even-minded regardless of external circumstances, which is a key quality of liberation.

Like the tortoise able to withdraw its limbs into its shell, the liberated easily resist the allure of worldly riches. They instead turn within to enjoy the completeness, Wholeness and Bliss of their own eternally present, ever-shining Self.

Tattva Bodha says that by realising the Divinity and unity of all things, the individual becomes what we call a *jivan muktah*, or one who is "liberated while living." Such a soul is described as follows:

> Most people cling to limiting beliefs, such as "I am a man or woman," "I am a body and mind," "I am a certain age and of a certain profession." The liberated, however, whose understanding is transformed by the Knowledge of Truth, have negated such false identities and ascertained that "I am free from attachment to form, for I am of the nature of Existence, Consciousness and Bliss, being the effulgent, self-shining light dwelling in the heart of all beings." By this direct knowledge, "I am Brahman, the Self alone", one is no longer bound by karma.

On the subject of liberation, Panchadasi states:

> A liberated person is mindful of the difference between his former life and his present life. He or she thinks, "Let samsaris chase objects. I am fullness itself." What is there to gain in this world?" Let the spiritual types seek high states of consciousness. Neither high nor low, I pervade all states.

A Gradual Unfoldment

Enlightenment, freedom from suffering, tends to be a gradual unfoldment. Don't expect it to happen in a sudden, dramatic flash of light. It's pretty safe to assume that the ground won't shake, nor angels appear with trumpets.

Furthermore, don't expect anyone else to notice the change in you. They may, or they may not. The fact is human beings generally relate to each other through a screen of mental concepts; a kind of mental overlay. They don't see what's there as much as what they think is there. So, others will continue relating to you as they've always done. If they do notice any changes, it'll be the fact you no longer exhibit the same stress, anxiety, fear and craving.

Don't expect your outer life to suddenly change simply because you know who you are. Your bank account won't suddenly skyrocket. People won't be falling over themselves to bask in your glory. Finally, the karma allotted for this lifetime will continue to play itself out until such time as it's exhausted.

The real change occurs within, in terms of how you relate to life, yourself and others. You no longer see yourself as a helpless little person frantically sifting through the rubble of samsara, trying to find whatever you believe will make you feel whole and complete.

When you are Self-Realised, you know that the happiness, peace and security you sought is already there as the light of your own being.

The mind will continue ticking away and you may find yourself habitually responding to certain things and situations according to old ignorance-based conditioning. That will resolve itself in time as you continue practising Vedantic meditation and contemplation upon your identity as Awareness and not the person.

Even once you unearth a precious jewel, it takes time and effort to clear away the dirt and debris and to polish it into something that sparkles and shines. The mind is no different.

Not that you're trying to improve yourself as such. Vedanta is not about self-improvement. It's about Self-Knowledge. It reveals to you the Self that doesn't need to, and, in fact cannot, be improved.

At this stage, avoid the temptation to be complacent. Until the Knowledge is fully assimilated, and even after that, you want to enjoy the full benefits conferred by this Knowledge.

Therefore, it's advisable to keep the mind pure and refined by observing dharma (which will become as natural to you as breathing), performing your actions as karma yoga, managing the three gunas and worshipping Ishvara in whatever form pleases you.

In other words, keep your life holy.

Teaching and Enlightenment Sickness

Some people have the idea that if they "crack" things spiritually, they must automatically become teachers.

This is a fallacy. Some will go on to become teachers of Vedanta, but only if it's in alignment with their personal dharma.

Teaching Vedanta is tricky and, unless your Knowledge is extremely solid and your mind sufficiently pure, it also runs the risk of inflating the dreaded "spiritual ego", leading to enlightenment sickness.

That's why it's probably unwise to jump into teaching right away.

It's better to spend time purifying the mind through the continuous application of Self-Knowledge. Rest assured, if you are meant to teach, the students will come.

Otherwise, it's enough to simply follow dharma and enjoy life with your newfound freedom. You don't need to change your job and you certainly don't need to parade your Self-Knowledge unless someone is genuinely open and interested. Most people won't be and are liable to misunderstand you. The Bhagavad Gita cautions against sharing this wisdom with the worldly, who tend to criticise and attack what they don't understand.

Stay vigilant with the mind and ego. The idea "I'm enlightened now" is tantalising to the ego. Never let the ego claim such a status.

After all, the notion of "an enlightened person" is actually a contradiction in terms. Enlightenment is the knowledge that you aren't a person, so "enlightened person" is an oxymoron.

What you are is, simply, a knower of the Self, or one who knows they are the Self.

Beyond All Sorrow

Tattva Bodha concludes with the following:

> The scriptures affirm that the knower of the Self goes beyond all sorrow. Whatever happens in the remainder of their bodily lifetime, he or she is liberated and freed from all karma.

How are you freed from karma? By recognising that karma belongs to Ishvara and the body-mind-sense complex. You are the Existence/Awareness in which these have their being.

As the sun illuminates the entire world, allowing all life to grow and flourish, while remaining unaffected by any of the things it shines upon, so, too, does the Self.

The body and mind exist in the space-time of duality. As such, they will always be subject to the play of the opposites; the good and the bad, pleasure and pain, happiness and sorrow.

Fortunately, the Knowledge "I am Awareness" neutralises suffering.

As the saying goes, pain is unavoidable in life but suffering is optional. Self-Knowledge reveals that you transcend any and all experience.

Regardless of what's happening to the body and mind and whether your state of mind is calm and sattvic, agitated with rajas or dulled with tamas, the Awareness that you are is free.

As Awareness, you don't modify to experience. You are untouchable. Like the space pervading a glass jar and the entire universe around it, you are that in which experience happens but experience doesn't contain you. It may affect the body and mind which, like all things in maya are subject to change, but it doesn't change *you*.

If sorrow, anger or any other troubling emotion should arise, you gently and lovingly take care of your body and mind, recognising that all such emotions are simply weather fronts passing across the vast open sky of your being. They come and go but you, Awareness, are constant and imperturbable.

Stage 7: Complete Fulfilment

What might be described as the highest stage of enlightenment is when the seeds of Self-Knowledge have fully blossomed, bringing a sense of complete fulfilment and satisfaction with oneself and life.

This satisfaction isn't derived from the achievement of certain goals and ends. It's not a state that can be manufactured. Anything that can be manufactured will be limited and subject to cessation. In other words, anything that has a beginning will have an end.

The fulfilment and satisfaction spoken of in the scriptures comes from the full realisation of your being as self-existent, self-luminous, ever present Awareness/Consciousness—which is without beginning and end.

Self-Realisation leads to life's highest goal. When you realise your Self and continue reeducating the mind with this Knowledge until it finally sinks in, you have accomplished all that is to be accomplished in life. You have found and taken ownership of the ultimate treasure, hidden in plain sight all along—the light of your own Awareness.

This satisfaction is present regardless of the emotional fluctuations of the mind and will last forever, because the Self lasts forever.

It is experienced as the polar opposite of samsara's aching sense of lack, inadequacy and discontent. Indeed, the Bliss of your own true nature, Awareness, confers abiding Wholeness, absolute adequacy and complete contentment.

This is perhaps best expressed in the Isha Upanishad with the following mantra:

That is Whole. This is Whole.
From Wholeness comes Wholeness.
When Wholeness is taken from Wholeness,
Wholeness still remains.

Like using a bucket to try to empty the ocean of water, no matter how much you take from Wholeness, Wholeness must remain.

Why? Because it is Whole.

In other words, Non-dual.

There is only a single thing in the entirety of existence and that is Existence itself; the Self—you!

Because you, the Self, are Non-dual, no matter what appears to happen, nothing can rob you of your inherent completeness and infinitude. This Knowledge is the key to liberation.

The End of Seeking

A sure way to know that you've attained your goal is when all seeking, specifically spiritual seeking, ends.

While you may have spent the best part of your life seeking enlightenment or that elusive "don't know quite what" from this path or that, you reach a point where the need to seek further simply falls away.

When you know who you are and fully internalise that Knowledge, there's simply no need to keep seeking.

After all, when you find your Self, which is everything, what more can you seek? What more can you ask for than *everything*? What more exists than the Absolute Wholeness and completeness of your own immediate, ever shining Awareness?

Some seekers make the mistake of abandoning their quest prematurely. A clear sign that you haven't yet assimilated your Self-Knowledge is when you find yourself getting restless and deciding to explore other avenues; other spiritual traditions and teachings. You succumb to that old familiar sense of "maybe that wasn't quite *it*".

While there are other enlightenment traditions, none worth their salt will tell you anything different. You are not the body-mind! You are the Awareness or Consciousness that animates the body-mind! You are, in essence, formless, Non-dual, whole and utterly complete!

Some call this the perennial philosophy, although it's not a philosophy, as such. It's Knowledge. It's the thread of Truth binding together all the various religious and spiritual traditions. For, unless they've been irredeemably distorted, as can happen, they are all expressions of the same basic Truth about Reality.

You don't need to look elsewhere. Vedanta is unparalleled in its vision, comprehensiveness, logic and sheer clarity. The wheel has been invented and it doesn't need to, and cannot, be bettered.

All that you need to do is stick with it.

It's virtually impossible to skip from stages one to three of the enlightenment process all the way to stage six or seven. Even if you intellectually understand the teaching, for most people it must be rigorously and consistently applied to the mind before it eventually reroutes and reorients one's innermost sense of identification.

Panchadasi states:

> Direct Knowledge is not firmly established immediately. Therefore, repeated listening, reflection and contemplation of Self-Knowledge is necessary. Until the meaning of the knowledge "I am Awareness" is firmly established, one should continue applying Self-Knowledge to the mind and practice self-control and the other virtues.

Vedanta is telling you that you are Divine. You are the intelligence and light that illumines the stars and weaves entire galaxies and universes; that all-pervading substratum in which all forms and beings have their existence.

Rather than adopting a godlike ego, however, it's best to live with humility. Stick with the threefold process of hearing, understanding and contemplating Self-Knowledge as long as you need to. Use this sharpened axe of spiritual Truth to chop down the forest of ignorance in which you've wandered, lost and suffering, for so many lifetimes.

Keeping the mind qualified, contemplate the Knowledge "I am Awareness" until you realise it as the heart of all Truth.

The word Vedanta literally means "the end of knowledge". It is the Knowledge that ends the need for any other knowledge; the missing key, the secret to existence; the one thing, by knowing which, you come to know all things in essence.

Remain steadfast and consistent until Self-Knowledge becomes ironclad conviction. You'll know when this happens. Your seeking ends when, regardless of your worldly circumstances and the condition of the body and mind, you come to abide in the unparalleled freedom, contentment and wholeness of your own being as Awareness/Consciousness.

Live Your Life As An Offering

So, what's left to do when you get to the end of the spiritual path? When Self-Knowledge has liberated you from the misdirected quest to find wholeness in the world of objects?

You may have spent years or even decades devoted to spiritual realisation and then, one day, the search is over and the need to seek simply vanishes. This generally frees up a tremendous amount of time and energy.

So, what do you do with the rest of your life?

When you realise the intangible, ever-changing and dreamlike nature of the phenomenal world, you find yourself in a somewhat desireless state. While some desires may still arise, they exist more as wispy preferences than compulsive yearnings.

From the Isha Upanishad:

> When you see the Self in all things and all things in the Self you know no fear. When you see the Self in all things and all things in the Self you know no grief. How can the multiplicity of life delude the one who recognises its unity?

Once again, it's always a good idea to keep the mind pure and sattvic by living in accordance with dharmic values, practising karma yoga, maintaining a devotional spirit and managing the three gunas.

Of course, it's not necessary for the Self that the mind be sattvic. Awareness is impartial and just as happy if the mind is conditioned by rajas or tamas.

For the sake of the body-mind, however, it's always preferable to proportion the gunas in a way that maximises sattva. A sattvic mind is a happy mind; a mind with clarity, contentment and joy.

Your outer life may be just as it was before; the same family, the same job, the same friends and pastimes. If, however, you find yourself with additional time, energy and space (and even if you don't), here's a suggestion.

Live your life as service; as an offering to God. Make your life stand for something. Make it a monument to the Divine; something beautiful, sacred and true. Whatever you're doing, do it with love. Do it to honour the Divinity in all things; the one Self in all beings; the glory shining at the heart of all life.

Life lived in ignorance is a burden; a succession of successes and failures, threaded by a pervasive sense of lack and insufficiency.

Self-Knowledge, which grants you Divine vision, the ability to see the Self in all things and all beings, transforms life from a burden to a blessing. When you are able to appreciate the Self everywhere and in everything, as the very heart of Existence, wherever you go is sanctified and whatever you do is a blessing.

The greatest gift you can give another being is to see who they truly are; beyond their body and mind, their words and ideas, their conditioning and ignorance, to the Self shining within.

What better gift can you bring to the world than to recognise the beauty and light within all things, however well it may at times seem hidden?

Until you know who you are, your every action is motivated by the desire for happiness. Once you know who you are, and feel, believe and intuit that with the entirety of your being, you know that happiness already exists abundantly within you and can never be exhausted.

That's why the liberated act not for happiness, but from happiness.

Life becomes an exercise in appreciation and joy; an expression of the sublime greatness that you are as pure, simple, ordinary, actionless, ever-present, ever-shining Awareness.

Summary

- Panchadasi outlines seven stages of the spiritual path, leading us from ignorance to liberation. The first three stages, which are samsara, are ignorance, veiling or concealment and projection. Stages four and five relate to Self-Realisation and are indirect and direct knowledge. Stages six and seven relate to liberation and are freedom from limitation and, finally, complete fulfilment.
- The first three stages are the product of maya, which, as ignorance, veils the true nature of Reality and the Self from us, causing us to project a reality and a personhood that isn't actually real.

- When a person seeks Self-Knowledge, this generally begins as indirect knowledge: knowledge of the Self. In order to yield liberation, this must be converted to direct knowledge; the knowledge that I am the Self.
- The scriptures unanimously proclaim the Self to be free. You are the Self. Therefore, you must be free.
- The Self alone is the source of all fullness, peace, happiness and fulfilment. When your sense of identity shifts from the body-mind/ego-self to the true Self, you begin to experience the boundless riches of your own true nature.
- All action, all doership and the results of action, belong to Ishvara and not you. This removes the burden of doership. You are free to simply enjoy life, content in yourself and your own innate Wholeness.
- There is no end to the Wholeness of your nature as the Self, because there is no end to the Self.
- Enlightenment is unlikely to be an earth-shaking moment of heavenly trumpets and blinding light. Instead, liberation tends to be a gradual unfoldment as you continue applying Self-Knowledge to the mind.
- Self-Knowledge leads you to see that you are free regardless of what is happening to the body and mind. It is advisable, though, to maintain a pure and sattvic mind, to enable you to fully enjoy the benefits of this Knowledge.
- The final stage of enlightenment is a sense of total fulfilment and satisfaction; the sense that you are completely whole and complete and have achieved all that is to be achieved in life. With this, comes the end of all seeking.
- When you have realised your nature as pure Awareness/Consciousness, the remainder of your individual karma for this lifetime will continue to play itself out. You are free, however, regardless of all extraneous factors.

- When you truly know the Divinity of all things and all beings, wherever you go is sanctified and whatever you do is a blessing.
- The liberated don't act for happiness. They act from happiness. For the liberated, life becomes an offering to the Divine and an expression of appreciation and joy.

Appendices

Appendix 1.
Tattva Bodha: Knowledge of Truth

Tattva Bodha by Adi Shankaracharya is an introductory Vedantic text which neatly and concisely outlines most of the key concepts and terminology.

Keeping the mind qualified, contemplate the Knowledge "I am Awareness" until you realise it as the heart of all Truth.

It has been referenced throughout this book, serving as a loose framework for the structure and topics. Here is the full text, which has been rendered in plain and simple language to ensure accessibility.

Invocation

Salutations to the Eternal Self! With eternal gratitude and reverence to the Vedantic lineage of teachers, Tattva Bodha, "Knowledge of Truth", is shared for the benefit of all sincere seekers of liberation.

We shall describe the method of enquiry into Truth, which is the means for liberation for those endowed with the fourfold mental qualifications.

A Qualified Mind

1.0. What are the fourfold mental qualifications (for gaining liberation)?

The fourfold mental qualifications are the ability to discriminate between the permanent and impermanent, dispassion towards sense objects and worldly seeking and attainment, the six qualities of inner wealth, and the burning desire for liberation.

1.1 What is meant by discrimination between the permanent and the impermanent?

This discrimination is the conviction that the Eternal Self alone is permanent and all else is impermanent.

1.2 What is dispassion?

Dispassion means freedom from attachment to sensory enjoyment and to the fruits of all desires, actions and attainments.

1.3 What are the six qualities of inner wealth?

These are control of the mind, control of the senses, withdrawal of the mind, endurance, faith and the ability to concentrate the mind.

1.3. a. The ability to control or master the mind is a prerequisite for all seekers.

1.3. b. The ability to control or master the external sense organs, such as the eyes, etc, is also necessary.

1.3. c. Withdrawal of the mind includes the strict observance of one's own duty towards oneself, one's family, community and religion while keeping universal values (dharma).

1.3. d. Endurance is the ability to endure the dualities of life, such as the pleasant and unpleasant, heat and cold, joy and sorrow.

1.3. e. The seeker also must have faith in both the teacher and the teaching pending the result of their own investigation.

1.3. f. Single-pointedness of mind is the ability to concentrate the mind at will.

1.4 Finally, intense desire for liberation is essential to the success of the student.

1.5 Upon cultivation of these qualities of mind, the seeker is qualified and ready for enquiry into the nature of Reality.

Enquiry Into the Nature of Reality

2.1 What is enquiry into the nature of Reality?

It is the firm conviction that the Self alone is Real (satya) and all else is only apparently real (mithya).

This knowledge of what is Real (the Self) and what is unreal (the not-Self) is the essence of enquiry into the nature of Reality.

2.2 What is the Self?

The Self is that which exists beyond the gross, subtle and causal bodies, beyond the five sheaths, is the witness of the three states of consciousness, is changeless and timeless, and is of the nature of Existence, Consciousness and Bliss.

The Three Bodies

3.0 What are the three bodies?

The three bodies are the gross body, subtle body and causal body.

3.1 What is the gross body?

The gross (physical) body is that which is made up of the five elements having undergone the process of grossification. It is born of the good actions (karma) of the past, is the vehicle by which one gains experience in the world, both pleasurable and painful, and is subject to the six modifications; to exist, be born, to grow, mature, decay and to die. That is the gross body.

3.2 What is the subtle body?

The subtle body is that which is made up of the five elements which have not undergone the process of grossification. It is born of the good actions (karma) of the past and is an instrument for subtle experience. It consists of seventeen components: five sense organs, five organs of action, the five physiological functions, the mind and the intellect.

3.3 What is the causal body?

The causal body is inexplicable, beginningless and of the nature of ignorance. It is that which causes the gross and subtle bodies to come into being, is the source of self-ignorance and is free from duality.

The Sense Organs

4.0 What are the five sense organs of perception ?

4.1 The five sense organs of perception are the ears, the skin, the eyes, the tongue and the nose.

4.2 The organs of perception evolve out of the properties of the five material elements; space for the ears, air for the skin, sun for the eyes, water for the tongue, and earth for the nose.

4.3 The functions of the organs of perception are cognition of sound for the ears, cognition of touch for the skin, cognition of form for the eyes, cognition of taste for the tongue and cognition of smell for the nose.

5.0 What are the five sense organs of action?

5.1 The five organs of action are the organ of speech, the hands, the legs, the anus and the genitals.

5.2 The organs of action are associated with the properties of the five elements: fire for the organ of speech, air for the hands, space for the feet, water for the genitals and earth for the anus.

5.3 The function of speech is to communicate, the function of the hands is to grasp, the function of the legs is movement, the function of the anus is elimination and the function of the genitals is procreation.

The Three States of Consciousness

6.0 What are the three states of consciousness?

The three states of consciousness are waking, dream and deep sleep.

6.2 What is the waking state?

The waking state is that state of experience in which sense objects such as sound are perceived through the sense organs such as the ears. The Self, identified with the gross body in the waking state is termed *vishwa*, the "waker".

6.3 What is the dream state?

The dream state is the subtle world projected while in sleep from the impressions gathered in the waking state. The Self, associated with the subtle body in this dream state is termed *taijasa*, the "shining one".

6.4 What is the deep sleep state?

The deep sleep state is the state about which one can only say, "I had no knowledge of anything; I simply enjoyed a good sleep". The Self, associated with the causal body in the deep sleep state is termed *prajna*, meaning "almost enlightened".

The Five Sheaths

7.0 What are the five sheaths?

The five sheaths are the food sheath, the vital air sheath, the mental sheath, the intellect sheath and the bliss sheath.

7.1 What is the food sheath?

The food sheath is that which is created from the essence of food and which merges into the earth. It is also termed the gross body.

7.2 What is the vital air sheath?

The five physiological functions (breathing, the evacuation of waste, the circulation of blood and nourishment to the cells, digestion and assimilation and the body's ability to reject unwanted objects) and the five organs of action (speech, hands, legs, anus and genitals) together constitute the vital air sheath.

7.3 What is the mental sheath?

The mind and the five organs of perception (ears, skin, eyes, tongue and nose) together constitute the mental sheath.

7.4 What is the intellect sheath?

The intellect and the five organs of perception together constitute the intellect sheath. Together, the vital air sheath, mental sheath and intellect sheath comprise the subtle body.

7.5 What is the bliss sheath?

Correlating with the deep sleep state and thus ignorance, the bliss sheath relates to the the causal body, is of impure sattva and, through the association with desired objects, is experienced as the bliss of the Self.

Beyond the Five Sheaths

7.6 My possessions, whether my house, my bracelet, or my clothing, may belong to me but, clearly, that which belongs to me must be other than myself, who am the knower of those things. In the same way, while the five sheaths may seemingly belong to me—"my body", "my mind", "my intellect" and "my ignorance"—they must clearly be other than myself, who am the knower. Therefore, the Self must be other than the aggregates of the five sheaths.

The Nature of the Self

8.0 What, then, is the Self?

The Self is of the nature of Existence, Consciousness and Bliss.

8.1 What is Existence?

That which remains unchanged in the three periods of time (past, present and future) is Existence.

8.2 What is Consciousness?

Consciousness is of the nature of pure Knowledge.

8.3 What is Bliss?

Bliss is of the nature of limitless Wholeness.

8.4 Thus, one should know oneself to be of the nature of Existence, Consciousness and Bliss.

The Universe and Maya

9.0 Now we shall explain the nature of the phenomenal universe.

9.1 Maya, a power dependent upon Brahman (the Self), consists of the three qualities of sattva, rajas and tamas.

9.2 From this (Brahman plus maya), space is born. From space, air is born. From air, fire is born. From fire, water is born. From water, earth is born.

9.3 From these five great elements, out of the sattvic aspect of space, the organ of hearing, the ear, evolved. From the sattvic aspect of air, the organ of touch, the skin, evolved. From the sattvic aspect of fire, the organ of sight, the eyes, evolved. From the sattvic aspect of water, the organ of taste, the tongue, evolved. From the sattvic aspect of earth, the organ of smell, the nose, evolved.

9.4 From the total sattvic aspect of these five elements, the inner instruments of the mind, intellect, ego and memory are born.

9.5 The mind is of the nature of indecision. The intellect is of the nature of decision. The ego has the notion of doership. Memory is of the nature of thinking or recollection.

9.7 Among these five elements, from the rajas aspect of space, the organ of speech is born. From the rajas aspect of air, the organs of grasping, the hands, are born. From the rajas aspect of fire, the organ of locomotion, the legs, are born. From the rajas aspect of water, the organ of procreation, the genitals, are born. From the rajas aspect of earth, the organ of excretion, the anus, is born.

9.8 From the total rajas aspect of these five elements, the five vital airs, the pranas, are formed.

9.9 From the tamas aspect of these five elements, the grossified five elements are born. This is called the process of panchikarana, or the grossification of subtle elements into matter. The tamas aspect of each of the five elements divides into two equal parts. One half of each remains intact. The other half divides into four equal parts. To the intact half of one element, one-eighth portion from each of the other elements gets joined.

9.10 From these five grossified elements, the gross body is formed.

The Relationship Between the Individual and God

10.0 The microcosm and the macrocosm, the individual and God, exist in total unity.

10.1 The reflected consciousness of the Self (Brahman), which identifies with the gross and subtle bodies, is called an individual, or jiva. This jiva ignorantly considers God (Ishvara) to be separate and different to him or herself.

10.2 The Self, when seemingly conditioned by ignorance at the microcosmic level, is called the jiva, or individual. The Self, when seemingly conditioned by maya at the macrocosmic level, is called God, or Ishvara. The difference is due to the differing adjuncts.

10.3 As long as the notion that the individual and Ishvara are different remains, there can be no redemption from samsara, the cycle of worldly suffering and rebirth. Therefore, the notion that man and God are separate and essentially different must be removed.

Enquiry Into the Statement "I Am That"

11.1 The jiva is endowed with ego and its knowledge is limited, whereas Ishvara is without ego and is omniscient.

11.2 Given these seemingly contradictory characteristics, how can the two share the same essential identity, as stated in the great Upanishadic statement "I Am That"?

11.3 There can be no doubt. The literal meaning of the word "I", in this case, is the one identified with the gross and subtle bodies. The implied meaning of the word "I" is pure Consciousness which is free from all conditionings and which can be recognised through Vedantic meditation.

11.4 The literal meaning of the word "That" is Ishvara, which is endowed with omniscience and all-knowledge. The implied meaning of the word "That" is pure Consciousness which is free from all conditionings.

11.5 Therefore, there is no contradiction regarding the essential oneness of the individual and Ishvara from the standpoint of pure Consciousness.

The Self-Realised Soul

12.1 Heeding the words of Vedanta and the guidance of the teacher, those who come to realise the Divinity and unity of all beings are liberated while living.

12.2 What can be said about such a soul? Most people cling to limiting beliefs such as "I am a man or woman", "I am a body and mind", "I am a certain age and of a certain profession".

12.3 The liberated, however, whose understanding is transformed by the Knowledge of Truth, have negated such false identities and ascertained that "I am free from attachment to form, for I am of the nature of Existence, Consciousness and Bliss, being the effulgent, self-shining light dwelling in the heart of all beings."

12.4 By this direct Knowledge, "I am Brahman, the Self", one is no longer bound by karma.

Action, Karma and Freedom

13.1 There are three types of karma: agami, sanchita and prarabdha.

13.2 The results of actions, good or bad, performed by the body of a Self-Realised person after the dawn of Self-Knowledge, is known as agami, or future, karma.

13.3 The results of actions, good or bad, performed in previous births which are in seed form and which give rise to endless rounds of future births, are called sanchita, or accumulated, karma.

13.4 Having generated the present body, the past actions which are fructifying in this present lifetime, both good and bad, are called prarabdha, or current life, karma. Only by going through an experience does prarabdha karma exhaust.

13.5 For the Self-Realised, sanchita karma is destroyed by the firm knowledge that "I am Brahman alone."

13.6 For the Self-Realised, agami karma is also destroyed by Self-Knowledge and the liberated is not affected by it any more than the lotus leaf is affected by water upon it.

13.7 Those who praise, serve and support the wise, receive the fruits of their good actions. Those who criticise, hate or cause pain to the wise, also receive the fruits of their bad actions.

The Results of Self-Knowledge

13.8 The knower of the Self, having crossed the ocean of samsara, attains complete Wholeness and Freedom. The scriptures affirm that the knower of the Self goes beyond all sorrow. Whatever might happen in the remainder of their bodily lifetime, he or she is liberated and freed from all karma.

13.9 Here ends the Tattva Bodha, Knowledge of Truth.

Om Tat Sat. Salutations to the Self!

Appendix 2.
Nirvana Shatkam

It's said that when Adi Shankara was only eight years old, he met the sage Govindapada, who would later become his guru.

Govindapada asked the young boy, "Who are you?"

The story goes that Shankara spontaneously recited the following six verses, which later became known as *Nirvana Shatkam*.

Nirvana means complete peace and equanimity, and shatkam refers to the number of verses. Needless to say, Govindapada immediately accepted the boy as his disciple! Wouldn't you?

This succinct yet powerful composition negates our misidentification with the body-mind and its aggregates. It reveals Self-Knowledge as a shift from false identification with the material components of our being to the all-pervading Existence/Consciousness/Awareness in which all things appear and have their being.

What follows is a somewhat loose translation, designed for clarity and ease of reading. You may find these verses make an excellent tool for meditation and deep contemplation. Read each verse slowly and thoughtfully, allowing yourself to fully contemplate the meaning of each sentence as you do.

Nirvana Shatkam

I am neither the mind, the intellect, the ego nor thought.
I am neither the ears, the tongue, the nose nor the eyes.
I am neither fire, water, air nor earth.
My nature is the Bliss of Unbound Consciousness.
I am the Self, I am the Self!

I am neither the vital energy nor the body's physiology.
I am neither the elements nor the five sheaths.
I am neither the internal organs, nor the hands, nor the feet, nor tongue.
My nature is the Bliss of Unbound Consciousness.
I am the Self, I am the Self!

I am free of greed and delusion, aversion and attachment.
I am free of pride and ego, seeking and attaining.
I have neither desires of mind nor craving for objects.
My nature is the Bliss of Unbound Consciousness.
I am the Self, I am the Self!

I am free of virtue and vice, pleasure and pain.
I am free of religious duty and observance.
I am neither the one that eats nor that which is eaten.
My nature is the Bliss of Unbound Consciousness.
I am the Self, I am the Self!

I have neither fear nor death, nor distinction of caste.
I have neither father nor mother, nor even birth.
I have neither friends nor comrades, disciples nor guru.
My nature is the Bliss of Unbound Consciousness.
I am the Self, I am the Self!

I am without form or limitation, for I pervade all.
I exist everywhere but am subtler than the body and senses.
I have no need of salvation, for I am already free.
My nature is the Bliss of Unbound Consciousness.
I am the Self, I am the Self!

Appendix 3.
Resources

What follows is a list of recommended Vedanta teachers, including associated websites and audio/visual resources. Though by no means exhaustive, it nevertheless provides a range of excellent material for all seekers of liberation.

There are a great many traditional Vedanta teachers out there, from various lineages. I have generally only included those whose teachings and material I'm familiar with and can personally vouch for. This is, therefore, only a shortlist of recommended teachers, which can, and most likely will, be added to.

I unreservedly recommend teachers from the Swami Dayananda Saraswati/Arsha Vidya lineage (listed at **arshavidyasampradaya.in**). Dayananda's approach arguably aligns the closest with Shankara's teaching.

In the centuries since Shankara, a range of other interpretations and schools of thought have arisen, each with subtle and not so subtle divergences from what we call traditional Vedanta. Modern teachers often tend to modify the teaching and inject new concepts and ideas, as has happened with what is often termed Neo-Vedanta, or "New Vedanta", not to mention Neo-Advaita and other non-traditional approaches adopted by various teachers.

This is not to say that value cannot be found in the non-traditional approach, which includes such revered sages as Ramana Maharshi and Nisargadatta Maharaj, whose lives and teachings have inspired seekers for generations now.

An entire book could be written on the various branches of Vedanta and its teaching. Suffice to say, I have only included those teachers I am familiar with and whose teachings are as closely aligned with Shankara's traditional Vedanta as possible. Any divergences that I'm aware of are noted.

My own website can be found at **unbrokenself.com**. It includes a range of articles, scriptural translations and a number of questions and answers on the topic of Vedanta.

Recommended Teachers and Audio/Visual Resources

James and Sundari Swartz — shiningworld.com. One of the best and most complete Vedanta resources on the internet. James is an American teacher who became a close disciple of the late, great Swami Chinmayananda back in the 1960's. He has taught Vedanta for upwards of sixty years now, now along with his wife and fellow teacher Sundari, in a way that is easily accessible for Western seekers, while never compromising on fidelity. Their website is filled with content; articles, scriptures, multimedia and thousands of question and answer satsangs. Youtube channel @JamesSwartzShiningworld features an abundance of excellent content from seminars over the last couple of decades.

Shiningworld has a number of other teachers skilled at presenting the teaching in a clear, easily accessible manner. These include **Lucua Prakashini**, a teacher from South Africa who teaches with great clarity using a minimum of Sanskrit and whose work is available from her website and app at **vedanta4all.com**. **Ben de Silva** is an Australian student of James Swartz, Swami Dayananda and Swami Paramarthananda, who conducts excellent weekly classes via Zoom. While Ben does not have a website he can contacted at bmselfknowledge@gmail.com. Details of other Shiningworld endorsed teachers can be found on the website.

Swami Dayananda Saraswati of Arsha Vidya — **arshavidya.org**. Swami Dayananda (1930-2015) was a disciple of Swami Chinmayanda and is one of the greatest and most influential Vedanta teachers of the past century. His material is excellent, accessible and wide ranging, from simple introductory texts to his voluminous and monumental Bhagavad Gita Home Study Course, an essential for the advanced and committed student. Swami Dayananda trained a wide range of disciples who are now excellent teachers in their own rights. Some are listed below.

Swami Paramarthananda is a disciple of Swami Dayananda and unquestionably one of the greatest teachers of Vedanta alive today. The Swami's latest classes are available in audio at **yogamalika.org** with archives available to purchase in the app "Sastraprakasika". Transcripts of his many audio classes are available online from the Arsha Avinash Foundation at **arshaavinash.in**.

Swami Tadatmayananda is an American disciple of Swami Dayananda who established the Arsha Bodha ashram in New Jersey, USA. The Swami's teaching style, while traditional, its exceptionally accessible to Westerners. Archives of his classes and meditations can be found on his website **arshabodha.org** as well as his excellent YouTube channel @SwamiT.

Radha/Carol Whitfield is a senior student of Swami Dayananda, based in her native USA, who has been teaching since the 1970's. Radha is not only an excellent and highly accessible Vedanta teacher, but also a Jungian psychologist which adds an insightful extra dimension to her teaching. Again, she is particularly recommended to Western students. Classes can be live streamed on her website **arshakulam.org** which also boasts a comprehensive archive of past classes and retreats.

Swami Chinmayananda (1916-1993) was initially a journalist and atheist and who later discovered Vedanta courtesy of his teachers Swami Sivananda and Tapovan Maharaj. He went on to became a world-renowned teacher himself, bringing the teaching alive with passion and revolutionary zeal. Chinmayananda combined Vedanta with yoga and an appeal to experiential states of consciousness, which arguably deviated slightly from Shankara's approach; something later course corrected by his student Swami Dayananda. I nevertheless recommend Chinmayanda's books and material, which many find hugely inspiring. His work and legacy is maintained by the

Chinmaya Mission, which has branches around the world and can be found online at **chinmayamission.com**.

Swami Satchidanandendra Saraswati (1885-1975) was a celebrated Vedantic scholar who authored some two hundred works. The Swami's work was considered monumental in bringing the teaching back into clear alignment with Shankara's original intent. His works include Adhyatma Yoga and are recommended for more advanced students. More details of the Swami can be found at **adhyatmaprakasha.org**.

Neema Majmudar is another student of Swami Dayananda, based in Mumbai, who has spent the last couple of decades travelling the world teaching. Classes are available online, with details at her website **discovervedanta.com**. An archive or previous classes can be found on YouTube at @DiscoverVedanta1.

Swamini Atmaprakashananda runs the UK branch of Swami Dayananda's ashram. Details of classes as well as an archive of audio teachings can be found at **arshavidya.org.uk**.

Other Helpful Websites and Resources

Dennis Waite is a British author who has devoted the past two decades to the study and dissemination of traditional Vedanta. His books, comprehensive and accessible, are recommended reading and his website and blog are found at **www.advaita.org.uk**.

Shanti Sadan is a UK organisation formed by Vedantin Hari Prasad Shastri in 1933. A range of books including scriptural translations and original works are available from the website **shantisadan.org**, as is a quarterly journal titled "Self-Knowledge."

Explore Vedanta - explorevedanta.com. An simple and clear online course covering the basics of Vedanta.

Yes Vedanta - yesvedanta.com. Website of Andre Vas, who teaches from the Dayandana/Chinmayanda lineage.

Vedanta Brasil - www.vedantabrasil.com. Website of teacher Arlindo Moreaes, in Brazilian with English translation available.

Vedanta Hub - vedantahub.org. Helpful archive containing links to the teachings numerous key Vedanta teachers.

Indica Moksha - indicamoksha.com. Formerly Advaita Academy. Perhaps for advanced students.

Divine Life Society established by **Swami Sivananda**, guru to Swami Chinmayanda. Sivananda's approach merges yoga with Vedanta, so it isn't strictly traditional Vedanta, but many find Sivananda's material helpful and inspiring. Website available at **sivanandaonline.org**.

Ramakrishna Mission was established by **Swami Vivekananda** in 1897 honour of beloved 19th century sage **Ramakrishna**. There are now branches of the Ramakrishna Mission all across the world. A teacher a number of people have recommended to me is **Swami Sarvapriyananda** of the Vedanta Society of New York, online at **vedantany.org**. It should be noted that Vivekananda's presentation of Vedanta diverges in some areas from traditional Vedanta, as he sought to "modernise" the teaching and added some of his own ideas. The Mission is, nevertheless, responsible for a number of excellent publications.

About the Author

Rory Mackay, born 1979, is a Scottish author, artist and music producer. He began his career exploring the potential of fiction to inspire, uplift and convey spiritual ideas and knowledge. His first published work was the metaphysical sci-fi/fantasy novel "Eladria", released in 2013, followed by "The Key of Alanar" in 2015. Rory then shifted to non-fiction with the publication of his own interpretation and commentary of the "Tao Te Ching" (2017).

A Social Science graduate and long term student of Eastern spirituality and philosophy, Rory's life was transformed upon discovering and devoting himself to traditional Vedanta. His teachers include James Swartz, Swami Paramarthananda and Swami Dayananda.

He is now dedicated to sharing the teaching of Vedanta and helping keep the flame of knowledge alive and pure. His life journey is documented in the spiritual autobiography, "There Is A Light That Shines". His website is unbrokenself.com.

Other Titles by the Author:

Eladria (novel), 2013, new edition 2023.
The Key of Alanar (novel), 2015, new edition 2017.
The Tao Te Ching (including commentary), 2017.
Bhagavad Gita - The Divine Song (translation and commentary), 2019.
Vedanta - The Big Picture (editor), 2021.
Avadhuta Gita - Song of the Liberated Soul, 2022.
There Is a Light That Shines (Personal Reflections on Advaita Vedanta, Non-duality and Enlightenment), 2024.

www.ingramcontent.com/pod-product-compliance
Lightning Source LLC
Chambersburg PA
CBHW072144070526
44585CB00015B/994